LEADERSHIP
in a ***Diverse***
and
Multicultural
ENVIRONMENT

*I am very happy to dedicate this book to my family and
to all of the cultural teachers I have had throughout my life.
I want to thank my family for their support and encouragement.
I thank my cultural teachers for their patience, as I have learned that
achieving multicultural competence is a journey and not a destination.*

—MLC

*I dedicate this book to Richard Brislin, who first
invited me to Hawaii, introduced me to the field of
culture and psychology, and to whom I owe a great deal.*

—PBP

LEADERSHIP
in a Diverse
and
Multicultural
ENVIRONMENT

Developing Awareness, Knowledge, and Skills

Mary L. Connerley
Virginia Polytechnic Institute and State University

Paul B. Pedersen
Professor Emeritus, Syracuse University
Visiting Professor, University of Hawaii

Foreword by Geert Hofstede

SAGE Publications
Thousand Oaks ▪ London ▪ New Delhi

For information:

Sage Publications, Inc.
2455 Teller
Thousand (
E-mail: ord

Sage Public
1 Oliver's Yard
55 City Road
London EC1Y 1SP
United Kingdom

Sage Publications India Pvt. Ltd.
B-42, Panchsheel Enclave
Post Box 4109
New Delhi 110 017 India

Printed in the United States of America

Library of Congress Cataloging-in-Publication Data

Connerley, Mary L.
Leadership in a diverse and multicultural environment: Developing awareness, knowledge, and skills / Mary L. Connerley, Paul B. Pedersen.
    p. cm.
Includes bibliographical references and index.
ISBN 0-7619-8860-2 (Paper)
    1. Executives—Training of—United States. 2. Diversity in the workplace—United States. 3. Leadership—United States. I. Pedersen, Paul, 1936- II. Title.
HD38.25.U6C66 2005
658.4′092—dc22   2004024117
This book is printed on acid-free paper.

05   06   07   08   09   10   9   8   7   6   5   4   3   2   1

Acquisitions Editor:	Al Bruckner
Editorial Assistant:	MaryAnn Vail
Production Editor:	Diane S. Foster
Copy Editor:	Kristin Bergstad
Typesetter:	C&M Digitals (P) Ltd.
Proofreader:	Libby Larson
Indexer:	Judy Hunt
Cover Designer:	Glenn Vogel

Contents

Foreword

Like many human characteristics, leadership is in the eye of the beholder—in particular, of those led. Just as the consumer and not the producer is the proper judge of the quality of a product, so it is the followers and not the leaders themselves who know best about the quality and effectiveness of leadership.

Many people would like to be leaders, and there is a large and well-selling literature listing all the traits a leader should possess—combinations of eminent characteristics unlikely to be united in most of us mortals. Fortunately, in actual practice the effectiveness of leadership depends only to a limited extent on the leader's traits and to a much larger extent on who the subordinates are, what the task is, and what the environment is.

Mary Connerley and Paul Pedersen's book is about leading more than about leader*ship:* a process rather than a property. It is about leading in the more and more frequent situation where the subordinates and/or the environment can be characterized as multicultural and diverse.

Learning to become an effective leader is like learning to play music: Besides talent, it demands persistence and the opportunity to practice. Effective monocultural leaders have learned to play one instrument; they often have proven themselves by a strong drive and quick and firm opinions. Leading in a multicultural and diverse environment is like playing several instruments. It partly calls for different attitudes and skills: restraint in passing judgment and the ability to recognize that familiar tunes may have to be played differently. The very qualities that made someone an effective monocultural leader may make her or him less qualified for a multicultural environment.

Multicultural leaders need to be context-sensitive. They need a broad interest and an eagerness to absorb new signals, including inspiration from fields like history, geography, religion, literature, and art.

As any intercultural trainer knows and professes, intercultural effectiveness inescapably starts with awareness. Our natural tendency is to watch the world from behind the windows of a cultural home and to act as if people from other countries, ethnicities, or categories have something special about them (a culture) but home is normal. Awareness means the discovery that there is no normal position in cultural matters. This is an uncomfortable message, as uncomfortable as Galileo Galilei's claim in the 17th century that the earth was not the center of the universe.

Mary Connerley and Paul Pedersen's book undertakes the prime task to raise the readers' and students' awareness and enthusiasm for the subject. A book cannot turn one into a multicultural leader, no more than a book can teach one to play music. What a book can do is create awareness of what there is to be known, and motivate the user to find out what he or she will need to know in addition to what the book contains.

The student of this book will also discover the complexity of, and some of the value conflicts inherent in the multicultural environment. If he or she feels comfortable with this amount of intellectual and moral confusion, then maybe this is the first step to a productive career in multicultural leadership.

Geert Hofstede
Velp, the Netherlands

Preface

No matter how highly skilled, well trained, or intelligent you are, if you are making wrong or culturally inappropriate assumptions, you will not be accurate in your assessment, meaningful in your understanding, or appropriate in your interactions as a leader. The inaccuracy or misattribution resulting from wrong assumptions translates into defensive disengagement by leaders and those they lead, each trying to protect the truth as he or she perceives it. This will likely have a negative impact on meeting an organization's goals. Developing multicultural awareness is too often classified as a secondary or tertiary prevention strategy. This book addresses the implications of leading in a diverse environment with a culture-centered approach and examines multicultural awareness, knowledge, and skills training through a three-stage developmental sequence as a primary strategy in leadership.

It is difficult to know the cultures of others until and unless you have an awareness of your own culturally learned assumptions as they control your life. The importance of unexamined underlying culturally learned assumptions is frequently underestimated by failing to recognize that our assumptions reflect our own cultural context. All behaviors are learned in a cultural context and displayed in a cultural context. Leaders who disregard others' cultural contexts are unlikely to interpret their behavior accurately. The same behavior across cultures might have a very different interpretation, just as different behaviors might have the same interpretation. Therefore, developing multicultural awareness is a primary prevention strategy for leaders who want to interpret the meanings of cultural similarities and differences accurately.

An organizational leader has only two choices: to ignore the influence of culture or to attend to it. In either case, however, culture will continue to influence the behavior of others, with or without the leader's intentional awareness. Multicultural awareness provides a safe and accurate approach to managing

AUTHORS' NOTE: Portions of this book are reprinted from Pedersen, P. (2000). A Handbook for Developing Multicultural Awareness. 3rd Edition. American Counseling Association. Reprinted with permission.

differences across groups in our multicultural populations. The importance of culture has been most evident in minority groups' political struggle for equity. Culture has provided the rationale and "roots" for unifying and defining ethnic populations of African Americans, Asian Americans, Hispanics, Latinos, Native Americans, and, more recently, White ethnics. The same model has also coalesced support among the elderly, gender groups, the physically handicapped, gays, lesbians, and many other special populations. The importance of culture is broader than indicated by any one or two of these special interest groups. Culture provides a metaphor for better understanding how we are similar and how we are different across boundaries. Perhaps more important, multicultural awareness provides a metaphor for understanding different perspectives within each of us as our thousands of different, culturally learned social roles compete, complement, and cooperate with one another inside ourselves (Pedersen, 1977, 1997c).

We are making several assumptions as we write this book and state these assumptions directly and explicitly:

1. Culture is defined broadly and inclusively, in the tradition of Herskovits (1955) who defined culture as the human-made part of the environment and Hofstede (2001) who described culture as a collective programming of the mind that manifests itself in values, symbols, and rituals.

2. All leadership takes place in a multicultural context, given the complexity of ethnographic, demographic, status, and affiliation variables in every leader-other interaction.

3. Culture includes both the more obvious objective and verifiable symbols and the more subjective perspectives hidden within each of us, waiting their turn to become salient.

4. Cultural similarities and differences are both equally important in the multicultural perspective to protect against exclusionary stereotyping or power exploitation.

5. The most important elements of multicultural awareness can be learned but cannot be taught. Good training, however, can create the favorable conditions for multicultural awareness to occur and can provide the knowledge and skills necessary for effective interactions with ALL people.

Portions of this book are based on Pedersen's (2000) *Handbook for Developing Multicultural Awareness*, Third Edition, which was written by the second author for the field of counseling. The field of counseling has extensively examined the competencies associated with multicultural awareness, knowledge, and skills and provides a solid foundation for developing multicultural competencies for leaders. No further reproduction is authorized without written permission of the American Counseling Association.

The leadership literature is vast and expanding rapidly, and there are many sources of multicultural awareness, knowledge, and skill. Developing multicultural awareness, knowledge, and skill is complex. We wish to thank all of the authors of the sources cited in this volume; they deserve credit for their extensive and useful publications. No doubt other valuable authors have been inadvertently omitted from the rapidly growing literature on developing multicultural awareness, knowledge, and skills in leaders as the pool of resources grows and develops. Our hope is that this book will lead readers to find examples of how multicultural awareness, knowledge, and skills can make their leadership task easier rather than harder and can increase their satisfaction in working with others from dissimilar cultures and backgrounds. It is also our hope that individuals with whom leaders interact find the relationship more satisfying and that an organizational culture is established that embraces and celebrates differences. As we will discuss, this is, in our view, not only the "right thing to do," it also has the potential to lead to many organizational and individual benefits.

Acknowledgments

We wish to acknowledge the faculty and staff at the Summer Intercultural Workshop, Center for International Business Education and Research at the University of Hawaii at Manoa. It was here that we first met and the idea for this book was initiated. We also wish to thank the many publishers and authors who granted us permission to use figures, information, and exercises, especially the American Counseling Association. We also thank Al Bruckner, editor, and senior editorial assistant MaryAnn Vail at Sage for their encouragement and patience. Kristin Bergstad, our copy editor, also deserves recognition for her very sharp eyes. Finally we thank the reviewers who provided thoughtful guidance and constructive feedback.

1

Making the Business Case for Increased Awareness, Knowledge, and Skills

Major Objective

To identify the business imperative for developing multiculturally aware, knowledgeable, and skillful leaders

Secondary Objectives

1. To identify the impact of both global and domestic demographic changes on the workforce

2. To discuss the similarities and differences between diversity and multi-culturalism

3. To discuss the need for multicultural skills

4. To explore the international perspective on multicultural diversity

5. To identify the value added by multiculturalism and diversity

6. To discuss the importance of focusing on leaders

C ulture is a complex and dynamic topic that is very difficult for leaders, or anyone, for that matter, to deal with. It is often easier in the short run to ignore culture than to deal with its complexity, but leaders need to acknowledge their own cultural baggage as they understand the importance of gaining an awareness of culture. Ignoring culture is like driving down the highway and taking your hands off the steering wheel. You may have started out in the right direction, but the vehicle will quickly veer off in unintended directions.

National boundaries no longer define the world of organizations. The free movement of labor continues to intensify as organizations diversify geograph- ically. This necessitates the effective interaction with broader constituencies as never before (see Siebert, 1999). Nestlé leads the world in external employment with 97% of its employees working outside of Switzerland, while 82% of Philips's workforce is located somewhere other than the Netherlands. A multi- national company like German auto parts supplier Bosch employs more than 180,000 employees in 32 countries. Many U.S. companies such as Ford and IBM have more than 50% of their employees outside of the United States, and AT&T, General Electric, PepsiCo, and General Motors all have between one third and one fifth of their employees working beyond U.S. borders (*Workplace Visions,* 2000).

However, staying within the borders of the United States does not neces- sarily result in workforces that are less multicultural compared to companies spanning different countries. Often when the term *multicultural* is heard, images of international scenarios come to mind. While the world of expatriate managers obviously includes a wealth of cultural issues, domestic companies are facing similar cultural realities. For example, it is estimated that Chinese individuals constitute 3% of New York City's population, with 250,000 concen- trated in Manhattan Island's Chinatown (Swerdlow, 1998). A managing partner at one New York Life agency that has about 200 agents representing 21 nation- alities states that language and cultural differences are the primary challenges facing his ethnic (African American, Asian Indian, and Hispanic) recruits (Ahmed, 2002). In addition, on any given day the Hotel@MIT in Cambridge, Massachusetts, has between 140 and 150 employees who represent at least 40 countries of ori- gin ("Serving the Multicultural Customer," 2003), and at one Washington, D.C., hotel employees speak 36 different languages. It is important that more U.S. companies, and their leaders, recognize that if they find common ground by treating ALL employees, regardless of race, ethnicity, religion, culture, gender, or age with fairness, dignity, and respect, value will be added to the company. It is our contention that the majority of leaders want to treat employees, clients, coworkers, suppliers, and everyone else with respect, but may not have the tools to do so.

Multiculturalism and Diversity

Diversity by definition focuses on differences, while multiculturalism focuses on aspects of multiple cultures. Heated debates still occur in determining the "correct" definition of diversity. Some scholars (e.g., Grossman, 2000; Linnehan & Konrad, 1999) advocate a definition that addresses power imbalances and reflects historical disadvantages (race and gender based). Rijsman (1997) suggests a definition that encompasses all difference. Others (e.g., Fujimoto, Hartel, Hartel, & Baker, 2000; Hartel & Fujimoto, 2000) recognize the complementary nature of the views and advocate a definition that integrates aspects of both approaches. Some have bridged the gap with definitions of cultural diversity. Cox (1994) defines cultural diversity as "the representation, in one social system, of people with distinctly different group affiliations of cultural significance" (p. 6).

Diversity is often discussed in relation to legal requirements, equal employment opportunity (EEO), and affirmative action. Terms like *protected groups, adverse impact, compliance,* and *lawsuit* are also frequently associated with diversity programs. It was stated by Title VII of the Civil Rights Act of 1964 that employers could not discriminate on the bases of sex, race, color, ethnicity, or religion. These characteristics, along with more recent focus on disabilities, age, and sexual orientation, are commonly considered as part of organizations' diversity initiatives. However, similar to academic scholars, practitioners also struggle with different views on defining diversity (Wellner, 2000).

Regardless of how diversity is defined, the adjustments that employees will make within an organization depend on the organization's tolerance for ambiguity, the demand for conformity, and the value placed on diversity, cultural fit, and acculturation (Carr-Ruffino, 1996). Individuals can make one of four specific adjustments to an organization (Cox & Finley-Nickerson, 1991). Multiculturalism is often viewed as the most functional of four strategies or adjustments to deal with both cross-national and intranational diversity (Tung, 1993). A narrow view of multiculturalism focuses on being open to the positive aspects of all cultures and using this information to create new and meaningful ways of interacting. We posit that, while focusing on the positive is a great way to encourage a new relationship, acknowledging what one might consider the negative aspects of a culture is also important. This allows us to determine why we may view these specific aspects as negative, whether they are viewed as a negative characteristic by all, and how that might influence our relationship. For example, the indirect negotiating style of individuals from an Asian culture could be seen as a negative by an American leader. It may seem like a waste of valuable time, but not all see this as a negative. The context-rich style allows for many nuances that can be lost in a direct style and could provide important information for both the transaction and later dealings.

The least functional strategy or adjustment for dealing with diversity issues in companies is called separation. Separation involves rejecting all cultural values except your own. This can be thought of as a form of alienation. This of course causes a great deal of conflict between coworkers from different cultural backgrounds. Assimilation and deculturation fall between multiculturalism and separation. Assimilation is the adoption of the organization's culture. This is usually seen by subordinate groups as conforming to the values of the dominant group. This strategy often produces mistrust in the long run if the dominant group does not attempt to understand the values of the subordinate group (Tung, 1993). Finally, deculturation is viewed as a weak or benign form of separation that occurs when all groups maintain their own values without trying to influence anyone else (McFarlin & Sweeney, 2003). One example would be an expatriate who does not understand an employee's culture and has no desire to change that situation.

We recognize that cultural differences can arise from more than just geographic or ethnic differences. It is our premise that all the ways that make people diverse can also lead to cultural differences. Men and women raised in the same location experience the world in different ways, whether those differences are based on internal differences, external differences in the way they are treated by others, or a combination of the two. Generational differences can also reflect cultural differences. A 23-year-old middle-level manager for a parts distributor growing up in the same neighborhood that his 61-year-old boss was raised in will very likely represent a different culture compared to his boss. The same thing can be said for other sources of difference.

However, even though this book recognizes the many different influences on culture, we do not stray far from traditional views of multiculturalism, and want to bring into understanding that culture is influenced by much more than solely geographic location. Traditional views of multiculturalism suggest that it focuses on the many aspects of culture. This is no easy task for leaders as the number of major cultural groups is estimated to number at least 25, with several subgroups creating much diversity within each major cultural group (Conejo, 2002). The old idea of America representing a "melting pot" has been replaced by images of "stews" or "salads," where everyone keeps his or her identity, which adds richness and flavor to the dish.

Multiculturalism Is Inclusive and Broadly Defined

The multicultural perspective seeks to provide a conceptual framework that recognizes the complex diversity of a plural society while, at the same time, suggesting bridges of shared concern that bind culturally different persons to one another. During the past 20 years, multiculturalism has become recognized as a powerful force, not just for understanding exotic groups but also for understanding ourselves and those with whom we work.

By defining culture broadly—to include within-group demographic variables (e.g., age, sex, place of residence), status variables (e.g., social, educational, economic), and affiliations (formal and informal), as well as ethnographic variables such as nationality, ethnicity, language, and religion—the construct "multicultural" becomes generic to all leader relationships. The narrow definition of culture has limited multiculturalism to what might more appropriately be called "multiethnic" or "multinational" relationships between groups with a shared sociocultural heritage that includes similarities of religion, history, and common ancestry. Ethnicity and nationality are important to individual and familial identity as one subset of culture, but the construct of culture—broadly defined—goes beyond national and ethnic boundaries. Persons from the same ethnic or nationality group may still experience cultural differences. Not all persons of color have the same experience, nor do all Asians, nor all American Indians, nor all Hispanics, nor all women, nor all old people, nor all disabled persons. No particular group is unimodal in its perspective. Therefore, the broad and inclusive definition of culture is particularly important in preparing leaders to deal with the complex differences among and between people they interact with from every cultural group.

Just as differentiation and integration are complementary processes, so are the emic (culture-specific) and etic (culture-general) perspectives necessarily interrelated. The terms emic and etic were borrowed from "phonemic" and "phonetic" analysis in linguistics describing the rules of language to imply a separation of general from specific aspects. Even Pike (1966), in his original conceptualization of this dichotomy, suggested that the two elements not be treated as a rigid dichotomy but as a way of presenting the same data from two viewpoints. Although research on the usefulness of emic and etic categories has been extensive, the notion of a "culture-free" (universal) etic has been just as elusive as the notion of a "culture-pure" (totally isolated) emic.

The basic problem facing leaders is how to describe behavior in terms that are true to a particular culture while at the same time comparing those behaviors with a similar pattern in one or more other cultures. Combining the specific and general viewpoints provides a multicultural perspective. This larger perspective is an essential starting point for leaders seeking to avoid cultural encapsulation by their own culture-specific assumptions (Sartorius, Pedersen, & Marsella, 1984).

There is a strong argument against the broad definition of culture. Triandis, Bontempo, Leung, and Hui (1990) distinguished between cultural, demographic, and personal constructs. Cultural constructs are those shared by persons speaking a particular dialect; living in the same geographical location during the same time; and sharing norms, roles, values, and associations, and ways of categorizing experience described as a "subjective culture" (Triandis, 1972). This view contends that demographic-level constructs deal with these same topics but are shared by only particular demographic groups within a culture, such as men and women or old and young. Personal-level constructs belong to still another category of individual differences and cannot be meaningfully interpreted with reference to demographic or cultural membership.

The problem with this perspective is that it tends to be arbitrary in defining the point at which shared constructs constitute cultural similarity, because, as Triandis et al. (1990) pointed out, we cannot expect that 100% of a sample agrees with a position. We decided, arbitrarily, that if 85% of a sample shares the construct, it is cultural. Similarly, if 85% of the men share it, we consider it gender linked. If less than 85% shares the construct we might examine whether it is shared by the majority of a sample, but if less than 50% of a sample shares the construct, we definitely do not consider it shared (p. 304).

Likewise, C. C. Lee (1991) made a persuasive argument against the broad definition of culture. Lee argued that the term multicultural is in imminent danger of becoming so inclusive as to be almost meaningless. The broad definition includes all constituent groups that perceive themselves as being disenfranchised in some fashion. This has resulted in diffusing the coherent conceptual framework of multiculturalism in training, teaching, and research. The term has been increasingly stretched to include virtually any group of people who consider themselves "different" (Locke, 1990). In responding to Fukuyama's (1990) argument for a more universalist emphasis on culture for understanding the complex interacting systems of society, Locke (1990) suggested that the broad view of *multicultural* at best serves as a prologue for a narrow or "focused" perspective.

The distinction between individual differences and cultural differences is real and important. The cultural identities to which we belong are no more or less important than is our individual identity. Skin color at birth is an individual difference, but what that skin color has come to mean since birth is cultural. Although culture has traditionally been defined as a multigenerational phenomenon, the broad definition of culture suggests that cultural identities and culturally significant shared beliefs may develop in a contemporary horizontal as well as vertical historical time frame and still be distinguished from individual differences.

The Need for Multicultural Skills

Organizational viability depends increasingly upon the knowledge, skills, abilities, and attitudes of all workers. Management practices are needed that encourage innovation, high performance, and a learning culture that embraces all employees (Macdonald, 1995), regardless of the cultural similarity with their leaders. It is assumed, often incorrectly, that leaders with global skills will likely have multicultural awareness, knowledge, and skills. Unfortunately, 85% of Fortune 500 firms believe there are insufficient numbers of employees with global leadership skills. According to the Center for Global Assignments survey, even when employees do possess global leadership skills, 60% said they are inadequate for their organizations' needs (*Workplace Visions*, 2000). Interestingly, although leadership is seen as an important fact for global growth, only 8% of executives and managers rated their organization's overall leadership capacity as excellent, while nearly one half (47%) rated this capacity to be only fair or poor (Csoka, 1998). Thus, there seems to be a disconnect between the importance of leadership and culturally related issues and the current leadership capacity available.

Developing multicultural awareness, knowledge, and skills is not an end in itself, but rather a means toward increasing a person's power, energy, and freedom of intentional choice in a multicultural and diverse world. Multicultural awareness, knowledge, and skills increase a person's intentional and purposive decision-making ability by accounting for the many ways that culture influences different perceptions of the same solution. Increasing multicultural awareness has real, tangible outcomes. Research recently conducted by Marianne Bertrand and Sendhil Mullainathan found that résumés randomly assigned White-sounding names such as Emily Walsh and Brendan Baker resulted in 50% more interviews than résumés assigned African American–sounding names such as Lakisha Washington and Jamal Jones (Taylor, 2002). Apart from their names, the résumés, which depicted phantom job seekers, showed the same experience, education, and skills. Another finding was that the likelihood of being called back for an interview rose significantly with credentials like experience and honors for White-sounding names much more than for Black-sounding names. Having an awareness of unconscious biases that may be affecting the status of job applicants is the first step to a fair and equitable selection process that hires applicants based on true ability and not perceived ability.

Leaders need to develop multicultural awareness, knowledge, and skills to respond appropriately to the problems and opportunities of both domestic demographic changes and globalization. As we hope to show in this book, if there are problems in leading a multicultural workforce, there may be assumptions made due to a lack of awareness in the leader. If the problem does not lie there, it may be in missing information, knowledge, or facts about the context. If the problem does not exist within awareness or knowledge, then there is likely a skill deficit.

Addressing these issues for leaders is critical. One needs only to look at results of recent census reports to understand how the world is changing. In the United States, for example, minority groups grew 43% from 1990 to 2000. In fact, in many large U.S. cities, traditional "minorities" now out number traditional "majority" members. Hispanics alone grew 58% and now constitute 13% of the

U.S. population. Although often lumped together, it is critical to realize that this group of Hispanics is made up of Cubans, Mexicans, Puerto Ricans, Dominicans, Salvadorans, and many others (U.S. Census, 2000). In fact, the use of the term *Hispanic* as a blanket label for all who speak Spanish is very offensive to many from Latin American countries who often prefer the term Latino. The United States, however, is not the only country to see large changes in its population. For example, in Japan between 1990 and 1995 the number of nationalities represented rose from 150 to 179 (Ministry of Public Management, 1995). In Australia, the census figures for growth assume a net gain of one international migrant every 5 minutes and 50 seconds (Australian Bureau of Statistics, 2001). The impact that these population changes have on the way leaders interact with their employees and customers has large consequences.

Both legal outcomes and world events can also impact multicultural relations in the work place. Two recent affirmative-action–related lawsuits (*Gratz v. Bollinger et al.*, 2003 [undergraduate lawsuit]; *Grutter v. Bollinger et al.*, 2003 [law school lawsuit]) filed against the University of Michigan by the Center for Individual Rights on behalf of White students initially interpreted as a victory for affirmative action were viewed much more ambiguously 6 months later (Golden, 2003). The Supreme Court's rulings allowed universities to continue using race as one of many factors in admissions to achieve a diverse student body, but quotas or separate admissions tracks would not be used. One benefit of the filing of these cases has been the resulting research on the benefits of affirmative action. Patricia Gurin and her colleagues have shown that both minority and nonminority students on a more multiculturally diverse campus were more successful compared to those on a more homogeneous campus (Hebert, 2001).

The September 11, 2001, terrorist attacks on the World Trade Center and the Pentagon have also influenced multicultural relations. Using a new database code to track charges alleging employment discrimination related to the events of September 11, the Equal Employment Opportunity Commission reported 654 cases filed under Title VII between September 11, 2001, and September 10, 2002. The charges most frequently cited were issues of discharge and harassment based on national origin, race, and religion (EEOC, 2002). Many of these cases are considered backlash discrimination resulting from the terrorist attacks, but this certainly does not excuse the discriminatory behavior.

International Perspectives on Managing Diversity

Although the United States is often considered the most legalistic country in the world, many countries have laws that protect certain groups, and violation of these laws can result in both financial and reputational losses for companies. For example, in 1977 the Parliament passed the Canadian Human Rights Act, which forbids discrimination on the basis of race, gender, and certain other grounds. Although this Act covers only federally regulated industries, each Canadian province also has employment laws that must be followed by all organizations doing business in that province (Mentzer, 2002).

The Netherlands' diversity management initiative (Glastra, Meerman, Schedler, & De Vries, 2000) resulted from concerns about the increasing number of unemployed ethnic minorities who were largely to be found in the disappearing low skilled labor industries such as metal working. The Netherlands government responded with policy and incentive initiatives (e.g., immigration policy, employment equity act, job creation venues), but they all failed. As a result, as Glastra et al. state, both the government and employers have adopted diversity management as the foundation for a complete reexamination of identity and relationships in the workplace.

New Zealand was the first country to give women suffrage and still recognize the roles and rights of indigenous citizens (*Maoris*) and European settlers (*Pakehas;* Ashkanasy, Hartel, & Daus, 2002). While diversity management in the United States often refers to treating all employees the same, diversity management in New Zealand is viewed as individualized treatment aimed at shifting power relations through reducing the power differential between managers and employees (Pringle & Scowcroft, 1996). Pringle and Scowcroft suggest that the diversity initiative in New Zealand evolved from EEO initiatives that were encouraged by discrimination legislation and changing demographics.

Poland takes a societal view, setting agendas for leaders and managers to follow as they address cross-cultural differences (Todeva, 1999). Polish researchers focus on four distinct areas: social anthropology, international dimensions of organizational behavior (e.g., cross-cultural leadership, motivational issues), the way in which culture shapes organizational structures of multinational organizations, and international dynamics in management practices (e.g., communication and negotiation across cultures; Ashkanasy et al., 2002).

Regardless of the country, it is true that laws, and the resulting lawsuits, may encourage organizations to comply, but becoming cross-culturally aware, knowledgeable, and skillful reaps much greater rewards than simply attempting to comply with the law to avoid a lawsuit. As shown in the next section, there is much value to be gained for leaders and organizations in the quest for multicultural awareness, knowledge, and skills.

Value Added by Multiculturalism and Diversity

After decades of debate over whether or not diversity was "good" for organizations, the jury still appears to be out according to research, but as we will show below, corporate America seems to be sold on the idea. In a comprehensive review of 63 studies assessing the effects of diversity on team and organizational outcomes, Jackson, Joshi, and Erhardt (2003) found largely mixed results. They reported studies on sex diversity that showed positive effects on performance (Jackson & Joshi, 2003; Rentsch & Klimoski, 2001), negative effects on performance (Jehn & Bezrukova, 2003), and nonsignificant results related to performance (Watson, Johnson, & Merritt, 1998).

The pattern of mixed results held for Jackson et al. (2003) when examining studies of international diversity. Some studies found positive effects on performance (Earley & Mosakowski, 2000; Elron, 1997) while others found that international diversity was related to poorer performance over time (Watson et al., 1998).

Studies on racio-ethnic diversity have also been mixed, although Jackson et al. (2003) reported more studies that found a negative effect of racio-ethnic diversity on performance (Jackson & Joshi, 2003; Kirkman, Tesluk, & Rosen, 2001; Leonard, Levine, & Joshi, 2003; Townsend & Scott, 2001) as compared to a positive effect (Richard, 2000). However, Richard's study does offer a great deal of promise, showing that cultural diversity does add value, and that for companies using a growth strategy, diversity can lead to a competitive advantage. Others have argued for the positive impact that cultural diversity can have for organizations in terms of advantages in resource allocation, marketing, enhanced creativity, problem solving, and flexibility (Cox & Blake, 1991).

Although study results are mixed, evidence of value from multiculturalism and diversity is important because there is still backlash against many anti-discrimination programs given that some established majority members are concerned that they are losing ground to minority groups (see Grossman, 2000). As noted in Ashkanasy et al.'s (2002) review of the history of diversity research, some scholars suggest that one of the underlying drivers of modern racism is the assumption that minority groups are receiving a higher status and more recognition in society than they have earned (e.g., Brief, Dietz, Reizenstein Cohen, Pugh, & Vaslow, 2000; Brief & Hayes, 1997; Heilman, Battle, Keller, & Lee, 1998). However, it is also noted that individuals' reactions depend on both their own group membership and the group favored by a policy such as affirmative action (Crosby, 1984; Kravitz & Platania, 1993).

Although academic research provides mixed results as to the value of multiculturalism and diversity, most organizations in the United States appear to embrace the idea. For example, an examination of company Web sites provides a view of strong support:

General Motors is a strong supporter of the Global Sullivan Principles. These principles have their roots in the 1977 Sullivan principles developed for South Africa by the late Reverend Leon H. Sullivan. These principles provide guidance to companies worldwide "regarding core issues such as human rights, worker rights, the environment, community relations, supplier relations, and fair competition." Reverend Sullivan was the first African American to be appointed to the Board of Directors of a major U.S. company when he accepted General Motors' invitation in 1971.

The objectives of the Global Sullivan Principles are to . . . support human rights and to encourage equal opportunity at all levels of employment including racial or gender diversity on decision making committees and boards; to train and advance disadvantaged workers for technical, supervisory and management opportunities; and to assist with greater tolerance and understanding among peoples; thereby helping to improve the quality of life for communities, workers and children with dignity and equality. (http://www.gm.com/company/gmability/sustainability/reports)

Citicorp states,

With a presence in more than 100 countries, where some 98 percent of our employees are hired locally, Citigroup is perhaps the most diverse company in the world. The diversity has been a source of strength for Citigroup's 250,000 employees, for our clients and for the communities where we live and work. . . . Citicorp values a work environment where diversity is embraced, where people are promoted on their merits, and where people treat each other with mutual respect and dignity. (http://careers.citigroup.com/diversity)

McKinsey's Statement on Diversity states,

McKinsey aspires to be the leading professional services firm in attracting, retaining, developing, and advancing exceptional individuals from the global talent pool. We bring together men and women from a wide variety of backgrounds and experiences to serve our diverse client base. McKinsey's consultants come from 90 different countries and speak more than 65 languages. By encouraging mobility throughout our more than 80 worldwide offices, our firm ensures that the benefit of our diversity is available to clients around the world. Our firm is committed to creating a work environment that supports, inspires, and provides respect for our colleagues' individuality, regardless of race, ethnicity, gender, sexual orientation or other identities. (http://www.mckinsey.com/aboutus/careers/people/diversity/divstate.asp)

Colgate-Palmolive states,

Nearly 40,000 Colgate People reflect the diverse richness of cultures around the globe. As a company, we celebrate differences, promote an inclusive environment, and value the contributions of all Colgate people. Our concept of diversity goes beyond that of race, creed, ethnicity and gender. We look to promote an inclusive environment and support the diversity of thinking that results from the differences in experiences, knowledge and background of all Colgate people. Diversity of thinking will help us continue to encourage the creativity and innovation necessary for our Company to maintain a competitive advantage in the global marketplace. (http://www.colgate.com/app/Colgate/US/Corp/Careers/Diversity.cvsp)

Lee Raymond, CEO and Chairman, Exxon Mobile Corporation, wrote the following in a letter to employees about the company's diversity goals:

> Having a workforce that is as diverse as your business is a key competitive advantage. Our success is a direct reflection of the quality of our employees. We strive to attract the best people and to provide them the best career opportunities in our industry. In doing so, we've built a diverse global workforce that is focused on producing superior business results. (http://www.exxonmobil.com/Global-English/HR/About/HR_GL_What_diversity.asp)

Understanding the importance of instilling a multicultural view in its leaders, United Parcel Service (UPS) stands as a benchmark organization. In a speech given to the Southern Institute of Ethics Diversity Management Network, Cal Darden, senior vice president of U.S. Operations for UPS, discussed the benefits of diversity leadership. This is an important topic for UPS as 35% of this 360,000-member workforce, and 52% of their new hires, are members of minority groups. Darden believes that diversity leadership results in leaders who inspire loyalty and their employees' best efforts. Externally, diversity leadership can attract investors as more and more people desire to invest in socially responsible companies.

Darden (2003) describes UPS's Community Internship Program, which shows the relationship between diversity and multiculturalism. This selective program chooses 50 high-potential managers each year. The interns leave their jobs behind for one month and travel, not to a distant country, but to a distant community. In 2002, the interns were assigned to one of three locations:

The Henry Street Settlement, a social services agency in New York

McAllen, Texas, an immigrant border town

An Appalachian mountain community near Chattanooga, Tennessee

The one urban and two rural locations were chosen purposefully to allow all interns to be placed in an unfamiliar environment, removing them from their comfort zone. The interns participate in community projects day and night while living in very frugal conditions. The interns are required to keep a daily log of activities performed, and they discuss their experiences with each other and social workers.

Interestingly, this very timely, culturally rich program was started by UPS in 1968. The company has spent around $13 million ($10,000/intern) and feels that this investment has yielded a substantial return because the interns return to work more aware of societal conditions and why they exist. This results in leaders who are more sensitive to problems that can exist for employees and who listen to employees with more empathy.

As measurement becomes more important for justifying business expenditures, there have been attempts to quantify the dollar value of diversity training. In 2001, Nextel instituted diversity training to increase awareness with the objective of training to improve employee retention, satisfaction, and productivity

(Kirkpatrick, Phillips, & Phillips, 2003). Their All-Inclusive Workplace training session was attended by all 13,000 employees. After a comprehensive return-on-investment (ROI) study was completed, Nextel conservatively determined that their diversity awareness training program had saved the company $3,204,000 in one year in turnover costs alone. The ROI was calculated to be 163%. For every dollar spent on training ($1,216,836 in this case), Nextel received $1.63 as a net benefit. These figures are based on the tangible benefits alone. Although Nextel did not attempt to quantify intangible benefits of awareness training, managers reported improved relationships with employees and more cooperation and communication among staff, and employees reported better teamwork and improved relationships with their managers.

Why Focus on Leaders?

First we must clarify the distinction between leaders and managers. Many writers use the terms interchangeably, but there are important distinctions between the two. Managers are appointed, and they have legitimate power that allows them to reward and punish employees. The formal authority granted them by their position gives managers their ability to influence employees. Conversely, leaders may either be appointed or emerge from a group of employees, and they can influence others beyond their formal authority in an organization. When determining leadership capacity, however, we do not view leadership as the sole responsibility of the CEO or vice presidents. Leadership within an organization can be found at every level, as inferred by this definition of leadership: "The act of one person guiding another or others toward the attainment of an objective" (Rodrigues, 2001, p. 427). Adler (1999) suggests that a leader is "someone who sets ideas, people, organizations, and societies in motion; someone who takes the worlds of ideas, people, organizations, and societies on a journey. To lead such a journey requires vision, courage, and influence" (p. 51). Taking the definition of leadership a step farther, Gessner, Arnold, and Mobley (1999) state that

> leadership involves people in business settings whose job or role it is to influence the thoughts and actions of others to achieve some finite set of business goals . . . usually displayed in large, multicultural contexts; that is, not just from one's native perspective. (p. xv)

Obviously, leadership viewed in this way encompasses both traditional leaders and those at all levels of an organization's hierarchy who play a critical role in attaining business objectives working with others. The term *followers* will be used periodically in this book referencing those the leaders are leading, with the understanding that anyone in an organization could play the role of follower, depending on the situation.

Important questions related to managers and leaders that have been asked are: Should all managers be leaders? Should all leaders be managers? Given that it has never been demonstrated that leadership ability hurts managerial ability, it has been stated that all managers should ideally be leaders (Robbins & DeCenzo, 2004). However, although leaders must be able to direct employees, they do not necessarily have the capabilities to conduct the other functions related to management successfully (i.e., plan, organize, control).

How important is leadership? Few could deny the impact that a great leader (or, unfortunately, a poor leader) can have on an organization's performance and employee morale. Leadership pervades an organization, and leaders shape their organizational cultures according to their own preferences and beliefs (Schein, 1992).

For example, when John Mack took over troubled Credit Suisse First Boston (CSFB) in July 2001, rumors abounded about the company being a dead franchise that should be sold off. Analysts, however, predicted a $350 million net profit by the end of 2003 versus the $1.2 billion loss of the year before (Sellers, 2003). Part of Mack's formula for success included cutting costs by more than $3 billion, reducing the number of employees from 27,500 to 17,500, selling off some subsidiaries, persuading executives to give back $421 million in cash pay, and eliminating multiyear guaranteed-pay contracts, all while encouraging his people to get out of their comfort zones (Sellers, 2003).

When Jean Monty was CEO of Nortel (Northern Telecom), Ontario, Canada, he took the organization from a $1.03 billion loss to $473 million profit in less than 2 years. When Bob Moffat took over IBM's personal computer division in July 2000, it had lost $1.5 billion in the previous 3 years (during the same time Dell made $4.8 billion). The first thing Moffat did was promise profits for the first quarter he was in charge. His division was inspired and delivered $99 million in profits for his first two quarters (Fishman, 2001). Moffat has realized success by being a straight talker who provides his managers with a "playbook" to help execute IBM's strategy.

Albert Dunlap earned the nickname "Chainsaw Al" from the media because he often sells off assets and fires people when he takes over a company. But few can deny his leadership ability. In his first 603 days at Scott Paper Company in the mid 1990s, the stock increased in value by $6.5 billion. That works out to more than $10 million per day (Dunlap, 1996).

Another example can be found in A. G. Lafley, who took over Procter & Gamble (P&G) in 2000. Lafley is an unassuming leader who is known for his openness and authenticity (Useem, 2003). He led P&G, a $43 billion company, back to profitability while endearing himself to both Wall Street and his employees.

These are just a few of the thousands of examples that could be used to show that leadership makes a difference and impacts millions of lives every day.

However, one thing that was missing from the above examples was a stated leadership focus on culture.

> All business is global, yet all markets are local. This globalized, multicultural world needs leaders with a keen understanding of national cultures. By learning from other countries, these leaders develop the best thinking and best practices from around the world, enabling them to leverage culture as a tool for competitive advantage. (Rosen, Digh, Singer, & Phillips, 2000, p. 171)

We are not suggesting that the leaders mentioned above do not value culture. In fact, Schein (1992) states that leadership and organizational culture are two sides of the same coin. However, it is also important to point out that organizations, and their leaders, also reflect national cultures (van Oudenhoven, 2001). Below, we offer an example of two leaders who explicitly understand the importance of culture:

Leo van Wijk, CEO of KLM Royal Dutch Airlines, states that his company is a bridger of cultures, with 13 million passengers a year, many from a wide variety of cultures. KLM, established in 1919, is the world's oldest and fourth largest international airline with 26,800 employees in 350 offices in 94 countries. Van Wijk, a culturally literate leader who listens and shares what is learned from around the world, uses his knowledge of cultures to form alliances and connections with individuals and organizations, such as KLM's extensive partnership formalized with Northwest Airlines in 1997 (Rosen et al., 2000). Van Wijk shows that he truly considers the importance of culture by allowing employees in other countries to keep their own cultural elements intact as much as possible. "We understand that they do things differently other places; as long as it doesn't interfere with our overall objectives and image to the customer, that's fine with us" (Rosen et al., 2000, p. 193). Van Wijk also understood that in dealing with different cultures, leaders need to recognize that they are dealing with different "fabrics of meaning" (Geertz, 1973). In his interactions with Americans, he realized that even though both parties spoke English, there was still ample room for misunderstandings even though the words were the same:

> We tend to think the values being created on the other side are exactly the same because we speak the same language, but that's not the case. It takes a long time to understand the mental and cultural setting of a statement, even if the words are the same. (Rosen et al., 2000, p. 193)

T. Fujisawa, cofounder of Honda Motor Co., states, "Japanese and American management is 95 percent the same, and differs in all important respects" (quoted in Dorfman, 2004, p. 265). Andre Laurent (1986) makes the following observation about the influence of one's nationality based on his studies of multinational corporations in the 1980s:

> Overall and across 56 different items of inquiry, it was found that nationality had three times more influence on the shaping of managerial assumptions than any of the respondents' other characteristics such as age, education, function, type of company . . . etc. (p. 93)

Thus, Laurent suggests that multinational companies do not and cannot submerge the individuality of different cultures, since the template for behaviors isn't from the company—but from the national culture.

Peter Ma is CEO of Ping An, an insurance company founded in 1988 as China's first partially employee-owned company. During its first year, Ping An had 10 employees and $30 million in assets. Today it has more than 130,000 employees and $30 billion in assets. Ma claims that much of Ping An's success comes from its ability to keep one foot in traditional Chinese culture and one foot in the world while constantly learning and modernizing Chinese culture (Rosen et al., 2000).

Unpublished data from a Conference Board Survey (Berman, 1997) show that 91% of surveyed CEOs rated leadership as the most critical factor for global growth and more important than business, management, and environmental factors (reported in Csoka, 1998). As we show in Chapter 4, many of the competencies necessary for successful global assignments are also necessary for successful domestic interactions in a diverse environment. Competencies such as creating a shared vision, developing and empowering people, appreciating cultural diversity, sharing leadership, living the values, and embracing change (Stewart, 1999) are just as appropriate for global leaders as for domestic leaders working in a multicultural environment.

This book is aimed at leaders because they set the tone for the climate of the organization. Leaders set the expectations for the company. It is common knowledge that the quickest way to a failed human resource implementation is to attempt to execute it without leader support. In addition, "The leader, being in the forefront, is usually the first to encounter the world outside the boundaries of the organization. The more you know about the world, the easier it is to approach it with assurance" (Kouzes & Posner, 2002, p. 392). Thus, the more leaders know about cultural influences, the better able they will be to direct the organization by understanding the behaviors of both their own employees and others outside the organization.

Focusing on behaviors is important because behaviors have no meaning outside their cultural context. Leaders need to understand each culturally learned behavior in the context of where that behavior was learned and is displayed. Attempting to change behavior that was learned in one context, in a culturally different context is unlikely to succeed, causing negative consequences for the organization, the leader, and the employee.

The focus is also on leaders because they can make or break a company. Warren Bennis studied 90 of the most effective and successful leaders in the United States and found that they had four common competencies: They had a compelling vision or sense of purpose; they could communicate that vision in clear terms that their followers could readily identify with; they demonstrated consistency and focus in the pursuit of their vision; and they knew their own strengths and weaknesses (Bennis, 1984). Many of these characteristics are similar to those of transformational leaders who pay attention to the concerns and developmental needs of individual employees, help employees look at problems in new ways, and excite and inspire employees to put forth extra effort to achieve goals (Bass & Avolio, 1990).

Conclusion

Chapter 1 should give the reader a better sense of the importance of being multiculturally aware, knowledgeable, and skillful. Demographic changes will continue at a rapid pace, making the need for these competencies more critical than ever. The principles presented in this book are not solely for top-level CEOs, but for all employees who influence others in the workplace, whether this influence is based on formal authority or informal norms. Being multiculturally competent can help every employee to get more out of every relationship in the workplace. To give a better understanding of both diversity and multiculturalism, the next chapter focuses on the complexity of culture, which plays a large role in both diversity and multiculturalism efforts.

CHAPTER 1 DISCUSSION QUESTIONS

1. What type of influence will a leader likely have if he or she does not consider culture when making decisions?

2. Are *diversity* and *multiculturalism* distinct terms, or do you believe that they are really talking about the same concept? How would you define each one using your own words?

3. What factors influence the strategy (multiculturalism, separation, assimilation, or deculturation) most prevalent in U.S. organizations in dealing with diversity and multiculturalism?

4. Beyond demographic changes stated in the Census 2000 report, is the need for multicultural skills higher today than 10 years ago?

Critical Incident: Culture and Performance Feedback

"No one said it was going to be easy," thought Stan as he slumped down in his chair, reading the memo that requested his presence in his boss's office. Stan was recently promoted to Vice President of Manufacturing at a large automobile assembly plant in the Midwest. One of his first encounters with his new staff had not gone well. When Stan was a manager of line workers, he learned that his employees from a Hispanic culture reacted differently to feedback than did his employees raised in an American culture. The American employees who received positive performance reviews would often improve their subsequent performance, whereas his Hispanic employees' performance would usually remain stable. After several years of similar outcomes, Stan realized that the Hispanic employees were much less likely than their American counterparts to exceed the informal work goals established by their peers as an acceptable level of output, regardless of the feedback they received. Based on his experience, Stan began to alter the type of feedback he gave to his Hispanic employees compared to the American employees. For the American employees, he would give the traditional individual level performance feedback, but for his Hispanic employees, he would give group level feedback and let them know where they stood as a group in relation to other employees grouped for this purpose only. He achieved the results he was looking for and everyone seemed pleased with the outcomes. Now he had a new problem. With his recent promotion, he was in charge of conducting performance evaluations on the managers of the assemblers. Knowing that his CEO was expecting results quickly, or his job could be on the line, Stan figured he would use his knowledge of his previous evaluations with employees from different cultures and rate his American managers individually, while rating his Hispanic managers collectively. Stan was quite pleased with himself, figuring he saved himself some valuable time until a parade of angry Hispanic managers came through his office. They could not have been more upset. All of them were accusing Stan of being biased and threatening lawsuits against the company and Stan personally.

CRITICAL INCIDENT DISCUSSION QUESTIONS

1. Did Stan make appropriate assumptions based on his knowledge of his Hispanic employees?

2. Was it appropriate for Stan to provide individual level feedback to his American assemblers and group level feedback to his Hispanic assemblers?

3. How should Stan have handled the performance evaluations of his managers?

4. What should Stan do now?

Exercise 1: Coalitions and Trust Formation

OBJECTIVE

This experience examines the importance of trust in the creation of lasting coalitions for a mixed group.

DESCRIPTION

Coalition formation is an important process in multicultural societies. This activity looks at how coalitions might be predicted among three individuals dividing up a sum of money. Normally the group will begin by dividing the sum in approximately equal amounts within the first minute and declare the experiment completed. The facilitator will remind them that the experiment must last 5 minutes. The three parties will then sit quietly for about another minute or two. Finally one of the three people will ask the facilitator if majority rule means that any two of the parties could divide the money as they wished. The facilitator will agree that these are the rules. Then one of the parties will suggest to one other party that they split the money 50-50, cutting the third party out completely. At that point the person being cut out will offer to give up three quarters in exchange for keeping the fourth quarter and cutting out the person who originally suggested a 50-50 split. The person who suggested the 50-50 split will be left out of the final coalition in most instances because, presumably, he or she cannot be trusted, and the final coalition will typically be a 75-25 split between the other two parties.

Time required: 30 minutes or less

Risk/expertise level: Low

Participants needed: Any number of participants plus one facilitator

PROCEDURE

1. Recruit three volunteers representing different cultural groups, broadly defined, for a 5-minute experiment.

2. Seat all three people around a table, with the other participants seated or standing so they can hear what is happening.

3. Lay four 25-cent coins in front of the three persons and instruct them that the distribution of the total sum of money will depend on majority rule by the three parties in this experiment.

4. The amount of money cannot be divided into smaller units such as dimes and nickels.

5. Typically the three people will divide the money as equally as possible and declare the activity over.

6. At that point you remind them that the activity is to last a full 5 minutes, and you sit quietly and wait.

7. Within a minute or two one of the players will suggest a two-way split of the money and the other person will agree.

8. Within another minute the third person will agree to a 75%-25% split rather than lose everything, and that coalition will last, cutting out the first person, who suggested a 50-50 split.

DEBRIEFING

In the debriefing the facilitator may want to explore the logic behind whatever distribution of the four quarters occurred during the 5 minutes and why. Some discussion questions may include the following:

1. Why was the first person to suggest a 50-50 split cut out of the lasting coalition?

2. What strategy would you use to end up with the most money?

3. Would the same dynamics occur in all cultures?

4. If the negotiation were not about money, would the outcome be different?

5. What feelings did you have during the activity?

INSIGHT

Lasting coalitions across different cultures and individuals depend on each party trusting the other party or parties.

SOURCE: Pedersen, P. B. (2004). *110 experiences for multicultural learning.* Washington, DC: American Psychological Association Press.

2

The Complexity of Culture

Major Objective

To demonstrate the benefits of defining culture inclusively

Secondary Objectives

1. To demonstrate the importance of both similarities and differences

2. To demonstrate the necessity of accepting cultural complexity

3. To demonstrate the ever-changing dynamic characteristics of culture

---

B efore identifying specific multicultural competencies and describing specific avenues to increase awareness, knowledge, and skills, a deeper understanding of multiculturalism would benefit leaders by providing a context for the complexity of culture. The word *culture* was first used in its anthropological and sociological context by E. B. T. Taylor (1871/1924) defined as "that complex whole which includes knowledge, belief, art, morals, law, custom, and any other capabilities and habits acquired by man as a member of society" (p.1).

Before we were born, cultural patterns of thought and action were already being prepared to guide our lives, influence our decisions, and help us take control of our lives. We inherited these cultural patterns from our parents and teachers, who taught us the "rules of the game." As we developed awareness of other people and cultures, we learned that "our" culture was one of the many possible patterns of thinking and acting from which we could choose. By that time most of us had already come to believe that our culture was the best of all possible worlds. Ethnocentrism, the belief that one's own culture is inherently superior to other cultures, is a natural tendency of most individuals (Haight, 1990), and leaders are no exception.

Even when we recognized that the new ways were better, it was not always possible to replace our cultural habits with new alternatives. The primary enemy of multiculturalism, therefore, is our exclusive reliance on the "self-reference criterion" by which we measure the goodness or badness of others exclusively according to ourselves and our own "natural" perspectives. George Bernard Shaw (1919), in his script for *Man and Superman: A Comedy and a Philosophy*, pointed out, "Do not do unto others as you would that they should do unto you. Their tastes may not be the same" (p. 227). Another twist on the Golden Rule is, "Do unto others as they would have you do unto them," suggesting again that others may have different, although valid, preferences for how they would like to be treated. In an organization with rules, regulations, and ever-looming deadlines this will not always be possible. Acknowledging the cultural background of the individuals who established the rules is nevertheless an important consideration.

The diversification of the United States is changing the complexion of society. In March 2000, 28.4 million foreign-born individuals lived in the United States, which is 10.4% of the U.S. population (U.S. Census, 2000). Recent migrations are different from earlier White European migrations that were oriented toward assimilation. The current foreign-born consist primarily of individuals from Latin America (14.5 million total; 9.8 million from Central America, including Mexico; 2.8 million from the Caribbean; and 1.9 million from South America). Asians accounted for 7.2 million (one quarter of the foreign-born), and Europeans accounted for 4.4 million or about one seventh of the foreign-born. In addition to the need for cross-cultural awareness for those doing business internationally, these population changes have obvious implications for leaders domestically.

Cultural Similarities and Differences

Multiculturalism presents us with a paradox because it requires us to look at how we are the same and how we are different at the very same time. The multicultural perspective is one of the most important ideas in this century because it emphasizes both the ways that we are each unique and the ways that we share parts of our identity with others. Alternative views of culture have made three serious mistakes.

1. The "melting pot" metaphor made the mistake of overemphasizing the ways we are the same and ignoring differences. This has usually resulted in the more powerful groups imposing their perspectives on everybody else.

2. The overemphasis of differences has resulted in stereotyped and disconnected "special interest" cultural groups in an exclusionary perspective while ignoring the common ground of shared interests that makes the welfare of each group important to each other group.

3. The assumption that you must select either a universalist or a particularist viewpoint has resulted in a false choice, because both are important to defining the cultural context accurately and comprehensively. A universalist perspective represents an all-embracing, all-reaching perspective. A particularist perspective represents adherence to one particular interest or system. Each cultural perspective is unique, but each perspective also shares overlapping features with each other group like overlapping fish scales. We can best understand the cultural perspective by focusing one eye clearly on the part that is shared and the other eye on the part that is unique in a cross-eyed but accurate perspective.

A Test of Reasonable Opposites

We are moving toward a future culture that promises to be so different from what we presently know that we hardly can imagine what it will be like. Furthermore, those who cannot adapt to that future culture will not survive. We are left with the alternative of learning adaptive skills through contact with cultures whose assumptions are different from our own. The means for learning those adaptive skills are through contact with different cultures, developing new ways of thinking, and challenging our unexamined assumptions.

Most of our educational emphasis is on examining the rational and reasonable process of a single culturally learned viewpoint. We suggest reexamining the starting point assumptions that determine the trajectory of those viewpoints. Many viewpoints, however similar, disagree because they have different starting points that lead them toward divergent assumptions. Looking at reasonable opposites will enlarge our repertoire of adaptive skills. A "test of reasonable opposites" provides a means of examining those basic assumptions that frequently escape examination in our educational system.

The test begins with identifying a basic but unexamined truth and the assumption(s) behind those truth statements. Second, it asks what the alternative policy positions are that would reverse those assumptions and provide a policy based on opposite or contrary assumptions. Finally, it compares the two statements and their assumptions to determine which alternative is more reasonable. In a surprisingly large number of instances, the opposite assumption seems at least as reasonable, and sometimes even more so, as the original assumption. For example, stating that the sun rises every day does not hold true for those few scientists living in darkness for six months at the South Pole. In applying the test of reasonable opposites we have found (1) that our thinking is usually so ambiguous that it is difficult to identify the opposite of what we say is true; (2) that once an opposite truth statement has been generated, it is often as reasonable as what we originally accepted; and (3) that the generation of reasonable opposites results in new and creative alternatives that otherwise might not have been discovered. Some examples of opposites might be: (1) Differences are important versus similarities are important; (2) Great leaders have followers versus great leaders teach others to lead themselves; (3) You are right versus you are wrong.

The reasonable opposite provides a stimulating alternative to unexamined assumptions. It is urgent that we distinguish between multicultural disagreements (e.g., where the assumptions are different) and interpersonal conflict (e.g., where the assumptions are similar). By challenging our assumptions we can develop adaptive skills for working with a wider range of different perspectives, and we can learn more about our own environment from other viewpoints. In the course of our social and professional evolution, these adaptive skills will be very important.

One Size Does Not Fit All

It is an interesting phenomenon that stereotypes guide our behavior with or without our permission. "Stereotyping is a process by which individuals are viewed as members of groups and the information that we have stored in our minds about the group is ascribed to the individual" (Cox, 1994, p. 88). Historically, race has been a commonly stereotyped characteristic. The concept of racism has broadened as we have become more aware of its complexity in recent years. Every attempt to reduce culture and cultural differences according to skin color alone has resulted in simplistic, stereotyped, or polarized alternatives that disregard the necessary complexity of multiculturalism. In 1996 on the television show *Oprah*, golfer Tiger Woods referred to himself as a "Cablinasian," a combination of Caucasian, Black, Indian, and Asian. For the first time in U.S. history, the 2000 census allowed people to describe themselves by checking more than one race, offering 126 categories and combinations. Nearly 7 million Americans (2.5% of the population) identified themselves as belonging to two or more races. However, the creation of the mixed race category was deeply opposed by some because it would dilute the population numbers for some traditionally underrepresented races, which many believed would also dilute their power base. Finally, many applicants to universities have decided to leave the question of race blank on the application. For example, in fall, 2004 at Virginia Tech, 14% of the 17,764 applicants who applied for admission did not declare a race. This sends a statement (left open to interpretation) to leaders of the university and makes it difficult to assess levels of diversity on campus.

Regardless of the exact numbers, though, racism is still a problem worldwide. In France, violent attacks against synagogues and other Jewish buildings have revived the cry of anti-Semitism. In the United States, an employee for Lockheed Martin arrives at work to find a hangman's noose sitting on his desk (Bernstein, 2001). Multimillion-dollar settlements of racial discrimination or harassment claims at companies such as Coca-Cola Co. and Boeing Co. reflect racism, but also give victims hope that a remedy is available.

Ridley (1989) points out some underlying assumptions about modern racism that demonstrate its pervasiveness. First, racism is reflected in behavior, in what the person does rather than how that person feels or thinks, although attitudes are important in motivating people to behave differently. Second, racist acts can be performed by prejudiced as well as nonprejudiced persons. There is no causal relationship in which racism depends on prejudice as its antecedent. Well-intentioned but misinformed persons can still behave in racist ways. Third, racism is not the sole responsibility of any single ethnic group. Anyone can be racist. Fourth, the criteria for judging an act as racist lie in the consequences rather than the causes of the behavior. Consciousness raising is not enough to eliminate racism and will not by itself prevent racist acts. Fifth, racism is perpetuated by the power or powerlessness of groups with respect to one another.

Miles (2003) links racism to the process of seeing history in racial terms, where the powerful are separated from the powerless and where those in power are presumed to have the right or even the responsibility to exclude the powerless from consideration. Because racism is an ideology, leaders must acknowledge its complexity and avoid simplistic applications to historical events. Because racism is a political and economic force, leaders should also view it with regard to its consequences in that some are included and others are excluded from positions of power. Racism may often include contradictory and multidimensional ideas in an unthinking and unexamined justification for action.

The Multicultural Perspective Has an Upside

The upside of the multicultural perspective: Culture continues to be one of the most important and perhaps one of the most misunderstood constructs in organizations. Culture may be defined narrowly as limited to ethnicity and nationality or defined broadly to include any and all potentially salient ethnographic, demographic, status, or affiliation variables. Given the broader definition of culture in this book it is possible to identify at least a dozen assets that are exclusively available through developing multicultural awareness (Pedersen, 1999).

1. Accuracy. Because all behavior is learned and displayed in a cultural context, accurate assessment, meaningful understanding, and appropriate interventions are culturally contextual constructs. When colleagues who oppose multiculturalism are asked if they consider accuracy to be important, they always respond in the affirmative. Thus, we are on the same side in our search for accuracy.

2. Conflict Management. The common ground of shared values or expectations can be expressed by contrasting culturally learned behaviors so that reframing conflict in a culture-centered perspective will allow two people or groups to "apparently" disagree in their behaviors without disagreeing on their shared values. Not everyone who smiles is your friend, and not everyone who shouts at you is your enemy. If we judge other's behaviors prematurely and out of context, we are likely to turn potential friends into enemies. If we begin by increasing our awareness of the shared positive values and expectations, we can both teach and learn about which behavior is best in each cultural context. This is discussed in greater detail in Chapter 8.

3. Identity. A useful visual image of culture is the picture of a thousand people sitting with us in our chairs or following us around day and night. An articulate awareness of these thousand culture teachers, accumulated from relatives, friends, acquaintances, enemies, and fantasies, whisper advice, reward, and censure as they celebrate our accomplishments and mourn our failures. Our internal dialogue with these culture teachers is a frequently underutilized resource in our decision-making and hypotheses forming processes. These culture teachers are our identity.

4. A Healthy Society. A healthy socio-ecosystem requires a diversity of cultural perspectives just as a healthy biosystem requires a diverse gene pool. Utopian or cult groups that have cut themselves off from outside society have failed throughout history. Superpowers that have failed to recognize and acknowledge their interactive dependence on smaller nations have inevitably fallen. Culture is a growing, changing, and always emerging force that resists capture and incarceration by language, powers, or influence.

5. Encapsulation-Protection. A culture-centered perspective protects us from inappropriately imposing our own culturally encapsulated self-reference criteria in the evaluation of others. It has been stated that culturally encapsulated

counselors define everyone's reality according to their own cultural assumptions, minimize cultural differences, impose self-reference criteria in judging the behavior of others, ignore proof that disconfirms their perspective, depend on techniques and strategies to solve their problems, and disregard their own cultural biases in a "culturally encapsulated" perspective (Wrenn, 1962). We suggest that culturally encapsulated leaders are defined in the same way.

6. Survival. Contact with culturally different groups provides an opportunity to rehearse adaptive functioning for our own future survival in the global village. We know the future is so different that it is beyond our imagination, and we know that some of us will not survive because we will not be ready. By seeking out people and groups who do not think, dress, eat, play, work, or talk like ourselves and by learning to interact with people or groups who are different, we will learn the facility for our own survival in that beyond-imagination future.

7. Social Justice. Understanding social justice and moral development in a multicultural context helps us differentiate necessary absolutes from culturally relative principles. Social justice typically requires an inclusive rather than an exclusive perspective, and moral exclusion has consistently resulted in classifying society according to the oppressed and the oppressors (Opotow, 1990). Cultural relativism has failed because it prevents discussion of social justice across cultures. Cultural absolutism has also failed, because those who are in power are not always right. Multicultural awareness offers a more interactive and relational perspective.

8. Right-Thinking. A culture-centered perspective reflects the complementarity of the quantum metaphor of Niels Bohr (1950; that light may be regarded as a particle and sometimes as a wave at the same time so that both quantum and wave theories are necessary to explain the real nature of light). Emphasizing both the similarities and the differences between and among us creates a balance of opposites. Overemphasizing differences will erect barriers and lead to hostile disengagement. Overemphasizing similarities will result in a melting pot where the person or group that is in power will make the rules.

9. Personalized Learning. All learning and change involves some degree of culture shock to the degree that it influences our basic perspectives and much can be learned through the culture-shock of active learning that could not be learned in any other way. The really important things we have learned are not abstractions but are profoundly personal internalized changes in our lifestyle. Culture-shock provides a metaphorical model for education and the personalized learning process generally, recognizing and accepting the pain or discomfort and reframing the experience in a positive and lasting perspective.

10. Spirituality. A culture-centered perspective enhances our spiritual completeness by linking culturally different spiritual perspectives to the same

shared reality. In many cultures the only really important questions are the questions about where we came from before birth and where we are going after death. Even if one has an unshaken faith in a single religion, exposure to and awareness of other religious perspectives can be used to understand other cultures, as well as one's own, better.

11. Political Stability. A culture-centered perspective builds pluralism as an alternative to authoritarianism or anarchy in our social organization. However, pluralism has never really been tried successfully. We have not developed the skill, or perhaps the ultimate necessity, to survive with one another. With population growth, pollution, and rapid utilization of limited global resources we will be forced to make one of these three choices, and learning to live together will be much preferred to the alternatives.

12. Strengthening Leadership Theory. A culture-centered perspective will strengthen contemporary theories of leadership rather than weaken or displace them. The only reality we have is the one we learn to perceive through our senses, and the rules for perception are themselves culturally learned. By making culture central rather than marginal to our leadership theory of choice, that theory will function more effectively in a variety of different cultural contexts.

Culture Is Complex, Not Simple

Complexity is our friend and not our enemy because it protects us from accepting easy answers to hard questions. This process is most apparent in our use of scientific theories. In attempting to understand complexity we develop simplified models that can be explained and understood but that reflect only selected aspects of reality. Our embedded rationality requires that we construct simplified models of complex reality in order to explain things. If we behave rationally with regard to the model, we assume the behavior is appropriately explained in the real world. The danger is that we confuse simple explanations and labels with a more complex reality. There is a natural tendency to "keep things simple." We normally have little tolerance for the confusion of aggregate, mixed-up, unsorted, undifferentiated, unpredictable, and random data. We naturally move quickly to sort, order, and predict simplified patterns from the chaos (Triandis, 1975).

By perceiving the world from a narrow or rigid frame of reference, we ignore the complex reality around us through the illusion of simplicity. Theories of cognitive complexity suggest that people who are more cognitively complex are more capable than others of seeing these multiple perspectives. Research in adult development likewise suggests that cognitive complexity is related to broader and more advanced levels of development. Thus, leaders who are more cognitively complex are more likely to employ greater vision when developing strategic plans for their organization. They are also more likely to have a better understanding of the complex nature of culture and its many implications in the workplace.

Diversity is valuable. Science has long accepted genetic diversity as essential to the survival of a species. Some persons are able to tolerate complexity better than others. These people are either better at differentiating and perceiving several dimensions in a range of alternatives or at integrating and seeing complex connections between different sources. People who are more complex are able to see many different dimensions, classifications, theories, or alternatives to explain a situation. Because reality tends to be complex, those who are able to identify more alternatives are more likely to see correctly and make more appropriate decisions, although this process requires a high tolerance for ambiguity.

Culture's complexity is illustrated by the hundreds or perhaps even thousands of culturally learned identities, affiliations, and roles we each assume at one time or another. The dynamic nature of culture is demonstrated when one of those alternative cultural identities replaces another in salience. Complexity involves the identification of multiple perspectives within and between individuals.

Ten examples of how a complicated culture-centered perspective of leading can be more useful include the following:

1. Identify multiple but conflicting culturally learned viewpoints in the employee's context.

2. Identify multiple but conflicting culturally learned viewpoints within the individual employee.

3. Explain the actions of employees from their own cultural perspectives.

4. Listen for information about cultural patterns that can be shared at an appropriate time with the employee.

5. Learn to shift topics in culturally appropriate ways.

6. Reflect culturally appropriate feelings in specific and accurate feedback.

7. Identify culturally defined multiple support systems for the employee.

8. Identify alternative solutions and anticipate the consequences for each cultural context.

9. Identify culturally learned criteria being used by the employee to evaluate alternative solutions.

10. Generate accurate explanations for the employee's behavior from the employee's cultural context.

It is important to view the multicultural perspective of leadership as being applicable to all areas of leadership, and not as a special case or to be used in special circumstances only.

Culture Balance Is Dynamic, Not Static

Cognitive balance is a search for consistency in an otherwise volatile situation and has traditionally been achieved by changing, ignoring, differentiating, or transcending inconsistencies to avoid dissonance (Triandis, 1977). However, there are more complicated and even dissonant definitions of balance demonstrated through a tolerance for inconsistency and dissonance where differences are not resolved but are managed in a dynamic, ever-changing balance (Pedersen, 1988).

In many non-Westernized systems, there is less emphasis on separating the person from the presenting problem than in Western cultures. There is less tendency to locate the problem inside the isolated individual than to relate that individual's difficulty to other persons or even to the cosmos. Balance describes a condition of order and dynamic design in a context where all elements, pain as well as pleasure, serve a useful and necessary function. The non-Western emphasis is typically more holistic in acknowledging the reciprocal interaction of persons and environments in both their positive and negative aspects.

Success is achieved indirectly as a by-product of harmonious two-directional balance rather than directly through a more simplistic one-directional alternative. In a one-directional approach, the goal is to make people feel more pleasure, less pain; more happiness and less sadness; more positive and less negative. In the two-directional alternative the goal is to help people find meaning in both pleasure and pain; both happiness and sadness; both negative and positive experience. In the Judeo-Christian tradition, God not only tolerates the devil's presence but actually created demonic as well as angelic forces in a balance of alternatives.

The restoration of value balance provides an alternative goal to the more individualized goal of solving social problems. In the context of value balance, social change is perceived as a continuous and not episodic process, taking place independently both because of and despite our attempts to control that change. Value balance is a process rather than a conclusive event or events. In a similar mode, the problems, pain, and other negative aspects of education provide necessary resources for creating a dynamic value balance.

Balance as a construct for leading in a multicultural context involves the identification of different or even conflicting culturally learned perspectives without necessarily resolving that difference or dissonance in favor of either viewpoint. Healthy functioning in a multicultural or pluralistic context may require a person to simultaneously maintain multiple, conflicting, and culturally learned roles without the opportunity to resolve the resulting dissonance.

Ten examples of observable and potentially measurable leader behaviors demonstrate the elusive construct of dynamic and asymmetrical balance:

1. Identifying positive implications in a negative experience
2. Anticipating potentially negative implications from an otherwise positive experience
3. Integrating positive and negative events as part of a holistic perspective
4. Avoiding simplistic solutions to complex problems
5. Recognizing both the collectivistic and individualistic perspective in others
6. Adjusting for the follower's changing level of empowerment across topics and time
7. Avoiding stereotyping of others
8. Recognizing that the same person can change identity across that person's life-roles
9. Adjusting the influence of the leader to match the strengths and weaknesses of the follower
10. Maintaining harmony within interactions

Although the construct of dynamic balance is elusive, the preceding 10 examples of observable leader behaviors describe some of the essential aspects as applied to leading in a multicultural context.

The Dangers of Ignoring Culture

The tendency to depend on one authority, one theory, and one truth has been demonstrated to be extremely dangerous in the political setting. It is no less dangerous in an organizational context. Few business students make it through college without hearing about major marketing mistakes that have embarrassed companies and hurt sales when introducing a product in a new country. Often the misunderstanding is due to a problem of translation. As we will see, however, the legends that are widely cited as part of the challenge in marketing across cultures are often urban legends that cannot be confirmed or can be proven incorrect. For example, it is widely cited by diversity consultants and marketing experts that when Gerber began selling its baby food in Africa, it used the same packaging as was used in America, featuring a White baby on the label. Because products in Africa were typically packaged in containers reflecting the contents on the label, it is reported that African consumers were appalled because they assumed the jars contained ground-up babies. Representatives from Novartis Consumer Health, the maker of Gerber products, were unable to confirm or deny the story due to the length of time that has passed since they began marketing baby food in Africa (Johnson, 2004). However, Snopes.com, an online urban legends resource, suggests that, due to a lack of specifics, the story is suspect. No specific country or city in Africa is named, "as if the entire continent–from Tunisia to South Africa, from Senegal to Somalia–were home to a homogeneous mass of people, all of whom share a single culture and therefore all think and act alike." The site goes on to state,

> This tale is cultural prejudice at its worst; an apocryphal anecdote based on the premise of a whole society of illiterates who don't know what baby food is [and] are credulous enough to believe that someone would sell ground-up babies as food.

Another well-known story focuses on General Motors' introduction of the Chevy Nova in South America, which reportedly reflected weak sales. It is stated that GM failed to realize that "no va" means "it won't go" in Spanish and once discovered they quickly renamed the car Caribe in Spanish markets. According to urbanlegends.com, another Web site dedicated to researching urban legends, this is also an urban legend. This site suggests that the sales were reasonably good in Latin American markets and even though "no va" does mean "doesn't go" in Spanish, that "nova and no va don't sound alike and are unlikely to be confused, just as 'carpet' and 'car pet' are unlikely to be confused in English" (Johnson, 2004).

This is not to suggest, of course, that all stories relating to marketing across cultures are legends. There seem to be endless examples of marketing fiascos resulting from misunderstandings or ignoring culture that have caused problems for American companies. For example, an American TV commercial for deodorant flopped in Japan. The ad showed an octopus putting antiperspirant under each arm. However, it wasn't until after the ad ran that the Americans learned that in Japan, octopuses do not have eight arms, they have eight legs (Rosen, Digh, Singer, & Phillips, 2000). This example seems funny now, but you can be assured that when the company paying for the ad campaign realized that their investment was not going to produce many sales, a leader somewhere along the line was held accountable.

Obviously, leaders with an increased multicultural awareness, knowledge, and skill base are necessary to interact effectively with those who are different from themselves in both domestic and multinational companies. One of the most recognized names in the fast food industry provides an excellent example of organizations' need for multiculturally competent leaders. McDonald's recognizes the importance of valuing diversity:

> One of our guiding principles is that our restaurants should always be a reflection of the communities they serve—not only the individuals we employ and the culture and ethnicity of those communities, but also the employment practices. . . . While there may be some specific differences worldwide in local labor laws of employment practices, our philosophy is the same whether we're in Beijing or Budapest. . . . Our global perspective is that whatever market or country we're going into, we always employ the most positive people practices and exceed the expectations of our employees. (Solomon, 1996, p. 48)

Of course, McDonald's learned the hard way. When they opened restaurants in India, it is reported that it took them 13 months to realize that Hindus (who make up more than 85% of India's population) do not eat beef. When McDonald's starting making hamburgers out of lamb, sales skyrocketed. Today they serve beer in Germany, wine in France, and kosher beef just outside of Jerusalem (Rosen et al., 2000). More recently, when McDonald's proudly displayed several Middle Eastern flags on their bags to show the global nature of their restaurant, Muslims from Saudi Arabia were very offended. The Saudi Arabian flag has a quote from the Quran, and they were throwing away both their national flag and a passage from the Quran. There is now a law that makes it illegal to use the Saudi Arabian flag for advertising purposes and trademarks. Reflecting their sensitivity for the culture of Saudi Arabia, however, McDonald's has a restaurant there that has two dining rooms, one for men and one for women and children.

There are also examples of companies attempting to implement manufacturing techniques across cultures with unintended results. For example, General Motors recently implemented Japanese production techniques (Just-in-time [JIT] and *kanban*) throughout its expansive manufacturing system. In 1998, two plants were shut down due to strikes involving more than 9,200 workers. In just a few weeks, over 125 factories closed, putting more than 170,000 workers out of work in five countries. The direct and indirect costs of the strike to the U.S. GNP (gross national product) were estimated to be $2 billion per week of lost production (Holden, 2002a). The devastating loss cannot be blamed on not understanding the technical aspects of JIT and *kanban*, but on GM's failure to understand the culture of the systems in the society in which they evolved (Holden, 2002b). General Motors continues to struggle with cultural issues. In fall 2003, the Buick division embarrassed itself by not paying attention to the French Canadian culture and their local slang. Buick gave its new vehicle a name that, in the local slang, refers to masturbation (Lopez, 2003). However, in spite of the negative press that General Motors has gained based on cultural missteps, whether urban legends or not, their support and implementation of the Global Sullivan Principles and the ethical treatment for all people from all countries (see Chapter 1) shows that they are headed in the right direction.

Encapsulated leaders are trapped in one way of thinking that resists adaptation and rejects alternatives. By contrast, a broader definition guides leaders toward a more comprehensive understanding of alternatives and a more complete perspective of their individual beliefs. The broader inclusive perspective offers liberation to culturally encapsulated leaders. Leaders who ignore cultural differences risk being inconsistent.

There is a history of moral exclusion, when individuals or groups are perceived as nonentities, expendable, or undeserving (Opotow, 1990). This exclusionary perspective has been described as a form of encapsulation. Wrenn (1962, 1985) first introduced the concept of cultural encapsulation in the counseling field; however, this perspective is just as valid for leaders as it is for counselors. This perspective assumes five basic identifying features. First, we define reality according to one set of cultural assumptions and stereotypes, which becomes more important than the real world. Second, we become insensitive to cultural variations among individuals and assume that our view is the only real or legitimate one. Third, each of us has unreasoned assumptions, which we accept without proof and that we protect without regard to rationality. Fourth, a technique-oriented job definition further contributes toward and preserves the encapsulation. Fifth, when there is no evaluation of other viewpoints, there is no responsibility to accommodate or interpret the behavior of others except from the viewpoint of a self-referenced criterion.

Defining culture broadly rather than narrowly helps avoid the problems of encapsulation. First, the broad definition allows and forces leaders to be more accurate in matching followers' intended and culturally learned expectation with their behavior. Second, a broad definition helps leaders become more aware of how their own culturally learned perspective predisposes them toward a particular decision outcome. Third, a broad perspective helps leaders become more aware of the complexity in cultural identity patterns, which may or may not include the obvious indicators of ethnicity and nationality. Fourth, the broad definition encourages leaders to track the ever-changing salience of a follower's different interchangeable cultural identities within an interaction.

White Privilege Is Real

It is sometimes difficult for the dominant culture to recognize the privileges that come with membership. It is easy to assume that everyone is on the same level playing field from the perspective of advantage. Many of the opponents of affirmative action take this perspective, saying affirmative action is at best unnecessary and at worst a racist policy. The Multi-City Study of Urban Inequality completed a 5-year study of Boston, Atlanta, Detroit, and Los Angeles, sponsored by the Russell Sage Foundation and the Harvard University Multidisciplinary

Program in Inequality and Social Policy (O'Connor, 2001). In this 5-year study, 50 researchers interviewed 9,000 households and 3,500 employers. They found that race is deeply embedded in the cultural landscape of the United States and that racial stereotypes and attitudes heavily influence the racial inequality in the labor market. This suggests that White privilege is real.

White privilege refers to the invisible systems that confer dominance on Whites (McIntosh, 1989) through being socialized in a racist society, even though none of them may have chosen to be racist or biased or prejudiced. There is a need to accept responsibility for the consequences of White privilege, however unintentional it may be, and to understand the anger that might well be a consequence of not having that privilege. Peggy McIntosh (1988/2002) has developed specific examples illustrating White privilege in a list of 46 statements about ordinary decisions of daily life that can be routinely done by a member of the dominant culture, but not as easily done by a member of a minority culture. Examples include, "My culture gives me little fear about ignoring the perspectives and powers of people of other races," "I can avoid spending time with people whom I was trained to mistrust and who have learned to mistrust my kind or me," "If I have low credibility as a leader I can be sure that my race is not the problem." "White priviledge, recognized or not, will influence workplace relations."

Conclusion

The development of multicultural awareness begins with an awareness of culturally learned assumptions. The assumptions highlighted in this chapter are the following:

1. Multicultural perspectives emphasize each group's similarities and differences at the same time

2. Multicultural perspectives are necessarily complex

3. Multicultural perspectives are dynamic for each person, place, and time

The inclusive multicultural perspective of emphasizing both similarities and differences has inhibited research on multicultural aspects of leading because our measures of culture are currently inadequate. It is easier to ignore culture or to limit the cultural perspective to either similarities or differences. Breaking this first rule of multiculturalism has resulted in false and inadequate/incomplete choices. The controversy over "political correctness" reflects the inadequacy of this false dichotomy where both sides of the argument are wrong. The argument supporting an objectively "correct" view of each culture rightly protects the unique and different perspectives of each cultural group against insult but wrongly presumes that culture is defined by these objective guidelines. The argument against political correctness rightly emphasizes the need to find common ground across cultures but wrongly presumes that cultural differences are unimportant.

Borrowing from the counseling literature, in order to escape from what Wrenn (1985) calls cultural encapsulation, leaders need to challenge the cultural bias of their own untested criteria. To leave our assumptions untested or, worse yet, to be unaware of our culturally learned assumptions, is not consistent with the standards of effective leadership.

CHAPTER 2 DISCUSSION QUESTIONS

1. How can organizations encourage leaders not to rely solely on a self-reference criterion when making strategic decisions?

2. What are some previously unexamined reasonable opposites that have influenced your thinking?

3. Do you believe that applicants failing to declare a race on university admissions forms are making a statement, and if so, how do you interpret that statement?

4. How do leaders avoid overemphasizing differences and overemphasizing similarities at the same time?

5. How can leaders encourage their employees to have a multicultural perspective at all times, and not just during a diversity training workshop or some other specific situation?

Critical Incident: Is It White Privilege?

"How dare she!" Jane was furious with her colleague Linda. "How dare she accuse me of sticking my head in the sand on the issue of White privilege," Jane said to her friend Paul. Jane, a Caucasian, and Linda, an African American, had been colleagues and friends ever since they were hired as entry-level managers 8 years earlier. They have both followed the same promotional path and have treated each other as confidants, or so Jane thought. This is the first time the issue of race has come up, and it has blindsided Jane. She has no idea why Linda would bring up race in such a negative way now. "What were the two of you talking about?" Paul asked. "Nothing much," said Jane. "Linda and I were brainstorming on how we could work in an extra meeting for our teams and she suggested we have a luncheon meeting. I just mentioned that I thought that it was weird that all African Americans eat together in the cafeteria. I didn't mean anything by it, I was just making an observation, but Linda abruptly stood up and as she left the room she angrily said that I wouldn't know White privilege if it bit me in the rear and I think I heard her mumble something about racism. How could she call me a racist after eight years of friendship. That's ridiculous!" "What are you going to do about it?" Paul asked. "I don't know," Jane replied. "I want to talk with her about it, but I don't know if she wants to be alone, or if she was mad about something else, but all I know is that I saw a side to her that I had never seen before."

CRITICAL INCIDENT DISCUSSION QUESTIONS

1. Why do you think Linda reacted so negatively to Jane's comment?

2. Should Jane bring up Linda's comment the next time they see each other, or should she let Linda be the one to bring it up?

Exercise 2: The Test of Reasonable Opposites

OBJECTIVE

To challenge one's prevailing culturally learned assumptions

DESCRIPTION

This activity provides an opportunity to challenge culturally learned assumptions about a topic or issue and to evaluate the opposite view as possibly as rational as what you have always believed. It is difficult to get beyond our culturally learned assumptions because they are pervasive.

Time required: 30 minutes or less

Risk/expertise level: Higher

Participants needed: Any number of participants and one facilitator

PROCEDURE

1. Ask participants to identify a culturally learned assumption that they suspect to be true.

2. Ask them to identify an alternative position that would reverse that assumption and provide an "opposite" position.

3. Ask them to compare the two statements to see which alternative is more "reasonable."

4. Some examples of opposites might be:

    Differences are important versus similarities are important

    Employees should follow current procedures versus employees should be creative

5. The facilitator then leads a debriefing discussion.

DEBRIEFING

Assumptions are usually so fuzzy that it is hard to find an opposite to what you assume.

Once an opposite truth statement has been generated it is often as reasonable as the original statement. The test of reasonable opposites forces one to generate new and creative alternatives that would never have been considered. Some discussion questions may include the following:

1. Were you able to find the opposite of something you always believed to be true?

2. What makes an idea reasonable?

3. What are the implications of two opposites both being reasonable?

4. Is our thinking nonrational?

5. Might two people from different countries disagree without either one being "wrong"?

INSIGHT

We need to escape from our own self-reference criteria to see other cultural perspectives.

SOURCE: Pedersen, P. B. (2004). *110 experiences for multicultural learning.* Washington, DC: American Psychological Association Press.

3

Cultural Frameworks and Their Importance for Leaders

Major Objective

To identify and describe models of culture and their relationship to leader actions in the workplace

Secondary Objectives

1. To identify several models of the various dimensions of culture

2. To discuss intercultural sensitivity

3. To outline a three-stage developmental sequence for developing multi-cultural awareness, knowledge, and skills

---

Culture has been defined as the source of ties that bind members of societies through an elusive "socially constructed constellation consisting of such things as practices, competencies, ideas, schemas, symbols, values, norms, institutions, goals, constitutive rules, artifacts, and modifications of the physical environment" (Fiske, 2002, p. 85). These internalized rules create traditions that often go deeper than reason (Stuart, 2004). Using Kelly's (1955) terms, cultural orientation could be thought of as the master plan behind superordinating constructs that covertly influence manifest cognitive content.

> Because much of the strength of cultural influences stems from the fact that they operate in the background of behavior at the value, linguistic, and construct levels, people often have difficulty defining their cultural influences, and social scientists have difficulty measuring them. (Stuart, 2004, p. 4)

This chapter identifies several models of culture before introducing the three-stage developmental sequence that will be used as the foundation for the rest of the book.

Leaders and Culture

The culture that we are embedded in inevitably influences our views about leadership (Hofstede, 1993). To make sense of the different types of cultural influence, Gardenswartz, Rowe, Digh, and Bennett (2003) developed the three cultures model, which posits three cultural influences at work in corporations: personal culture, national culture, and organizational culture. They state that the model is based on work in global corporations, but it is our premise that it captures cultural influences in both global and non-global corporations.

Personal culture is the shared combination of an individual's traits, skills, and personality formed within the context of his or her ethnic, racial, familial, and educational environments. Every one has a unique personal culture.

National culture is a shared understanding that comes from the combination of beliefs, values, attitudes, and behaviors that have provided the foundation for the heritage of a country. Although national culture is a shared understanding, as is well known, individuals within a nation still have a very wide range of beliefs about their nation.

Corporate culture is a combination of widely shared institutional beliefs, values, and the organization's guiding philosophy that is usually stated in its vision, mission, and values statements (Gardenswartz et al., 2003). Similar to national culture, individuals within an organization often view their organization differently. These varying views often align themselves with individuals' levels within the company hierarchy. This results in leaders often having different views about their corporate culture compared to those in the lower levels in the organization. Keeping in touch with how these views differ is an important part of every leader's job.

For interactions within organizations, culture is a mix of personal, national, and corporate culture. The focus of this book is on the personal culture that has developed within the national culture that takes place within the corporate culture. Culture is not external but is "within the person"; it is not separate from other learned competencies. Developing multicultural awareness, knowledge, and skills should be seen as a professional obligation as well as an opportunity for a leader. With the millions of employees living and working in diverse environments, there are abundant opportunities for enhancing multicultural awareness, knowledge, and skills. People who live in an unfamiliar culture are likely to become more multicultural in their awareness of alternative values, habits, customs, and lifestyles that were initially strange and unfamiliar. Sometimes they have learned to adjust even more profoundly and effectively than they themselves realize. They have learned to respond in unique ways to previously unfamiliar situations and come up with the right answers without always being aware of their own adjustment process. Again, as stated earlier, given demographic changes, understanding culture has great implications both domestically and internationally.

Seminal Work on Culture

Differences in culture can significantly affect leadership practices. One of the earliest identifications of the dimensions of culture was developed by Kluckhohn and Strodtbeck (1961).

- Basic nature of human beings: Good—left to their own devices, individuals are basically good and will act in a reasonable and responsible manner; Evil—individuals are basically evil and are not to be trusted; Mixed—individuals are a mixture of good and evil.

- Relationships among people: Individualistic—the primary responsibility of an individual is to him- or herself. Individual abilities and characteristics are the primary consideration; Group—responsibility to family and groups is most important. Ability to fit into the group is more important than individual ability; Hierarchical—Similar to the group orientation with the addition that distinct differences in status are expected and respected.

- Activity orientation: Being—the point of life is to live and experience an understanding. Activity for activity's sake is unimportant. Doing—the point of life is actually to do things, be involved, and accomplish goals.

- Relation to nature: Subjugation—nature and the environment determine human activities; Harmony—humans should live in harmony with their environment; Domination—Humans can exert domination over their environment while they control their own destinies.

• Time orientation: Past—history is important in determining our present actions; Present—the current situation should determine what we do as we focus our energy on the present; Future—our actions should concentrate on the future and the attainment of future goals.

The power of national cultures can also be understood by examining seminal research conducted by Geert Hofstede (1984, 1985, 2001). Hofstede conducted research on IBM employees in 40 countries and discovered that cultural values strongly influenced relationships both within and between organizational divisions. Four of the significant cultural dimensions that Hofstede defined have been examined by many researchers. Understanding the way these dimensions influence culture is of increasing importance for both global leaders and those managing a diverse workforce.

• Power Distance refers to whether individuals accept inequality in power, including within an organization. Low power distance means individuals expect equality in power and do not accept a leader's authority just because of the leader's position.

• Uncertainty Avoidance refers to the feeling of comfort or discomfort associated with levels of uncertainty and ambiguity. Low uncertainty avoidance means that individuals easily tolerate unstructured and unpredictable situations.

• Individualism and Collectivism refer to the social frameworks in which individuals prioritize individual or group needs. In individualistic societies, individuals are expected to take care of themselves; in collectivistic societies, individuals are expected to look out for one another, and organizations protect their employees' interests.

• Masculinity and Femininity refer to the emphasis a culture places on emotional and social roles and work goals. A masculine culture reflects a preference for assertiveness, achievement, and material success. A feminine culture values relationships, cooperation, and quality of life. Despite the label for this dimension, both men and women subscribe to the dominant value, whether it is masculine or feminine.

Additional Important Research Related to Culture

It must be noted that although Hofstede's landmark work is widely cited, it also has its critics (see Dickson, Hanges, & Lord, 2001, for a review of literature defining culture, including a section on criticisms of Hofstede's work). In addition to the work done by Hofstede, many other influences on behavior have been classified. Trompenaars and Hampden-Turner (1998) also focus on cultural differences and how they affect business and management. They present data from more than 30,000 participants of training programs and describe seven dimensions of cultural difference:

- Universalism versus Particularism: In a Universalist culture, rules are more important than relationships; legal contracts are drawn up and are seen as trustworthy, you must honor them; In a Particularist culture, whether a rule applies "depends" on the situation and relationships evolve.

- Individualism versus Communitarianism: Essentially the same as Hofstede's Individualism versus Collectivism dimension.

- Neutral versus Affective (Emotional): Individuals in a Neutral culture hide their thoughts and feelings while maintaining a cool self-control. Speech is often monotone, and individuals do not touch each other. In an Affective culture, individuals express their thoughts openly while using gestures and dramatic expressions. There is often a great deal of passion in discussions, and individuals often touch.

- Specific versus Diffuse: In Specific cultures, individuals are direct, clear, blunt, and to the point while examining the facts. In Diffuse cultures, individuals are more indirect and tactful. The context of a situation matters, and they tolerate ambiguity.

- Achievement versus Ascription: In Achievement-oriented societies, there is little focus on titles, which are used only when they reflect competencies. Leaders are judged on what they do and know. In Ascribed-status societies, titles are important; the boss is the boss, regardless of the situation. Leaders with authority are usually older males.

- Attitudes toward time: Past versus Present versus Future—Essentially the same as Kluckhohn and Strodtbeck's time orientation dimension.

- Internal versus External control: Essentially the same as Kluckhohn and Strodtbeck's subjugation and domination orientations in the sense of being able or not being able to control what happens in the environment.

Ten distinct types of motivational values have been derived from the universal requirements of human existence and verified in cross-cultural research by Schwartz (1992) and colleagues (e.g., Sagiv & Schwartz, 1995; Schwartz & Bilsky, 1987, 1990; Schwartz & Huismans, 1995; Schwartz & Sagiv, 1995).

The 10 types of motivational values are as follows:

Power: Social status and prestige, dominance or control over people and resources

Achievement: Demonstrating competence according to social standards

Stimulation: Challenge, excitement, and novelty in life

Self-Direction: Independent thought and action

Hedonism: Pleasure and sensuous gratification for oneself

Security: Harmony, stability, and safety of society, relationships, and self

Conformity: Restraining actions or impulses that would likely upset or harm others and violate social expectations

Tradition: Commitment, respect, and acceptance of the ideas and customs that traditional culture and religion provide

Benevolence: Preserving and enhancing the welfare of all people with whom one is frequently in contact

Universalism: Being broadminded and having an appreciation, understanding, and tolerance for the welfare of all people and for nature

Understanding values is important in cross-cultural interactions. Research has shown that personal values accounted for a large proportion of individual variation in readiness for contact with others from a different group (Sagiv & Schwartz, 1995).

Ronen and Shenkar (1985) clustered countries based on patterns of similarity in employees' attitudes toward work and how well it met their needs. Eight country clusters, with four countries remaining independent of any cluster, were identified. The clusters include Near Eastern, Arab, Far Eastern, Latin American, Latin European, Anglo, Germanic, and Nordic. As an example, the Anglo cluster is made up of the United States, Canada, Australia, New Zealand, the United Kingdom, Ireland, and South Africa. The four independent countries are Brazil, Japan, India, and Israel, which have unique religions, languages, and/or histories. Cluster classifications were made after a comprehensive review of previous research that included assessments of how thousands of employees in close to 50 countries responded to questions about the importance of various work goals, the extent to which work satisfies certain needs, organizational and managerial issues, and the nature of work roles and interpersonal relationships (e.g., how well managers relate to subordinates).

Although there are limitations to Ronen and Shenkar's approach (many countries are not included), leaders can use the clusters to determine where broad similarities and differences of values and attitudes may exist between the countries that are listed. Because business practices often reflect values and attitudes, this can help leaders to be more effective in their interaction with those from cultures not similar to their own.

GLOBE Research

Perhaps the most comprehensive research conducted to date on national cultural dimensions has been made available by the GLOBE (Global Leadership and Organizational Behavior Effectiveness) Project Team. This project team is made up of 170 researchers who collected data over 7 years on cultural values, practices, and leadership attributes from 18,000 managers in 62 countries representing a wide variety of industries and organizational sizes. The GLOBE team identified nine cultural dimensions distinguishing one society from another and having implications for managers (Javidan & House, 2001). Four of the GLOBE dimensions identified (Uncertainty avoidance, Power distance, Institutional collectivism vs. individualism, In-group collectivism) overlap with Hofstede's dimensions and are described above.

Five GLOBE dimensions are different from Hofstede's dimensions:

- Assertiveness, which refers to the extent a society encourages individuals to be tough, confrontational, assertive, and competitive versus modest and tender. Germany and Austria are highly assertive countries that value competition compared to New Zealand and Sweden, which value warm and cooperative relations and harmony.

- Future orientation, which refers to the level of importance a society attaches to future-oriented behaviors such as planning, investing, and delaying gratification. Singapore and Switzerland scored high on this dimension, signifying their propensity to save for the future and have a longer time horizon for decision making. This is compared to Russia and Argentina, which tend to have a shorter time horizon for decisions and place more emphasis on instant gratification.

- Performance orientation, which measures the degree to which a society encourages and rewards group members for performance improvement and excellence. Singapore, Hong Kong, and the United States score high on this dimension. This reflects the value of training and development and initiative taking along with a preference for a direct and explicit style of communication. Countries like Russia, Italy, and Argentina scored low on this dimension, reflecting an emphasis on loyalty and belonging. More value is placed on one's family and background as opposed to performance. Feedback is often viewed as discomforting for individuals from low performance orientation countries.

- Humane orientation, which is the extent to which a society encourages and rewards people for being fair, caring, generous, altruistic, and kind. The Philippines, Ireland, Malaysia, and Egypt scored highest on this dimension, reflecting a focus on sympathy and support for the weak. Spain, France, and the former West Germany scored lowest on this dimension reflecting more importance given to power, material possessions, and self-enhancement.

- Gender differentiation, which refers to the extent to which a society maximizes gender role differences. Hungary, Poland, and Denmark report the least amount of gender-differentiated practices, meaning that women have a higher status and role in decision making. Men and women in low gender-differentiated cultures tend to have the same amount of education, and a higher percentage of women are in positions of authority compared to countries scoring high on this dimension, such as South Korea, Egypt, and China, where more men tend to have higher social status and few women hold positions of authority.

Research cannot pinpoint which cultural dimensions are most important for leadership behavior. Triandis (1993) suggests that Individualism/Collectivism may be one of the most important dimensions of cultural variation. Collectivist cultures would expect successful leaders to be supportive and paternalistic, whereas individualist cultures would more likely value an achievement orientation and participative leadership. It has also been suggested that power distance is particularly important for leaders (Dorfman, 2004). In low power distance cultures, subordinates expect to be consulted, while in high power distance cultures, subordinates expect leaders to act more direct and autocratic.

Research results from Hofstede and GLOBE can be very helpful to leaders in multicultural interactions. For example, it may be inappropriate to train leaders in very high power distance cultures to use participative decision making, since the leaders in these countries are supposed to have all the answers. By inviting subordinates to become involved, the leader may be viewed as weak and incompetent. In addition, in cultures with a long-term time orientation, subordinates may be more likely to accept development plans that have a longer time frame compared to those in short-term time orientation cultures. By developing awareness and anticipating cultural similarities and differences, leaders can develop the knowledge, skills, and behaviors necessary to interact with dissimilar others in a way that leads to mutual appreciation. This type of appreciation can lead to a more productive and enjoyable work setting.

Leader behaviors that lead to beneficial results in one culture do not necessarily lead to positive results in another culture. For example, one of the first things Robert Eckert, CEO of Mattel, did when he started his job was to meet with employees in the cafeteria. He did this to build trust into the relationships with employees. This makes sense in a low power distance culture like the United States, but in a high power distance culture like Malaysia, this behavior would likely weaken the relationship between employees and their leader.

Culture and Context

Hall (1976) argues that cultures vary in terms of how contextual information is viewed and interpreted. The context of a situation is crucial to communication, often heavily influencing not only what is said and how it is said, but more important, how the information is perceived. Although the need for context in understanding information is universal, Hall states that some cultures rely more heavily on context in their perceptions and interactions with others. In high context cultures, such as China, Korea, Japan, France, Greece, and many Arab countries, what is unsaid but understood carries more weight than what is actually written down or said. In addition, trust is relied upon during negotiations and agreements, and personal relations are often a central part of the interaction. In low context cultures, such as the American, Scandinavian, German, and Swiss, the focus is on the specifics of what is written or said, and trust is gained through legal agreements. Handshakes, while often given, are not sufficient to establish a contractual agreement, and personal relationships detract from business.

Hall argues that many cross-cultural problems can be understood by examining differences in how context is viewed. Leaders would be well advised to consider context in their interactions with those from a culture with a different context. Consider the experiences of a French manager working in a German company and a German manager working in a French company. After one year the German manager was let go because of alleged performance deficiencies. The German was taken by surprise because no one had told him what was expected in terms of performance. The French manager resigned from the German company because of frustration over constantly being told what to do, which threatened both his pride and his intelligence (McFarlin & Sweeney, 2003). Obviously context must be a consideration in all business dealings with those from cultures that differ on this important construct.

Developing Intercultural Sensitivity

The developmental model of intercultural sensitivity (DMIS) was created as a theoretical framework to explain the reactions of people to cultural differences (Bennett, 1986, 1993b). There are six orientations. The first three are more ethnocentric, which means that one's own culture is experienced as central to reality, while the later three are viewed as more ethnorelative, which means one's own culture is experienced in the context of other cultures (Hammer, Bennett, & Wiseman, 2003).

ETHNOCENTRIC STAGES

Denial of Differences: One's own culture is experienced as the only real one. There is no recognition of cultural differences unless a difference is seen as impinging on him or her, in which case he or she acts aggressively to eliminate the difference. In an extreme form of Denial, those who are different are only seen as tolerable or exploitable and are usually dehumanized.

Defense Against Difference (Reversal): In this stage, one's own culture is experienced as the only viable one. Other cultures are viewed negatively. The level of threat felt from other cultures is higher than that found in the Denial stage because other cultures are recognized and the perspective is "Us" versus "Them." A variation of this stage is Reversal, where an adopted culture is viewed as superior to one's primary culture. Reversal is similar to Defense because it also polarizes the worldview to Us versus Them; however, it does not view the other culture as a threat.

Minimization of Differences: This stage represents the acceptance of superficial cultural differences. People are viewed as similar biologically (physical universalism) and/or religiously, economically, or philosophically (transcendent universalism). Universal absolutes may obscure deeper cultural differences, trivializing or romanticizing other cultures. For those from dominant cultures, minimization tends to mask recognition of their own culture and the institutional privilege that it often provides to its members.

ETHNORELATIVE STAGES

Acceptance of Difference: This stage represents the view that one's own culture is experienced as just one of a number of equally viable alternatives. Those from different cultures are viewed as different, but equal. Cultural relativity marks this stage.

Adaptation to Difference: Here we begin to develop communication skills that allow us to interact with those who are culturally different from ourselves. Individuals at this stage have empathy, which allows them to take the perspective of those from other cultures. This stage represents those who can shift their frame of reference to understand and be understood across cultures.

Integration of Difference: This stage is represented by an internalization of bicultural or multicultural frames of reference. Individuals construe their identities at the margins of two or more cultures. Bennett (1993a) suggests that cultural marginality may have two forms: an encapsulated form, where alienation is experienced as part of the separation; and a constructive form, where movements through different cultures are a positive part of one's identity. Hammer et al. (2003) point out that Integration is not necessarily better than Adaptation in situations that demand multicultural competence, though it describes a growing number of individuals.

It is often stated that knowledge is power. If leaders understand their own intercultural sensitivity, they can use this information as a point of reference as they assess their own multicultural awareness.

Cognitive, Affective, and Behavioral Components

In learning to interact with those from a wide variety of cultures, leaders can find a very rich pool of information in the area of intercultural communication. The field of intercultural communication has seen a proliferation of theories, research methods, and training models (Milhouse, 1996). An important issue that frequently comes up in the teaching of intercultural communication is how best to present the material and address learning goals. It has been recommended that instructors use a combination of cognitive, affective, and behavioral components of teaching and learning goals (Gudykunst, Ting-Toomey, & Wiseman, 1991). Cognitive goals focus primarily on understanding how communication is both different and similar across cultures. Affective goals focus on the motivation to communicate with others from different cultures and on issues of sensitivity. Behavioral goals relate to actually obtaining the skills necessary to communicate with people from other cultures (Gudykunst et al., 1991).

Cognitive, affective, and behavioral attitudes have also been proposed as three components that effect attitudes toward change (Dunham, Grube, Gardner, Cummings, & Pierce, 1989). It is often asked which attitude is most important or which one should come first (Rashid, Sambasivan, & Rahman, 2003). Given that information gathered during the cognitive stage is used to form feelings and actions, it makes sense that cognitive attitudes set the stage for affective and behavioral attitudes. Although the cognitive-affective-behavioral framework is a popular three-pronged model within intercultural communication, it is not the only three-stage framework. Below, we present a three-stage developmental sequence that can be used by leaders who desire to enhance their ability to interact with individuals from all cultures.

A Three-Stage Developmental Sequence

At this point, we introduce the three-stage developmental sequence that provides the foundation for developing multicultural awareness, knowledge, and skills that is presented throughout this book. As Bhawuk and Brislin (1992) suggest, "To be effective in another culture, people must be interested in other cultures, be sensitive enough to notice cultural differences, and then also be willing to modify their behavior as an indication of respect for the people of other cultures" (p. 46). Given the impact that diversity and culture play for leaders, their decision making, and their relationships, the three-stage developmental sequence we describe moves from multicultural awareness to knowledge/comprehension to skill/applications. This process will guide leaders to competency without diminishing the ambiguous and dynamic complexity of diversity and cultures. First, auditing the assumptions being made by leaders and increasing the level of cultural self-awareness by both the leaders and those being led challenges culturally encapsulated conventions about management. Second, documenting facts and knowledge for increased comprehension is essential to meaningful understanding of how to present a problem in its cultural context and will provide or construct a receptive site for research, training, and direct intervention. Third, generating appropriate intervention skills for bringing about suitable and effective change will match the skill to the cultural context. The same shared values and expectations—common ground—may be expressed differently in each cultural context. By developing multicultural awareness, the leader is able to interpret employee or customer behavior in the cultural context where that behavior was learned and is displayed.

The three-stage developmental sequence of awareness, knowledge, and skills is based on work done by Sue and colleagues (1982) to develop interculturally skilled counselors. As will be evident, however, there are many relevant aspects of this framework that apply directly to the role that leaders must play within their companies. As part of this process, multicultural training programs that had failed were examined. Programs seemed to fail for three reasons. The first reason for failure was a program's overemphasis on awareness to the point that participants were sick and tired of being made aware of cultural bias in an effort that seemed nonproductive as an end in itself. The second reason for failure was a program's overemphasis on knowledge, facts, and information to the point that participants—lacking awareness and skill—could not see how all that information was relevant. The third reason for failure was a program's jumping directly to teaching skills, but the participants—lacking awareness and knowledge—could not tell if their skills were making things better or worse! For that reason this three-stage developmental sequence from awareness to knowledge to skill was developed as an evaluation framework (Pedersen, 1981).

Much training skips over the primary stage of developing multicultural awareness about our underlying assumptions. It is difficult to know the culture of others until and unless we have an awareness of our own culturally learned assumptions as they control our life. We dare not assume that we, or those within our fields, have already achieved a high level of cultural self-awareness because this is an ongoing incomplete developmental process. The importance of these unexamined underlying assumptions is frequently underestimated. Once we have achieved some degree of self-awareness, both as we perceive ourselves and as we are perceived by others, it is appropriate to move to the second level.

The second level involves accumulating information that will result in comprehension. Increased awareness will help us ask the right questions about the facts and information we will need. Increased awareness will also help us find the similarities and differences between and among the populations being led. Once we have accomplished both cultural self-awareness and accumulated the facts, information, and knowledge necessary to that comprehension, we are ready to identify the appropriate skills we will need.

The third level involves developing culturally appropriate skills. A skill that is appropriate in one culture may be completely inappropriate in another culture. Because every test and theory was developed in a specific cultural context, it is likely to reflect assumptions implicit in that context and, to a greater or lesser extent, be biased. Culture-centered skill is the ability to use data from culturally biased tests or theories and still apply them appropriately, meaningfully, and helpfully in a variety of different cultural contexts.

This book reviews the development of multicultural awareness, knowledge, and skills and applies them to the critical role that leaders fulfill within their diverse and multicultural firms every day. Readers—whether leaders or business students who are our future leaders—should benefit from this development in two ways. First, reviewing the influence of their own multicultural identity will help readers to better understand their own constantly changing viewpoint, and, second, they will be able to anticipate the right questions to ask as they adapt their lifestyle to multicultural alternatives.

Conclusion

The numbers of different country and cultural classifications available may create an overwhelming feeling of confusion about which one is "right." Instead of feeling overwhelmed, leaders who know that culture influences the assumptions that individuals have as to what makes an effective leader should embrace the various aspects of culture as opportunities to educate themselves on the many dimensions of culture and what they mean for leaders in a multicultural environment. Multicultural development, as presented in this book, is a continuous learning process based on the three stages of development. The AWARENESS stage emphasizes assumptions about cultural differences and similarities in behavior, attitudes, and values. Increased awareness provides more freedom of choice to those who become more aware of their own multiculturalism. The KNOWLEDGE stage expands the amount of facts and information about culturally learned assumptions. The SKILLS stage applies effective and efficient action with people of different cultures based on the participants' clarified assumptions and accurate knowledge. Leaders need to be trained in awareness, knowledge, and skills to develop multicultural competency.

CHAPTER 3 DISCUSSION QUESTIONS

1. Is understanding cultural dimensions as important for leaders of domestic companies as it is for leaders of multinational firms? Why or why not?

2. Should differences in culture affect leadership practices?

3. The three cultures model posits three cultural influences at work in corporations. What contextual factors do you believe influence which cultural influence—personal, national, or corporate—has the strongest impact on behavior?

4. Although many different cultural dimensions were presented, are there any work-related goals in your field that could be considered universal? What is the most important work-related goal that differs by culture?

5. Should research on determining the dimensions of culture continue or should research shift its focus?

Critical Incident: Whose Holiday Is It, Anyway?

As a leader in a large Southeastern insurance company, you find yourself in the middle of a tense situation. Two years ago, the traditional yuletide decorations put up annually in your department were considered insensitive to the values of non-Christian employees. As far as you could tell, none of your employees complained, but a human resource manager said that out of respect for all religions, no holiday-related decorations should be put up if they didn't reflect all cultures. Last year, employees thought they had addressed the problem by putting up traditional Christmas decorations, along with a menorah and Kwanzaa-related decorations. Although they had not complained earlier, several Jewish employees explained that the menorah was a private symbol, and it was not intended for public display in an office lobby. All of the holiday decorations were ordered removed and several of your employees complained that the Grinch was alive and well in your company. You began to notice that divisions that had not existed earlier among your employees began to develop along religious lines, and you felt that overall performance levels were falling because of the conflict. This year you quietly tried to sidestep the entire holiday fiasco by telling your administrative assistant not to put up any decorations and not to mention it to anyone. However, a Hispanic group of employees noticed the absence of Christmas decorations and asked your assistant why there weren't any since no one had specifically complained about the tree in the past. Your assistant told them that it was your decision, and they filed a grievance claiming that their cultural values required that they be allowed to put up a tree with decorations.

CRITICAL INCIDENT DISCUSSION QUESTIONS

1. With no initial complaints, was it appropriate to remove the Christmas decorations in the first place?

2. What was the correct action in response to the Jewish employees who objected to the menorah being displayed publicly?

3. How should you address the resulting conflicts between religious groups in your organization?

4. What is the best response to the grievance filed by the group of Hispanic employees?

Exercise 3: Describing Cultural Identity

OBJECTIVE

To identify the complex culturally learned roles and perspectives that contribute to an individual's identity

DESCRIPTION

Participants are instructed to identify several of their personal identity groups affiliated with different cultures or social groups. Through this activity participants will become more aware of their multiple and simultaneous memberships in different cultural groups.

Time required: 30 minutes or less

Risk/expertise level: Moderate

Participants needed: Any number of participants plus one facilitator

PROCEDURE

1. In the blanks below, ask participants to please write answers to the simple question: "Who are you?" Participants should give as many answers as they can think of.

2. Ask participants to write the answers in the order that they occur to them.

3. Allow 7 minutes for them to complete the list.

4. Gather participants in small groups to discuss and compare their responses.

DEBRIEFING

1. If you had the time, would you be able to list a larger number of identities for yourself?

2. Which identities were most important to you?

3. How can these multiple identities be helpful to you?

4. Are all these identities equally strong for you?

5. Is there a maximum number of identities for an individual?

INSIGHT

Each of us belongs to many different, potentially salient cultural identities at the same time.

EXHIBIT

Identity list indicating the cultural roles of the participant:

I am _____

I am _____

I am _____

I am _____

I am _____

I am _____

I am _____

I am _____

I am _____

I am _____

(etc.)

SOURCE: Adapted with permission from Pedersen, P. (1997a). *Culture-centered counseling interventions* (pp. 25–26). Thousand Oaks, CA: Sage.

4

Where Does One Start on the Journey to Multicultural Awareness, Knowledge, and Skills?

◆

Major Objective

To provide a foundation for leaders to examine their own multicultural awareness, knowledge, and skills

Secondary Objectives

1. To discuss identity models and why they are important for leaders

2. To describe different types of intelligences

3. To identify different learning styles

4. To discuss Gagne's theory of instruction

◆

I n terms of the demographic makeup of leaders, the numbers are changing: According to *Fortune,* people of color make up 19% of boardrooms versus 18% in 2002 and 11% in 2001; currently, 26% of managers and officials are minorities, an increase from 24% in 2002 and up more than 50% compared to 1998 (Hickman, Tkaczyk, Florian, & Stemple, 2003). However, it is still a statistical fact that the majority of leaders in the United States are White and male. Becoming familiar with ethnic identity models can provide a foundation for building an awareness of multiculturalism, since racial or ethnic identity is seen as a precursor to awareness. However, as we discuss ethnic identity models, we must acknowledge that every individual belongs to multiple groups—nation, region, gender, religion, age, and occupation, for example—each of which exerts a different cultural influence that may be congruent, complementary, or may conflict with any of the others (Stuart, 2004). Research has shown that being a member of a disparaged group in society increases the salience of one's group identity (Phinney & Onwughalu, 1996). Because of the complexity of culture, leaders should never use stereotypes to infer an individual's personal cultural orientation solely based on the individual's group membership.

In order to be aware, leaders must first have an awareness of their own cultural values and biases. This means having a stronger self-identity. Identity is developed in a cultural context. Belonging to a cultural group means accepting the beliefs and symbols of that group as having meaning and importance in a profoundly personal sense. Identity includes personal elements such as one's name, social connections such as family, and cultural connections such as nationality and ethnicity. This combined description of identity has also been referred to as our personality. As we become more aware of how ethnographic, demographic, status, and formal/informal affiliations have shaped our lives we become more intentional in developing our own identity through multicultural awareness. We become more aware of our cultural identity through contact with persons from other cultures who are different from ourselves, and we see ourselves in contrast.

Cultural identity is complicated. Sometimes within-group differences seem to exceed between-group differences as we track the complex and dynamic salience of our own cultural self-identity across situations and times. Oetting and Beauvais (1991) developed a theory of cultural identification that does not polarize cultures but instead acknowledges the simultaneous multiplicity of coexisting identities in each of us. This "orthogonal" model recognizes that increased identification with one culture does not require decreased identification with other cultures. We can belong to many different cultures at the same time (Pedersen, 2000). The linking of the social with the individual perspective is essential to the development of multicultural awareness.

Culture is the context in which all behaviors are learned. Imagine yourself surrounded by thousands of people whom you have met, learned from, and come to appreciate in your lifetime. Each of these culture teachers has taught you something that you have incorporated into your identity. You do not have just one cultural identity; rather, thousands of different potentially salient identities are presented by ethnographic, demographic, status, and affiliation groups as they take turns whispering advice into your ear.

Imagine the thousands of culture teachers sitting in your seat with you, talking with you and talking among themselves about you as you interact with them or listen passively. These metaphorical voices are not a schizophrenic episode but the healthy and normal behavior of most thinking people. Spengler, Strohmer, Dixon, and Shivy (1995) define *thinking* as multidimensional: "We recognize that multiple world views of reality lead to multiple sources of evidence and ways of explaining and predicting human behavior" (p. 508). Developing a multicultural awareness of your identity means observing yourself, finding patterns in complex data, challenging faulty inferences, and being guided by individual others' cultural contexts.

Most stage development models of identity suggest that individuals experience three or four phases or stages of cultural identification. First, there is identification with the dominant culture in a pre-encounter, conformity, or traditional stage. This is true even if one is from the dominant culture. As is discussed below, dominant culture members are often unaware of issues of identity. Second, there is an awakening to the impact of racism in a transitional encounter or dissonant stage. Third, there is identification with one's own ethnic group. Fourth, there is an internalization and integration of both cultures.

Theories of identity development (e.g., Arce, 1981; Atkinson, Morten, & Sue, 1983, 1998; Berry & Kim, 1988; Cross, 1971, 1991; Erikson, 1968; Hardiman, 1982; Helms, 1984, 1985, 1990; Horney, 1967; Jackson, 1975; Kim, 1981; Kitano, 1989; Phinney, 1990; Ponterotto, 1988; Smith, 1991; Sue & Sue, 1972; Szapocznik, Kurtines, & Fernandez, 1980; Tajfel, 1978; Thomas, 1971) have long established the importance of the sociocultural context in identity formation. Until recently, measures of identity have been defined by the dominant culture, with minority populations either adapting to those dominant culture characteristics or suffering the consequences. The research on racial/ethnic/cultural stages of identity development has made a significant contribution to research on identity development generally.

Ethnic Identity Models

Where do we start in the examination of our own multicultural awareness, knowledge, and skills? Identity models are important because how group members relate to each other and how others relate to them is a critical part of their psychological well-being (Phinney & Onwughalu, 1996). *Ethnicity* refers to "social groups that distinguish themselves from other groups by sharing a common historical path, behavioral norms, and their own group identity" (Tseng, 2003, p. 7). There are two broad approaches to ethnic identity: the Acculturation Framework and the Developmental Framework. Acculturation focuses on contact between two cultures influencing changes in people's attitudes, values, and behaviors. Berry (1990) established four resolutions regarding acculturation: (a) assimilation—exclusive identification with a new culture; (b) separation—exclusive identification with culture of origin; (c) integration or biculturality—identification with both cultures; or (d) marginality—the absence of identification with either culture. How a person experiences his or her culture of origin in relation to a new culture, the factors that influence this adaptation, and the psychological adjustment that occurs have been examined (e.g., Abe-Kim, Okazaki, & Goto, 2001).

The developmental perspective focuses on stage models of ethnic identity development. A framework proposed by Phinney (1990) reflects a three-stage progression from (a) unexamined ethnic identity characterized by a lack of attention to ethnicity and unreflected preference for the dominant culture, to (b) an ethnic identity search involving immersion in the culture of origin that may or may not involve a rejection of dominant cultural values, to (c) ethnic identity achievement characterized by a true appreciation of one's ethnicity and the resolution of conflicts with the dominant group.

The salience of individuals' ethnic identity may be particularly important in relation to the context in which they find themselves. Distinctiveness theory assumes that people are most aware of social characteristics (e.g., age, gender, ethnicity) that distinguish them from others (McGuire, McGuire, Child, & Fujioka, 1978). In addition, self-awareness theory suggests that the aspect of self to which people attend is determined, in part, by external conditions that heighten the salience of different facets of themselves (Duval & Wickland, 1972). Individuals are more likely to be aware of their demographic characteristics when these attributes are underrepresented in a context or situation (e.g., Mehra, Kilduff, & Brass, 1998).

Recent research found that ethnic self-awareness has different meanings for European Americans and Asian Americans (Kim-Ju & Liem, 2003). Specifically, Asian Americans appeared to be more aware of their ethnicity across three vignettes compared to European Americans, who responded with virtually no awareness of their ethnicity. This is a common finding from members of a majority group. Since their culture is the dominant culture, they usually do not have to think about it or attend to it because it just is, whereas members of a minority group often must constantly consider their culture because there are cues everywhere to suggest to them that their culture is part of a subset instead of being part of the whole.

Racial Identity Models

One of the goals of racial identity models is to advance a healthy racial identity and a positive sense of self as a racial being (Pack-Brown, 1999). Another noted benefit of such models is that they recognize the reality of psychological heterogeneity within racial and ethnic groups (Robinson & Howard-Hamilton, 2000). More central to this book's focus, however, is that these models have assisted in fostering an understanding of how people move from relatively low levels of awareness regarding their racial selves to a more advanced understanding of both themselves and others as racial beings (Helms, 1984). Two of the best known models of racial identity were developed by Cross (Black racial identity 1971, 1991) and Helms (White racial identity 1990, 1995).

BLACK RACIAL IDENTITY

It is important to understand Black racial identity because compared to other minority groups, African Americans report feeling distinctly more separated from mainstream society (e.g., Phinney, DuPont, Espinosa, Revill, & Sanders, 1994; Sigelman & Welch, 1991). After two decades, Cross revised his original five-stage Nigrescence model (1971) into four stages of Black racial identities (Cross, 1991).

Stage 1—Pre-Encounter: This stage is characterized by two identities: Assimilation Identity and Anti-Black Identity. Individuals with an Assimilation Identity have a pro-American reference group orientation and race is not salient to them. Individuals characterized with an Anti-Black Identity have very negative views about being Black. Cross (1991) used the term *miseducation* to describe a negative mind-set that is based on stereotypes that Blacks have about the African American community.

Stage 2—Encounter: This stage depicts the experience of an event or series of events that encourages individuals to reexamine their reference group orientation.

Stage 3—Immersion-Emersion: Intense Black involvement, which characterizes a Black person's over-romanticized immersion into the Black experience, and Anti-White Identity, which manifests itself as rejecting everything from the White culture, are the two aspects of this stage.

Stage 4—Internalization: This stage is characterized by three identities. Black Nationalists work on empowering the Black community. Individuals characterized by the biculturalist identity have Black self-acceptance while also focusing on one other cultural orientation (e.g., gender, nationality, ethnicity). The multiculturalist, along with having a positive Black self-identity, focuses on two or more salient cultural identities.

Recent empirical research has shown support for Cross's revised model (Cokley, 2002). Research in the United States has consistently shown that young Black children prefer White over Black for dolls, pictures, and other stimuli (Aboud, 1988; Powell-Hopson & Hopson, 1992). Black Americans also see the benefits of living in America as less applicable to them, which increases with age and suggests a disillusionment with society (Phinney & Onwughalu, 1996).

WHITE RACIAL IDENTITY

Helms (1990) developed a White racial identity development model with six stages:

Stage 1: Contact—White people are unaware of themselves as racial beings and are misinformed about other races, especially African Americans. They are also unaware of White privilege.

Stage 2: Disintegration—White people experience dissonance regarding preconceived ideas about race and actual experiences with people who differ in terms of race.

Stage 3: Reintegration—White people attempt to protect their unearned White privilege status. This stage is marked by pro-White, anti-Black feelings.

Stage 4: Pseudo-independence—First stage in a positive White identity.

Stage 5: Immersion/Emersion—Misinformation and misconceptions about racial issues are replaced with accurate information.

Stage 6: Autonomy—Accomplishment of a positive White identity. White people can be proud of their racial identity while seeking to eliminate racism.

In 1995, Helms revised her White racial identity development model to include information processing strategies. It is important that leaders understand racial identity models because of the models' implications for workplace relations. For example, racial identity has been found to have a strong relationship with self-esteem (Phinney & Onwughalu, 1996).

Howard (2000) developed a conceptual model of White identity orientations that is helpful for leaders who desire to become more multiculturally aware. The three White identity orientations are Fundamentalist, Integrationist, and Transformationist. The Fundamentalist orientation leaders believe that their perspective is the only one and that it is the right one. They feel threatened by differences and lead with an autocratic/directive style while expecting that others who are different will assimilate. "Unaware fundamentalist whites often do not see themselves as racial beings at all but prefer to describe themselves as 'just American' or 'just Australian'" (Howard, 2000, p. 22). Leaders with an Integrationist orientation acknowledge diverse perspectives and have a beginning awareness. They will learn *about* other cultures while remaining tacitly Eurocentric. "[Integrationist Whites] are aware of the personal pain others have experienced because of white dominance, but they have not yet grasped the systemic and institutional nature of social inequities" (Howard, 2000, p. 22). Transformationist leaders learn from other cultures while acknowledging the legitimacy of diverse perspectives. Leaders with this orientation even attempt to dismantle the structure that supports White dominance, while Integrationists tacitly support it and Fundamentalists actively perpetuate it.

Combining race and gender issues, Scott and Robinson (2001) developed the key model, which focuses on White male racial identity. The key model assumes that initial phases of development involve minimal self-interrogation, while later stages of development reflect a personal crisis resulting in a resolution that leads to greater self-knowledge.

Type 1—Noncontact Type: Individuals have little or no knowledge of their own or other races. "The White male is functioning in society as he is expected to function and will either ignore, deny, or minimize the issues dealing with race and race relations" (Scott & Robinson, 2001, p. 418).

Type 2—The Claustrophobic Type: White men may blame "outsiders" (i.e., persons of color and women) if they feel the American dream is not a reality for them. "During this phase, the person secures power for those like himself while seeking to restrict women and people of color from gaining access to their privileges" (Scott & Robinson, 2001, p. 419).

Type 3—Conscious Identity Type: A White man reevaluates the extent to which his culture influences his attitudes about persons of color and women after an event, either positive or negative, that creates dissonance between his thoughts and his experiences. The White male may feel guilty about his unearned privilege.

Type 4—Empirical Type: "During this phase, the White man finally realizes that racism and sexism are real (i.e., not fabrications of people of color and women) and are involved in many aspects of his life" (Scott & Robinson, 2001, p. 420).

Type 5—Optimal Type: This person understands that working with all people regardless of race and gender is important for a meaningful existence. "There is an increased knowledge of race and gender relations and the roles they play. In this phase, the individual values all people for their intrinsic worth as human beings" (Scott & Robinson, 2001, p. 420).

Implications of Identity Models for Leaders

Although there are many other identity models available in the literature, the above models give readers a sense of the types of categorizations that may influence their own or others' thoughts, actions, and interrelationships. The models are not to be used as shortcuts with which leaders interact with someone who is different to quickly label that individual as being at a particular stage and to make judgments as to the person's motives. They are presented as a tool for leaders to use to become more self-aware about their own ethnic and racial identities.

Studies have suggested that more advanced levels of racial identity development are associated with higher levels of multicultural competency (Ottavi, Pope-Davis, & Dings, 1994; Vinson & Neimeyer, 2000). In addition, it is important to note that even though different models have been developed for ethnic identity, Black identity, and White identity, what constitutes perceptions of majority and underrepresented group status is not always based on ethnicity or race. For example, in a recent study on self-categorization and identity construction, approximately 15% of the White majority employees sampled felt that they were a member of an underrepresented group, even though they did not fit any of the traditional definitions (Day, Cross, Ringseis, & Williams, 1999). The results also revealed that these "nontraditional" underrepresented group members had lower reported job satisfaction, poorer perceptions of the psychological climate at work, worse relationships with leaders, and more negative attitudes toward diversity-related issues than either traditionally underrepresented employees or traditionally majority employees.

Different Types of Intelligence

Howard Gardner's (1983, 1999) theory of multiple intelligences can provide leaders in a multicultural environment with an awareness of the value of different types of intelligence. Gardner's theory suggests that all human beings have eight or nine basic intelligences (e.g., linguistic, logical-mathematical, musical, naturalist) and that no two individuals have exactly the same profile of strengths and weaknesses. He also states that strength in one intelligence does not predict strength or weakness in other intelligences. Thus, being a technically gifted engineer does not preclude someone from having good interpersonal skills.

People differ in their preferred intelligences, and knowing their own preferences can allow them to view themselves as a source of knowledge. They can also identify others as potential sources of knowledge (Martin, 2003). Using Gardner's theory as a framework, leaders can offer different developmental opportunities that tap a variety of talents that their employees possess.

Of course Gardner's theory of multiple intelligences is not the only theory of intelligence. In fact, it has been argued that it is surprisingly analogous to the theory of intelligence implied in the ancient Chinese "Six Arts" educational program (Chongde & Tsingan, 2003).

In addition, there has been a great deal of recent research examining the utility of emotional intelligence in predicting leader effectiveness (e.g.,

Dulewicz, 2000; Gardner & Stough, 2002; George, 2000; Goleman, 2000). Emotional intelligence "involves the ability to perceive accurately, appraise, and express emotion; the ability to access and/or generate feelings when they facilitate thought; the ability to understand emotion and emotional knowledge; and the ability to regulate emotions to promote emotional and intellectual growth" (Salovey & Mayer, 1990, p. 10). Mayer and Salovey (1993) argue that individuals do have differences in emotional intelligence relating to an ability to appraise the emotions of both the self and others.

A competency-based model of emotional intelligence developed by Goleman (1998) provides the four general abilities underlying emotional intelligence. These general abilities include

Self-awareness—ability to understand feelings and accurate self-assessment

Self-management—ability to manage resources, internal states, and impulses

Social awareness—ability to read both people and groups accurately

Relationship management—ability to encourage desirable responses in others

Leaders who are emotionally intelligent are thought to be happier and more committed to their organization (Abraham, 2000), perform better in the workplace (Watkin, 2000), and maybe most important in a multicultural and diverse environment, utilize emotions to improve their decision-making skills and to instill a sense of enthusiasm, trust, and cooperation in their employees by using interpersonal relationships (George, 2000).

Kolb's Learning Styles

While understanding ethnic identity models and different types of intelligences can help leaders as they develop a multicultural awareness, understanding different learning styles, and particularly the one that best represents their own style, can assist leaders as they attempt to gain multicultural knowledge and skill.

David Kolb, a well-known theorist on experiential learning, argues that the learning process is not the same for all people. Learning is a complex process, and individual differences influence learning styles. A learning style reflects the choices individuals make during the learning process, and the impact on information selected and how it is processed. Differences in learning styles help explain why some people are more comfortable with some training approaches than others (Kolb, 1984, 1999).

Kolb theorizes that a person's learning style is based on his or her preferred mode of learning, which is the individual's orientation toward gathering and processing information during learning. Kolb proposed four modes of experiential learning:

1. Concrete Experience. A preference for learning through direct experience, emphasizing interpersonal relations and *feelings* instead of thinking

2. Abstract Conceptualization. A preference for learning by *thinking* about an issue in theoretical terms

3. Reflective Observation. A preference to learn by *watching* and examining different points of view to arrive at a point of understanding

4. Active Experimentation. A preference for learning something by actually *doing* it and judging its practical value

Kolb argues that an individual's learning style often combines two modes of learning. Each style emphasizes some learning abilities and de-emphasizes others. Based on his own work and the work of pioneering theorists (such as Lewin, Dewey, and Piaget), Kolb identified four learning styles:

1. Convergent. A combination of abstract conceptualization and active experimentation (*thinking* and *doing*). Learning characteristics for this type of learner include decisiveness, practical application of ideas, and hypothetical deductive reasoning. This type of learner tends to prefer dealing with technical tasks rather than with interpersonal issues.

2. Divergent. A combination of concrete experience and reflective observation (*feeling* and *watching*). Learning characteristics include skill at generating ideas, ability to see a situation from multiple perspectives, and being aware of meaning and value. This type of learner also tends to be interested in people, culture, and the arts.

3. Assimilation. A combination of abstract conceptualization and reflective observation (*thinking* and *watching*). This type of learner is good at inductive reasoning, creating theoretical models, and combining disparate observations into an integrated explanation. This type of learner tends to be less concerned with people and more concerned with ideas and abstract concepts.

4. Accommodative. A combination of concrete experience and active experimentation (*feeling* and *doing*). This type of learner is good at implementing decisions, carrying out plans, and getting involved in new experiences. This type of learner also tends to be at ease with people but may be seen as impatient or pushy.

Kolb theorizes that learning styles are developed as a result of life experiences and hereditary influences. He also noted that while individuals have a dominant learning style, they may also use other learning styles in certain situations. One of the most recent studies on learning style preferences of those from different cultural backgrounds found that subjects from Puerto Rico and Columbia preferred to be trained using round robin, an experiential technique, whereas subjects from the United States also preferred an experiential technique, with role play receiving higher marks than other techniques (Franchi, 2003). Given that developing a globally literate workforce requires leaders to focus on business strategy, leadership strategy, culture strategy, and learning strategy (Rosen & Digh, 2001), more research is needed to discover additional information on how culture can influence learning style preferences. In the meantime, leaders would do well to consider their learning style and how that style supports or hinders their multicultural development.

Gagne's Theory of Instruction

To take the area of learning a step farther, the Gagne (or Gagne-Briggs) theory of instruction examines the kinds of things people learn and how they learn them (Gagne, 1972, 1984; Gagne, Briggs, & Wager, 1992). The theory suggests that there is no one best way to learn everything. The theory proposes two main components: what is being learned (learning outcomes) and the techniques used to teach what is being learned. Gagne proposed that human performance could be divided into five categories, each requiring a different set of conditions to maximize learning, retention, and transfer (DeSimone, Werner, & Harris, 2002).

1. Verbal Information: Also known as declarative knowledge; involves the ability to state or declare something, such as a fact or idea

2. Intellectual Skills: Also called procedural knowledge; consists of the rules, concepts, and procedures we follow while accomplishing tasks. These skills may be simple or complex.

3. Cognitive Strategies: Also known as strategic knowledge; makes up the skills we use to control learning, thinking, and remembering. Cognitive strategies allow us to figure out what procedural knowledge and declarative knowledge we need to complete a task.

4. Attitudes: Internal states of mind that influence which of several behaviors we choose. Attitudes are highly resistant to change and are not learned by simply hearing facts from someone else. Usually personal experience or some sort of reinforcement regarding the object of the attitude is needed for learning to occur.

5. Motor Skills: Using our bodies to manipulate something such as a pen while writing or a bicycle while riding. As individuals practice motor skills, the quality of the movement should improve.

Gagne et al. (1992) provide information on which types of training techniques or actions are best suited for implementing each of the five learning outcomes. Training scholars (DeSimone et al., 2002) and practitioners (e.g., Zemke, 1999) alike praise Gagne's framework for helping human resource development professionals and trainers increase the effectiveness of their training programs. This information is invaluable for training in multicultural awareness, knowledge, and skills.

Conclusion

People differ in many ways. Ethnic and racial identity models provide a framework for understanding how people may differ in terms of their racial identity and the implications of those identifications. Leaders who are familiar with both their own identity and that of others will benefit in their interactions with others. Individuals also differ in terms of their intelligences and preferred learning style. Leaders who are more emotionally intelligent are more likely to find developing multicultural skills easier compared to leaders who score lower on emotional intelligence. Also, leaders who are more aware of their own learning styles can better attend to the choices they make during the learning process. This information can also be used to help leaders step outside of the comfort zone of their learning style to help them see situations from other perspectives.

CHAPTER 4 DISCUSSION QUESTIONS

1. Why should leaders be familiar with ethnic and racial identity models?

2. How can leaders learn to appreciate all types of intelligence instead of the "school-based" intelligence that the corporate world tends to favor?

3. Given that there is no one best way to learn, should organizations offer different types of training covering the same topic to employees?

Critical Incident: A Celebration-of-Culture Picnic

Jon, an African American Vice President for Business Loans at a large southwestern bank, groaned as he read an interoffice memo over his Caucasian coworker, Laura's, shoulder. "What's wrong with you?" Laura asked. "A Celebration of Culture Picnic sounds like a fun idea." "Fried chicken and watermelon. That's what I'm going to bring," Jon said sarcastically. "That's what they want right? Some stereotyped food to label us with. What are you going to bring . . . what typifies a White girl from southern Minnesota?" "Well,"

Laura thought for a moment, "my great grandparents came from Germany, so some kielbasa could work." "Doesn't this bother you at all," Jon asked in disbelief. "Actually, I think it's a great idea," Laura said. "All of the employees at this bank represent so many different cultures, I think it's a chance to show pride in one's heritage and to share it with others." "If they want me to represent my heritage, I think I will just stop by McDonald's and drop off a couple of Big Macs . . . what's more American than that?" Jon asked. "At least we'll get some good Mexican food from the tellers," Jon said. "Do you hear yourself when you talk?" Laura asked. "What?" Jon asked defensively. "Are you going to tell me that the majority of our tellers aren't Hispanic?" "I just think you are missing the whole point of the picnic," Laura said. "I must be because I'm just going to stay home," Jon said as he walked out of the office.

CRITICAL INCIDENT DISCUSSION QUESTIONS

1. Is a picnic celebrating cultural differences a good idea in a multicultural workplace?

2. How could the memo be worded to avoid negative reactions like Jon's?

3. Why was Jon reacting so negatively to the idea of this picnic?

Exercise 4: Interpreting Policy in a Cultural Context

OBJECTIVE

To identify culture-specific patterns of common and variant interpretations as expressed in words added or left out of policy statements

DESCRIPTION

A number of key words or phrases are blanked out in a paragraph-length policy statement and the incomplete statement is given to participants with instructions to fill in the blanks. Participants are free to complete the policy statement as they see appropriate. By discussing the different variations of the "revised" policy statement, participants can become aware of how cultural patterns of special interest groups are reflected in policy statements.

Time required: 30 minutes or less

Risk/expertise level: Moderate

Participants needed: Any size group plus one facilitator

PROCEDURE

1. The facilitator selects one or more paragraphs drawn from a document describing the policies of an organization.

2. The facilitator then deletes at least 10 or 15 "key" words, keeping the space where these words were extracted blank for the participants to write in their own words, as they consider appropriate.

3. Each participant is given a copy of the paragraph and a pencil and asked to fill in the blanks to give the paragraph meaning.

4. After filling in the blanks to give the paragraph meaning, participants compare their interpretations and discuss them according to culture-specific variables.

DEBRIEFING

When participants compare the similarities and differences in how they filled in the blanks to complete the policy statement, consider the following discussion questions:

1. Does the way you filled in the blanks reflect your own cultural values?

2. How does your completed paragraph compare with the original paragraph?

3. Would you be willing to defend the policy statement in your completed paragraph?

4. Has this activity given you any new insights about the original policy statement?

5. What special interests are represented in the original policy statement?

INSIGHT

Cultural patterns are expressed through the words we choose to use and/or leave out in our writing.

SOURCE: Adapted with permission from Weeks, W., Pedersen, P., & Brislin, R. (1977). *A manual of structured experiences for cross-cultural learning*, Yarmouth, ME: Intercultural Press, p. 28.

5

The Development of Multicultural Competencies

◆

Major Objective

To identify the competencies necessary for multicultural awareness, knowledge, and skills

Secondary Objectives

1. To identify general global leadership competencies

2. To describe the race and culture specific attributes of multicultural competence

3. To describe the components of multicultural competence

4. To discuss the elements of individual, professional, organizational, and societal levels for multicultural competence

◆

A general understanding of competencies is important to provide a foundation for a deeper understanding of the complexity of developing competencies that go beyond lists based on individual samples. Competencies are the knowledge, skills, abilities, personal characteristics, and other person-based factors that help distinguish between outstanding performance and average performance (Pritchard, 1999). Competencies are then identified by examining star performers, surveying individuals who are familiar with the action being assessed (in our case, multicultural competency), and/or developing competencies based on good performers whose actions have been benchmarked in other companies (Kochanski, 1997). The next step is ensuring that the competencies relate to effective performance. It is important to verify that the competencies are necessary for successful leadership and that the level of proficiency is appropriate (Noe, 2005). Comparing the level of multicultural competency needed to be a successful leader with the current level that a leader possesses allows for both training and development plans to be determined.

Global Leadership Competencies

There has been a great deal of focus on the global leadership competencies needed for success in the rapidly changing global environment (e.g., Adler & Bartholomew, 1992; Brake, 1997; Dalton, 1998; Gregersen, Morrison, & Black, 1998; Kets de Vries & Mead, 1992; Mendenhall, 1999; Spreitzer, McCall, & Mahoney, 1997; Stroh & Caligiuri, 1998; Tichy, Brimm, Charan, & Takeuchi, 1992; Tung & Miller, 1990; Yeung & Ready, 1995). Obviously, developing competency lists for global leaders has become popular.

The competencies required for effective global leadership, whether domestically in a multicultural environment or abroad, are very similar. Aycan (1997) summarized key global leadership competencies based on several sources as: in-depth business and technical knowledge, managerial competency, ability to cope with uncertainties and conflicts, willingness and ability to embrace and integrate multiple perspectives, communication effectiveness, competence in developing and maintaining good interpersonal relations, willingness and commitment to succeed, ability to motivate and develop people with potential, ability and willingness to learn from experience, and competence in playing the role of a change agent.

When senior international human resource managers from eight large companies were asked, "What are the key global pressures affecting human resource management practices in your firm currently and for the projected future?" one of the top three that emerged was, "Identifying and developing talent on a global basis." In other words, identifying who can function effectively in a multicultural organization and developing his or her abilities (Roberts,

Kossek, & Ozeki, 1998, p. 94). The other two factors in the top three were deployment (easily getting the right skills to where they were needed regardless of geographic location), and knowledge and innovation dissemination (spreading state-of-the-art knowledge and practices throughout the organization regardless of where they originated). Obviously, dealing with multicultural pressures is very complex. Many companies, like Ford Motor Company, have a global human resources (HR) perspective that requires understanding different cultures and what motivates people from different societies (Solomon, 1998).

Global competencies are required for business success, but determining which competencies are most important is difficult. There is often a temptation to begin training without thoroughly analyzing the instructional needs of those to be trained. For leaders to be successful in multicultural interactions abroad and domestically, they must be globally literate. "To be globally literate means seeing, thinking, acting, and mobilizing in culturally mindful ways. It's the sum of the attitudes, beliefs, knowledge, skills, and behaviors needed for success in today's multicultural, global economy" (Rosen & Digh, 2001, p. 74). To be globally literate, leaders must possess the following competencies, according to Rosen et al (2000):

Personal literacy (understanding and valuing oneself)

Social literacy (engaging and challenging other people)

Business literacy (focusing and mobilizing one's organization)

Cultural literacy (valuing and leveraging cultural differences)

All of these competencies are both interrelated and interdependent. Together they form the foundation for the next literacy. How each of these literacies is expressed depends on the culture in which the leader is working, living, and conducting business.

Mai-Dalton (1993) posits a set of characteristics believed to be important to the successful leading of a diverse organization:

- A personal, long-range vision that includes employees of different ethnic and cultural groups
- An awareness of multicultural issues and a broad knowledge of diversity dimensions
- An openness to change in themselves by encouraging feedback from their employees, accepting criticism, and showing a willingness to change their behavior
- Mentoring and empowering those who are culturally different

To be successful, leaders must be aware of important cultural dimensions and understand how these dimensions can influence their working relationship with others from dissimilar cultures. Focusing specifically on the literature related to international selection, London and Sessa (1999) provide a review of five publications that have developed skill requirements, or competencies, for successful executives in a global environment.

Adler (2002):

- Able to employ cultural sensitivity and diplomacy
- Able to foster relationships that create respect for all parties
- Able to communicate clearly
- Able to solve cultural problems synergistically
- Able to negotiate across cultures

De Merode (1997):

- Motivating cross-cultural teams
- Conducting cross-cultural negotiations
- Recognizing cultural influences on business practices
- Selecting and staffing and evaluating staff in different cultural settings
- Managing information across multiple time zones and organization boundaries
- Building relationships among diverse groups
- Focusing on markets, consistently customizing offerings in relation to clients' needs in local markets across many local markets

Kanter (1995):

- Integrate knowledge
- Move capital, ideas, and people where needed
- Develop new communication routes
- Manage dispersed centers of expertise, influence, and production
- Learn from and leverage the world marketplace
- Use cultural differences to gain competitive advantage

O'Hara-Devereau and Johansen (1994):

- Ability to understand and communicate across multiple cultures
- Technological competence in a time of rapidly proliferating information
- Ability to create and sustain business teams in a global setting
- Ability to support the complex process of facilitating teamwork

Tung (1997):

- Ability to balance conflicting demands of global integration and local responsiveness
- Ability to work in teams from multiple functions and disciplines, companies, and industries
- Ability to manage and/or work with people from diverse racial and ethical backgrounds

London and Sessa (1999), in addition to providing the annotations above, also developed a nine-dimensional construct of intercultural sensitivity:

Dimensions of Intercultural Sensitivity
- Comfort with other cultures
- Positively evaluating other cultures
- Understanding cultural differences
- Empathy for people in other cultures
- Valuing cultural differences
- Open-mindedness
- Sharing cultural differences with others
- Degree to which feedback is sought
- Level of adaptability (p. 11)

Competency lists, while useful, do have problems. Much of the global leadership literature is based on U.S. samples without much thought given to its generalizability across cultures. Addressing this gap, Kuhlmann and Stahl (1996, 1998, reported in Stahl, 2001) used a sample of German expatriates to determine critical success factors. Their intercultural competencies were as follows:

- Tolerance for ambiguity
- Behavioral flexibility
- Goal orientation
- Sociability and interest in other people
- Empathy
- Nonjudgmentalness
- Meta-communication skills

Kuhlmann and Stahl's list differs from the majority of competency lists by offering individual and group exercises that help develop the competencies. For example, cross-cultural role plays would address issues of tolerance for ambiguity, empathy, nonjudgmentalness, behavioral flexibility, and meta-communications skills, whereas an international negotiating simulation would address all of Kuhlmann and Stahl's competencies. However, as stated, going to the next level of attempting to use the lists for developmental purposes is the exception rather than the rule.

A competency list recently developed by McCall and Hollenbeck (2002) is based on a survey of more than 100 global leaders from 16 companies in 36 countries. Their seven global competencies needed for success in international business are:

- Flexibility in strategy and tactics
- Cultural sensitivity
- Ability to deal with complexity

- Resilience and resourcefulness
- Honesty and integrity
- Personal stability
- Sound technical skills

However, many have shared the frustration with the competency list phenomenon and feel that there must be more to multicultural leadership than a list of competencies (Hollenbeck, 2001; Wills & Barham, 1994). One problem appears to be that although the lists overlap, they never converge. Furthermore, each writer seems to have his or her own methodology for determining competencies, which makes the lists difficult to compare.

We agree with Birchall, Hee, and Gay's (1996) statement in a study that cited many lists of international competencies that the best development strategy may simply be to teach people the basics and help them "learn how to learn." This is what we do in the next section of this chapter: Provide a developmental strategy that will help leaders to increase their multicultural awareness, knowledge, and skills for both international business and for leading a diverse and multicultural workforce at home. Developing competence, especially multicultural competence, is not easy, but leaders need to aspire to competence to be effective in a multicultural environment.

The Multidimensional Model for Developing Cultural Competence

As stated earlier, trying to define a leader's job by reading lists of competencies is unfulfilling. One has a sense of staying only at the surface level without being given the tools to work toward a deeper level of competence. We address this problem by introducing the multidimensional model for developing cultural competence (MMDC), developed by Derald Wing Sue (2001), a renowned leader in the counseling psychology field. As shown in Figure 5.1, the MMDC provides a conceptual framework for organizing three primary dimensions of multicultural competence: (a) specific racial/cultural group perspectives, (b) components of cultural competence, and (c) foci of cultural competence. The model is based on a $3 \times 4 \times 5$ design that allows for the systematic identification of cultural competence in several different combinations.

DIMENSION 1: RACE- AND CULTURE-SPECIFIC ATTRIBUTES OF COMPETENCE

As Sue (2001) states, one of the most troubling issues in defining cultural competence concerns the inclusive or exclusive nature of multiculturalism.

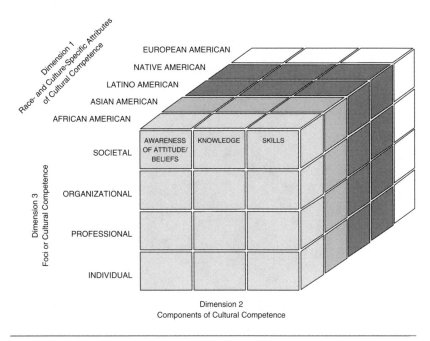

Figure 5.1   A Multidimensional Model for Developing Cultural Competence

SOURCE: Sue, D. W. (2001). Multidimensional facets of cultural competence. *Counseling Psychologist,* *29,* p. 792. Used with permission.

Some feel that an inclusive definition of multiculturalism (e.g., including gender, ability/disability, sexual orientation) can diminish the importance of race as a powerful dimension of human existence (Carter & Qureshi, 1995; Helms & Richardson, 1997). This is not to diminish the importance of the cultural dimensions of human identity, but to point out the greater discomfort that individuals feel in discussing issues of race compared to other sociodemographic differences (Carter, 1995). As stated by Cornell West (2000) in a presentation to the International Press Institute's World Congress in Boston, "Let us be very clear, let us not be deceived, race is the most explosive issue in American life, the most difficult dilemma in American society. It's America's rawest nerve." Yet if the focus is solely on race, other groups may feel excluded. Thus, increasing multicultural understanding and sensitivity requires balancing our understanding of the sociopolitical forces that dilute the importance of race with our need to recognize the existence of other group identities related to culture, ethnicity, social class, gender, and sexual orientation (Sue, Bingham, Porche-Burke, & Vasquez, 1999).

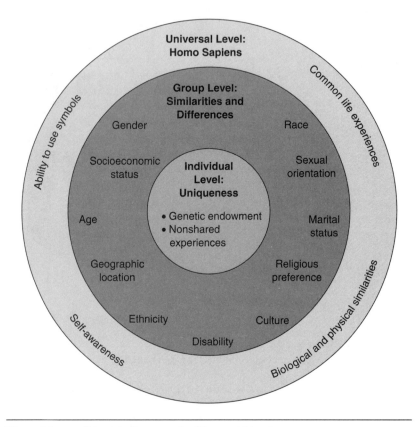

Figure 5.2   Tripartite Framework of Personal Identity

SOURCE: Sue, D. W. (2001). Multidimensional facets of cultural competence, *Counseling Psychologist, 29,* p. 793. Used with permission.

To help in exploring and understanding the formation of personal identity, Sue (2001) presents a tripartite framework made up of three concentric circles representing universal, group, and individual levels of personal identity (see Figure 5.2).

Because we are all members of the human race, and belong to the species *Homo sapiens,* we share many similarities, and the universal level can be summed up with the statement, "All individuals are, in some respects, like all other individuals." Because all of us are born into a cultural matrix of beliefs, values, rules, and social practices, group-level factors influence us. The group level of identity could be summarized by the following statement: "All individuals are, in some respects, like some other individuals." Some of the group-level factors are fixed and unchanging (e.g., race, gender, ability/disability, age), while others are relatively nonfixed (e.g., education, socioeconomic status, marital status, geographic location). As Sue (2001) points out, Figure 5.2 shows that individuals can belong to more than one cultural group (i.e., race, gender, and disability), some group identities may be more salient than others, and the salience of cultural group identity can shift from one to the other depending on the situation.

The individual level of identity can best be summed up with the following statement: "All individuals are, in some way, like no other individuals." A holistic approach to understanding personal identity requires that we recognize all three levels: individual, group, and universal. As Sue (2001) notes, although the concentric circles in Figure 5.2 may suggest a clear boundary, each level of identity must be viewed as permeable and ever changing in salience. In addition, even within a level of identity, multiple forces may be at work.

DIMENSION 2: COMPONENTS OF CULTURAL COMPETENCE

While the business literature struggles to make sense of all of the various competency lists, the field of counseling psychology provides a wonderful framework. The three-stage developmental sequence introduced in Chapter 2 and demonstrated in this book provides a convenient structure for organizing the necessary elements of multicultural training to provide leaders with the necessary awareness, knowledge, and skills to be effective in multicultural environments. This three-step approach is best known through the definition of multicultural counseling competencies (Sue et al., 1982). The "multicultural counseling competencies" have become widely used and have provided a stabilizing force for multicultural counseling development (Helms & Richardson, 1997). The multicultural competencies of awareness, knowledge, and skill have been endorsed by the Association for Counselor Education and Supervision as well as six other divisions of the American Counseling Association (Sue & Sue, 1999) as the most articulate examples of assessing counseling competencies across cultures. These competencies and their principles are appropriate for reframing the field of leadership competencies.

Adapting the philosophy underlying the multicultural counseling competencies to leadership leads to the understanding that all leader interactions are multicultural in nature. There are always sociopolitical and historical forces that influence the beliefs, values, practices, and worldviews of both leaders and followers; and ethnicity, culture, race, language, and other dimensions of diversity need to be factored into leader preparation and practice (Arredondo & Arciniega, 2001).

Awareness provides the basis for accurate opinions, attitudes, and assumptions. It is first essential to become aware of implicit priorities given to selected attitudes, opinions, and values. Awareness presumes an ability to compare and contrast alternative viewpoints accurately, relate or translate priorities in a variety of cultural settings, identify constraints and opportunities in each cultural context, and understand one's own limitations. A well-defined awareness is essential for leading and interacting with others. If the awareness stage is overlooked in multicultural leadership training, then the knowledge and skills—however accurate and effective—may be based on false assumptions. If, however, training does not go beyond awareness objectives, leaders will be frustrated because they can see the problems but are not able to change anything.

Developing awareness means observing objectively what is happening around us and receiving impressions from all of our surroundings. We then use this information to determine what to expect the next time we are in a similar situation. This may seem straightforward, but according to Storti (1989), "It is not as easy as it sounds: just as, by the laws of conditioning, we can't expect people to behave in ways we have never experienced, neither can we observe behavior we've never seen before" (p. 77). There are many behaviors exhibited by individuals from a culture other than our own "that we are not capable of seeing, or more accurately, that technically we may *see*, but that we do not recognize as having any significance or meaning. Needless to say, this can make observing what is happening around us—and learning therefrom—a tricky business" (Storti, 1989, p. 77). Thus, the attributions we put on certain behaviors are based on our limited ability to understand, not on the intentions of the actor.

Knowledge provides the documentation and factual information necessary to move beyond awareness toward effective and appropriate change in multicultural settings. Through accumulated facts and information based on appropriate assumptions, it is possible to understand or comprehend other cultures from their own viewpoint. Facts and information about other cultures are available in the people, the literature, and the products of each culture at the local, regional, and national levels. The second stage of gaining knowledge helps people access those facts and that information, directs people to where the knowledge can be found, and identifies reliable sources of information for a better understanding of the unfamiliar culture. If the knowledge stage is overlooked in training, then the cultural awareness and skill—however appropriate and effective—will lack grounding in essential facts and information about the multicultural context, and the resulting changes may be inappropriate. If, however, training does not go beyond the collection of facts and information about other cultures, those interacting with the leader will be overwhelmed by abstractions that may be true but will be impossible to apply in practice.

Skill provides the ability to build on awareness and apply knowledge toward effective change in multicultural settings. Trained people will become skilled in planning, conducting, and evaluating the multicultural contexts in which they work. They will assess needs of other cultures accurately. They will work with interpreters and cultural informants from the other culture. They will observe and understand behaviors of culturally different people. They will interact, advise, evaluate, and manage their tasks effectively in multicultural settings.

We believe that adapting the competencies cited in Sue, Arredondo, and McDavis (1992) provides a promising framework for leaders in a multicultural environment. Developing these competencies should be beneficial for leaders who interact with a multicultural workforce domestically and abroad.

Awareness Competencies

The first level of developing multiculturally skilled leaders requires developing an awareness of the culturally learned starting points in the leader's thinking. This foundation of multicultural awareness is important because it controls the leader's interpretation of all knowledge and utilization of all skills. The need for multicultural awareness is seldom addressed in the generic training of leaders. The multiculturally skilled leader does not take awareness for granted.

Proposed Cross-Cultural Competencies and Objectives

I. Leader Awareness of Own Cultural Values and Biases
   A. Attitudes and Beliefs
      1. Culturally skilled leaders have moved from being culturally unaware to being aware and sensitive to their own cultural heritage and to valuing and respecting differences.
      2. Culturally skilled leaders are aware of how their own cultural backgrounds and experiences and attitudes, values, and biases influence interactions with others.
      3. Culturally skilled leaders are able to recognize the limits of their competencies and expertise.
      4. Culturally skilled leaders are comfortable with differences that exist between themselves and others in terms of race, ethnicity, culture, and beliefs.

   B. Knowledge
      1. Culturally skilled leaders have specific knowledge about their own racial and cultural heritage and how it personally and professionally affects their definitions of what is considered normality.
      2. Culturally skilled leaders possess knowledge and understanding about how oppression, racism, discrimination, and stereotyping affects them personally and in their work. This allows them to acknowledge their own racist attitudes, beliefs, and feelings. Although this standard applies to all groups, for White leaders it may mean that they understand how they may have directly or indirectly benefited from individual, institutional, and cultural racism (White identity development models).

3. Culturally skilled leaders possess knowledge about their social impact on others. They are knowledgeable about communication style differences, how their style may clash or foster interactions with individuals from underrepresented groups, and how to anticipate the impact it may have on others.

C. Skills
    1. Culturally skilled leaders seek out educational, developmental, and training experience to improve their understanding and effectiveness in working with culturally different individuals. Being able to recognize the limits of their competencies, they (a) seek consultation from a diverse group, (b) seek further training or education, or (c) engage in a combination of these.
    2. Culturally skilled leaders are constantly seeking to understand themselves as racial and cultural beings and are actively seeking a nonracist identity.

SOURCE: Adapted from Sue, Arredondo, & McDavis (1992) p. 484.

These cross-cultural competencies and objectives will be discussed further in the next chapter. First, we will discuss Dimension 3 of Sue's (2001) multidimensional model for developing cultural competence.

DIMENSION 3: THE FOCI OF CULTURAL COMPETENCE

This dimension examines the individual level versus organizational/systems level of analysis (Sue, 2001). The work on cultural competence has typically focused on the individual level of analysis. However, for leaders, as well as all employees, the history and culture of the organization will influence the attitudes of employees and implementation of ideas. Studies on ethics have shown that the organizational ethical climate (Petersen, 2002) and leaders' behavior (what they pay attention to, how they react to crises, how they behave, how they allocate rewards, and how they hire and fire individuals; Sims & Brinkmann, 2002) can shape and reinforce ethical and unethical behavior in employees. Similarly, for leaders and employees to act with multicultural competence, the organizational system must support and reward those actions.

As Sue (2001) states, the obstacles at the individual level are biases, prejudices, and misinformation, which often manifest themselves as discrimination; at the professional level, culture-bound definitions and ethnocentric standards serve as obstacles; at the organizational level, monocultural policies, practices, and structure can be obstacles; and at the societal level, obstacles include the invisibility of ethnocentric monoculturalism, the power to define reality, and a biased interpretation of history. Barriers to cultural competence and possible solutions for overcoming them are discussed below.

Individual/Personal Level

Sue (2001) developed the MDCC with an underlying assumption; namely, that no one was born into our society with the desire or intention to be biased, prejudiced, or bigoted (Dovidio, 1997; Sue, 1999). Fearing and hating others is something that people learn. Misinformation about culturally different groups is imposed through a process of social conditioning and is not acquired through free choice (Jones, 1997; Sue, Carter, et al., 1998). Research suggests that biases and prejudices often express themselves unintentionally and at an unconscious level (Dovidio & Gaertner, 1999). Sue (2001) even suggests that people are taught from the moment of birth to be culturally incompetent.

As part of the MDCC, Sue (2001) suggests four major obstacles that block the path to attaining personal cultural competence. First, as individuals we find it difficult to acknowledge personal biases because we perceive ourselves as moral, decent, and fair (Sue, 1999). If we believe in justice and democracy, realizing that we do have biases threatens our self-image (Fine, Weiss, Powell, & Wong, 1997). Second, it is part of many individuals' nature to be polite, and we are not comfortable honestly examining, exploring, and discussing unpleasant racial realities such as prejudice, stereotyping, and discrimination in public (President's Initiative on Race, 1997). Third, being culturally competent at the personal level means accepting responsibility for actions (or inactions) that directly or indirectly perpetuate injustice. When we realize how our own biases and actions may contribute to inequities, we can no longer escape personal responsibility for change. Finally, addressing bias goes beyond an intellectual exercise and involves dealing with "embedded emotions" (fear, guilt, anger, etc.) that are often associated with painful racial memories and images (President's Initiative on Race, 1997). Most people avoid unpleasant situations and are tempted to avoid facing the reality of their fears (Sue, 2001).

As Sue (2001) states, understanding personal resistance to developing cultural competence is important for training because it suggests the type of activities and exercises likely to produce positive change (Carter, 1995; Helms, 1995; Sue, Carter, et al., 1998). The personal journey to overcoming multicultural incompetence represents a major challenge for leaders. Both trainers and trainees must be willing to address internal issues related to their personal belief systems, behaviors, and emotions when interacting with other racial groups (Dovidio, 1997; Sue, 1999). It is easier to address racism at an institutional and societal level than at the personal level, which requires acknowledging biases and preconceived ideas. It also means being open and honest with one another; hearing the dreams, fears, and concerns of all groups in society; recognizing how prejudice and discrimination hurt all people; and seeking common solutions that allow for equal access and opportunities for all people (President's Initiative on Race, 1997; Sue, 1999). To change, people must be willing to confront and unlearn biased conditioning that has occurred over their lifetime (Ponterotto & Pedersen, 1993).

Sue (1999, 2001) provides four principles that can be personally helpful in achieving individual cultural competence. First, to check the validity of their assumptions and beliefs, individuals must experience and learn from as many different sources as possible (not just the media or what their friends or neighbors say). Second, to gain a balanced view of any group requires that individuals spend time with people who represent that culture. Third, in order to understand a new culture, individuals must supplement their factual understanding with the experiential reality of individuals from that culture. Finally, individuals need a "have to" orientation and have to be constantly vigilant for manifestations of bias in both themselves and in the people around them (Sue, 1999). Leaders must go beyond simply attending workshops on multiculturalism and must take personal responsibility for developing personal growth experiences in the real world. Training programs can help by building in learning experiences for trainees that require personal growth experiences (Sue et al., 1999).

Professional Level

Evidence suggests that culture impacts values, beliefs, traits, and decision styles that are consistent with differences in management and leadership styles (Adler, 2002; Arvey, Bhagat, & Salas, 1991; Dowling, Welch, & Schuler, 1999). A wealth of leadership theories has been developed, and most of them have been criticized for being culture bound (Dorfman, 2004). Chemers (1994) identified how cultural differences in values likely impact three leadership functions—image management, relationship development, and resource utilization.

The way different cultures view leadership varies. American folk wisdom portrays a good leader as independent and forceful, whereas in Japan the attributes of fairness and harmony would likely be seen as important. In France, managers and leaders are thought to be experts and would lose respect if they did not know the precise answer to a subordinate's question. In the United States, managers and leaders are viewed as problem solvers, and it is usually perfectly acceptable for them to tell a subordinate that they will provide the answer to a question after they look it up (Dorfman, 2004).

In a study that showed that culture played a role in perceptions of successful leader behavior, O'Connell, Lord, and O'Connell (1990) found that for Japanese respondents, being fair, flexible, a good listener, outgoing, and responsible were important traits for effective leaders to exhibit. For the American respondents, the traits of intelligence, honesty, understanding, verbal skills, and determination were associated with effective leadership. These results suggest that different traits are valued in different cultures, and for leaders to be perceived as effective in a multicultural environment, they must have knowledge of the values held by the various cultures they are leading.

Organizational Level

If leaders are truly to value multiculturalism, they must be part of an organization that moves toward multiculturalism in how it treats all employees, suppliers, and customers. Organizations contain systems that create the majority of problems (Deming, 1986). If leaders in organizations expect employees to be multiculturally competent, then those organizations must support those competencies in their stated strategies, policies, procedures, and implementations. Much of the knowledge on multicultural organizational development was developed in response to the changing complexion of the workforce and marketplace as businesses were forced to reevaluate their organizational cultures (Sue, Parham, & Bonilla-Santiago, 1998). Multicultural organizational development suggests that organizations, like individuals, vary in their receptivity to cultural, racial, ethnic, sexual orientation, and gender issues. It has been suggested that organizations that value multiculturalism can often avoid the conflicts and misunderstandings characteristic of monocultural institutions (Thomas, 1990). They will also be in a better position to capitalize on a diverse marketplace and to attract a broader applicant pool. Determining what the organizational culture is like, what policies or practices either facilitate or impede multiculturalism, and how to implement change is crucial (Sue, 2001).

Multicultural researchers have identified three types of organizations on a continuum of multicultural implementation (e.g., Adler, 1986; Barr & Strong, 1987; D'Andrea & Daniels, 1991; Foster, Cross, Jackson, & Hardiman, 1988; Sue, 1991).

1. Monocultural Organizations. Organizations at this level are primarily Eurocentric and ethnocentric. They operate from the following statements and assumptions: (a) there is an exclusion, either explicitly or implicitly, of racial minorities, women, and other marginalized groups; (b) they are structured to the advantage of Euro-American majority members; (c) there is only one best way to manage, administrate, or lead; (d) culture is believed to have minimal impact on management, personality, or education; (e) employees should assimilate; (f) culture-specific ways of doing things are not valued or recognized; (g) everyone should be treated exactly the same; (h) there is a strong belief in the concept of the melting pot (Sue, 2001).

2. Nondiscriminatory Organizations. Organizations enter a nondiscriminatory stage as they become more culturally relevant and receptive. The following premises and practices represent these types of organizations: (a) there are inconsistent policies and practices regarding multicultural issues—though some departments and some leaders and workers are becoming sensitive to multicultural issues, it is not an organizational priority; (b) although leaders may recognize a need for some action, they lack a systematic program or policy that addresses the issue of prejudice and bias; (c) the changes that are made to address multicultural issues are often superficial and made for public relations purposes; (d) equal employment opportunities and affirmative action are implemented grudgingly (Sue, 2001).

3. Multicultural Organizations. Organizations at this level value diversity and attempt to accommodate continuing cultural change. These organizations (a) work with a vision that reflects multiculturalism; (b) reflect the contributions of diverse cultural groups in their mission, operations, products, and services; (c) value multiculturalism and view it as an asset; (d) engage in visioning, planning, and problem-solving activities that provide for equal access and opportunities; (e) understand that equal access and opportunities are not the same as equal treatment; and (f) work on diversifying the environment (Sue, 2001).

In order to move toward cultural competence, organizations must alter the power relations to minimize structural discrimination (Lewis, Lewis, Daniels, & D'Andrea, 1998). This may involve including minorities in decision-making positions and sharing power with them, and developing multicultural programs and practices with the same accountability and maintenance priorities as other valued programs within the organization. More important, programs that directly address the biases, prejudices, and stereotypes of leaders and all employees need to be developed (Sue, 2001). Although, as stated earlier, the fields of diversity and multiculturalism have often only tangentially acknowledged each other, evidence suggests that if a multicultural initiative does not contain a strong antiracism component, it will be much less likely to succeed (D'Andrea & Daniels, 1991; Wehrly, 1995).

Societal Level

Race is a part of our history and, as was stated earlier, is the most explosive issue in U.S. society (West, 2000). On June 13, 1997, President Clinton issued Executive Order No. 13050 creating a Race Advisory Board to examine race, racism, and potential racial reconciliation in the United States (President's Initiative on Race, 1997). This advisory board concluded that (a) bigotry and racism continue to be two of the most divisive forces in our society; (b) the need to address issues of race, culture, and ethnicity have never been more important; (c) most U.S. citizens appear to be ill equipped to deal with issues of race, culture, and ethnicity; (d) unfair disparities exist between racial/ethnic minorities and Euro-American groups due to racial legacies of the past; (e) these inequities are often so deeply ingrained in our society that they are nearly invisible; and (f) a constructive dialogue regarding race must occur in this nation. The recommendations of this advisory board included "looking at America through the eyes of others" (marginalized groups), searching for common values and goals shared by members of all groups, and developing and institutionalizing practices that allow for equal access and opportunity.

Although the report does not directly mandate increasing cultural competence, it does encourage people from all segments of society to become more culturally aware, sensitive, and respectful toward each other (Sue, 2001). As part of the MDCC, Sue (2001) identifies the three major barriers to attaining cultural competence in our society: (a) the invisibility of ethnocentric mono-culturalism (our strong belief in the superiority of our own cultural heritage), (b) the power to define reality from a singular perspective, and (c) a biased historical legacy that glorifies the contributions of one group over another.

Overcoming these barriers in all four levels is a monumental task. Leaders have the potential to change at the personal level, which can help with change at the professional and organizational level, which could then provide a foundation for change at the societal level.

Conclusion

Aligning a leader's competencies with the requirements of his or her job is necessary for superior performance. All leaders need competencies related to multicultural awareness, knowledge, and skills. The multidimensional model for developing cultural competence developed by Sue (2001) goes beyond the many lists of global competencies to provide an in-depth framework for the dimensions of multicultural competence. Chapters 6 and 7 integrate the development of multicultural awareness, knowledge, and skills with training issues to provide the tools necessary for leaders to develop their own multicultural competence.

CHAPTER 5 DISCUSSION QUESTIONS

1. What are the advantages and disadvantages of using a list of global leadership competencies to determine one's own multicultural competence?

2. In developing multicultural competence, should one have an inclusive or exclusive view of multiculturalism? What are the implications for each view?

3. Describe a time when you "saw" a behavior, but did not recognize it as having any significance even though it was meaningful to the one exhibiting the behavior.

4. How can leaders recognize their limits of multicultural competencies while still feeling confident in their interactions with diverse others?

Critical Incident: I Had Them Right Where I Wanted Them . . . I Thought

Stan was excited. It was his chance to show his CEO that he could be counted on for the important jobs. Stan was going to meet with an executive team that had flown in from Tokyo, Japan. This executive team represented a large computer company that could place enough orders to make up a quarter of Stan's company's current sales of microchips. Stan was supposed to close the deal to secure commitment from this company. When Stan entered the room where the Japanese executives waited, he didn't waste any time heading for his computer to start what he thought was his finest PowerPoint presentation ever. Before he began to speak, each executive handed Stan a business card held in both hands with a slight bow. Stan took out three of his own cards and handed them to one of the executives while keeping one hand on his computer. During the presentation, Stan was getting a good vibe from the executives as they continuously nodded their heads in agreement with what Stan was presenting about the quality and state of the art of the technology his company could offer them.

At the end of the presentation the executives asked Stan if he would like to join them for drinks, but Stan, who didn't have a high level of tolerance for alcohol, declined their offer. They bowed as Stan left, and he felt like he had just earned the respect of three international businessmen. Stan strutted through the office for the rest of the day, confident that he had just secured one of his company's largest orders. Later that day his boss called him in and asked him to sit down. Stan waited with anticipation and a slight curiosity as he noticed the vein on his boss's head throbbing. Stan's boss cleared his throat and surprised Stan with the next words that came out of his mouth. "Stan, I don't know what happened during your meeting with the Tokyo executive team, but all deals are off. They are flying back to Japan tonight and said that they would look for another supplier."

CRITICAL INCIDENT DISCUSSION QUESTIONS

1. Did Stan do anything wrong before his presentation?
2. Did Stan make inappropriate assumptions about the nonverbal behavior of the Japanese executives?
3. Is there anything that Stan or his company can do to rectify the situation?

Exercise 5: Double-Loop Thinking

OBJECTIVE

To analyze a cross-cultural situation from two perspectives.

DESCRIPTION

Participants are assigned a topic and divided into two teams that are instructed to take opposing viewpoints of the topic under discussion. After a period of time the two teams are instructed to reverse roles, each team taking the viewpoint originally held by its opponent. The participants will experience difficulty in switching roles but will learn from the challenge. By having argued for both opposite positions, the participants will be encouraged to see the situation from both viewpoints at the same time.

Time required: About an hour

Risk/expertise level: Moderate

Participants needed: Ten or more participants to form two teams plus one facilitator

PROCEDURE

1. Select a critical incident or brief case examples.

2. Assign the case or incident to one or more participants, asking them to discuss the incident from the perspective of one individual in the incident.

3. Ask one or more other participants to discuss the same incident from a contrasting perspective of another individual in the incident.

4. Critical incidents involving conflict between two individuals work best for this experience.

5. Each participant is asked to describe the perspective assigned to him or her according to (1) the behaviors displayed, (2) the expectations the individual had for consequences of the behavior, and (3) the value reflected by the behavior and expectation.

6. After the two groups of participants have discussed their contrasting perspectives for 10 minutes, a spokesperson from each group reports the behaviors, expectations, and values of the perspective assigned to his or her group.

7. The facilitator will then ask the two groups of participants to switch sides and repeat the above process, describing the behaviors, expectations, and values of the perspective of the contrasting individual in the critical incident.

8. As an additional experiment along the same line, take a newspaper article about an "enemy" group presumed to be hostile toward us. Wherever the article uses the word *they* substitute the word *we* to see how that perspective changes the meaning of the article toward *inclusiveness.*

DEBRIEFING

In debriefing, discuss the following questions:

1. Is there an area of common ground between the two parties?

2. Can a skilled individual see the same incident from different perspectives?

3. What is the advantage of being able to see both perspectives?

4. What is the disadvantage of being able to see both perspectives?

5. What cultures or special interest groups are most likely to be able to take both perspectives?

INSIGHT

It is possible to hold two opposing positions in one's mind at the same time.

SOURCE: Pedersen, P. (2004). *110 experiences for multicultural learning.* Washington, DC: American Psychological Association Press. Adapted with permission.

Pedersen, A. (n.d.) [unpublished workshop materials].

6

What Can We Do to Make Multicultural and Diversity Training More Effective?

Major Objective

To discuss basic issues related to multicultural and diversity training

Secondary Objectives

1. To highlight the need for a thorough needs assessment

2. To discuss the principles of learning

3. To identify conditions of practice

4. To describe the importance of the transfer of training

5. To discuss issues surrounding traditional diversity training

A ny training initiated without the proper preparation will result in less than optimal outcomes. Multicultural and diversity training is no different from other types of training in the preparatory work that must be done before the actual training begins. Organizations face the challenge of determining which competencies are most important, given their multicultural realities. It is a given, however, that to lead successfully in a multicultural environment, leaders must develop and possess a foundation of multicultural competencies. One way to do this is to conduct a needs assessment and, based on the results, provide training, or at least attend training, that addresses these multicultural needs.

Needs Assessment

The main objective of training is to improve the performance of both the individual and the organization. Before training begins, ensure that organizational support exists. As is true for every human resource function, if there is a lack of real or perceived top management support, no one will take the effort seriously.

Organizational Analysis. Once organizational support is established, the needs analysis moves to the organizational level. Analysis conducted at the organizational level uses the mission statement and relevant strategies that have been identified in a strategic plan that reflects where the organization wants to be. The organizational analysis determines where the organization currently is relative to its strategy (Blanchard & Thacker, 1999). This can be determined by examining the organization's short- and long-term goals as well as trends that are likely to affect these goals (Goldstein & Ford, 2002). It is also at this stage that decision makers must determine if training is the solution to their problem. In some situations, selecting individuals with the desired awareness, knowledge, and skills is more effective than training. However, given the shortage of leaders with multicultural competencies and the increasing international interactions that will occur, selecting leaders for these positions may not be possible, or at the very least more difficult than developing the leaders already employed by the organization.

Another aspect of organizational analysis is estimating the number of people who need to be trained immediately and in the future. This can be determined by using either employment planning or concept testing (Wexley & Latham, 2002). Employment planning involves determining the number of employees currently in each job classification and the number needed. It also entails reviewing age levels of employees in each classification to predict future retirements and the average turnover rate for the job. Other information includes the current level of knowledge and skill for each individual, and the ability to perform other jobs within the organization. Finally, information is included that highlights potential replacements and the amount of training time it would take for them to be able to perform the job satisfactorily.

Concept testing involves asking a sample of employees to fill out a survey that details the proposed training and asks if it addresses a barrier they face in their current job, if the training would add value, and how likely it would be for them to attend such training (Wexley & Latham, 2002). This allows the organization to determine if there is a big enough need for a specific type of training and where in the organization it is needed. However, if leaders have a lack of awareness about their organizations', their employees', or their own multicultural needs, they may need convincing about the importance of multicultural awareness, knowledge, and skills. As mentioned throughout this book, there are many important reasons, organizationally and personally, for leaders to possess the competencies that lead to enhanced multicultural awareness, knowledge, and skills.

Finally, organizations might use a culture survey to determine the way employees perceive specific aspects of their job and their membership in the organization (Wexley & Latham, 2002). This allows trainers to get a sense of the relationship between employees and their organizations. If there is a lack of trust, even the best training will fail. A culture survey can help determine where problem areas may exist. These types of surveys can be tailored for each organization's specific needs, and questions addressing the multicultural abilities of leaders can reveal a potential need.

Task Analysis. Next, in order to determine the content of a training program, an analysis is conducted at the task, or job, level. Job descriptions identify the tasks, duties, and responsibilities that leaders engage in as part of their job. For the majority of leaders, it would become quickly evident that interpersonal interactions make up a significant portion of their job. It would also likely become clear that a leader's tasks and duties necessitate cultural sensitivity when working with a multicultural workforce.

Individual Analysis. Finally, analysis is conducted at the individual level. A major focus of this chapter will be on assessment at the individual level of analysis. Specifically, we use the MDCC as a foundation as we focus on the assessment of a leader's level of multicultural (a) awareness, (b) knowledge, and (c) skill.

AWARENESS

Assessing the level of an individual's awareness is an important and crucial first step. Socrates has been quoted as saying, "Know thyself." More than

50 years ago Allport (1954) suggested that insight may be one path to tolerance. He also suggested that awareness of one's prejudices and feeling ashamed of them will likely lead to tolerance (Allport & Kramer, 1946). Awareness is the ability to judge a cultural situation accurately from both one's own and the other's cultural viewpoint. A leader should be able to describe a situation in each culture so that a member of that culture will agree with the leader's perception. Such an awareness will require a leader to have the following:

- An ability to recognize direct and indirect communication styles
- A sensitivity to nonverbal cues
- An awareness of cultural and linguistic differences
- An interest in the culture
- A sensitivity to the myths and stereotypes of the culture
- A concern for the welfare of persons from another culture
- An ability to articulate elements of his or her own culture
- An appreciation of the importance of multicultural teaching
- An awareness of the relationships between cultural groups
- An accurate criteria for objectively judging "goodness" and "badness" in the other culture

As discussed in Chapter 4, the theories of racial/ethnic identity development provide a structure for seeing identity development as a tool for building awareness. Developing an awareness of oneself starts with understanding one's identity and how it developed. The next step is to understand others' identities and how they developed.

KNOWLEDGE

In addition to awareness or insight, Allport (1954) also suggested that knowledge might be another road to tolerance. Knowledge is often considered to be composed of three distinct but interrelated parts: declarative, procedural, and strategic (Kraiger, Ford, & Salas, 1993). Declarative knowledge is an individual's store of factual knowledge about a specific subject matter. Facts are verifiable blocks of information, such as the population demographics for a certain country. Declarative knowledge is evident when the person is able to recall and/or recognize specific blocks of information. Procedural knowledge is at a higher level of understanding and refers to an individual's understanding how and when to apply the facts that have been learned. Thus declarative knowledge is the first step and procedural knowledge builds on the facts. Procedural knowledge involves the underlying relationships between facts and procedures. It allows individuals to consider the context of the situation so they can apply their factual knowledge correctly. The way factual knowledge is stored and the linkages that are made with other knowledge acquired by the individual are important for procedural knowledge. Strategic knowledge is the highest level of knowledge and is used for planning, monitoring, and modifying goal-directed activity. Strategic knowledge requires both factual and procedural knowledge and gives individuals the awareness of what they know and how and when to apply this knowledge.

Assessing the level of a leader's declarative knowledge becomes important once the leader's awareness, based on factual knowledge, has been corrected and judged to be adequate. If awareness helps the leader to ask the "right questions," then declarative knowledge provides access to the "right answers." The increased strategic knowledge available based on the factual and declarative knowledge should clarify the alternatives and reduce the ambiguity in a leader's understanding about a culture. Learning the language of another culture is an effective way to increase one's information. Anticipating preconceptions and stereotypes from another culture's viewpoint requires knowledge of the myths and widely "understood" perceptions from that culture's viewpoint. It is also important to know the right way to get more information about the culture in question so that the teaching/learning resources will be appropriate.

In a needs assessment to determine the leader's level of knowledge about a culture, the following questions provide guidelines for measuring knowledge awareness.

- Does the leader have specific knowledge about the culturally defined group members' diverse historical experiences, adjustment styles, levels of education, socioeconomic backgrounds, preferred values, typical attitudes, predictable behaviors, inherited customs, slang, learning styles, and ways of thinking?
- Does the leader have information about the resources for teaching and learning available to persons in the other culture?
- Does the leader know about his or her own culture in relation to the other culture?
- Does the leader have professional expertise in an area valued by persons in the other culture?
- Does the leader have information about teaching/learning resources regarding the other culture and know where those resources are available?

Leaders need a great deal of information before they can be knowledgeable about another culture. Some assessment of the leader's level of knowledge prior to training is essential so that the trainer can fill any gaps with accurate factual information that will allow the leader to proceed with an accurate and comprehensive understanding of the other culture.

SKILLS

Confucius has been quoted as saying, "I hear and I forget. I see and I remember. I do and I understand." This supports the value of learning through experience, which can be developed as skill building. *Skill* is defined as the capacities needed to perform a set of tasks that are developed as a result of training and experience (Dunnette, 1976). Skills are reflected in how well an individual is able to carry out specific actions such as communicating effectively, or fluently using a second language. A leader's job can be broken down into critical roles or skills (Katz, 1974; Mintzberg, 1980). Research has shown that effective managers or leaders must be competent in four difference skill areas (Pavett & Lau, 1983):

1. Conceptual Skills. The mental ability to coordinate all of the organization's activities and interests

2. Human Skills. The ability to work with, understand, and motivate other people, both individuals and groups

3. Technical Skills. The ability to use the tools, procedures, and techniques of a specialized field

4. Political Skills. The ability to enhance one's position, build a power base, and establish the right connections

Research has shown that for higher levels of leadership, such as the chief executive level, conceptual skills are required to a greater extent compared to the lower levels (Pavett & Lau, 1983). However, it has also been found that human skills—such as the ability to listen, to communicate, and to understand subordinates' needs—are most important for success at any managerial level (Robbins & Hunsaker, 2003). In addition, research supports the notion that training that focuses on human skills produces improvements in overall managerial performance (Burke & Day, 1986).

The focus on skills is an improvement over the traditional focus on awareness and knowledge. Related to multicultural skillfulness, human skills in assessing the level of a leader's skill become important once the leader's informed awareness is supplemented with factual data about the other culture. Thus, skills are dependent on knowledge, but there is a difference between knowing what to do when, and how well one is actually able to do it. Two levels of skill acquisition indicate differences in the degree to which a skill has become a routine behavior (Blanchard & Thacker, 1999). The compilation stage (lower level) reflects when an individual is learning, or has recently learned, a skill. The individual must still think about what needs to be done to perform the skill. The automaticity stage (higher level) signals that an individual has mastered a skill and has used it often. At this level skill use has become automatic.

In developing multicultural competencies in leaders, skill is the most important stage of all and therefore requires a great deal of preparation before teaching about awareness and knowledge. By teaching a skill, the trainer is enabling the leader to "do" something that he or she could not do before. It is possible to measure the things leaders now can do effectively that they could not do before training. Skill allows leaders to do the right thing at the right time in the right way and provides the final test of whether the training has been effective.

Skills are difficult to evaluate. Sometimes the suggested solution is not credible to all persons in the other culture. Skill requires the ability to present a solution in the other culture's language and cultural framework. Skill requires the leader to test stereotypes against real and present situations and to modify the stereotypes accordingly. Skill requires the leader to seek agreement on evaluation criteria and to implement change that will cause an improvement.

In a needs assessment to determine the leader's level of skill development, a trainer might examine several aspects:

- Does the leader have appropriate teaching/learning techniques for work in the other culture?
- Does the leader have a teaching/learning style that will be appropriate in the other culture?
- Does the leader have the ability to establish empathetic rapport with persons from the other culture?
- Is the leader able to receive and accurately analyze feedback from persons of the other culture?
- Does the leader have the creative ability to develop new methods for work in the other culture that will go beyond what the leader has already learned?

Transfer of Training

Very little of the training in multicultural awareness, knowledge, and skills will influence leaders' interactions and behaviors in the workplace if that training is not transferred to the workplace. Moreover, not just any transfer needs to take place; positive transfer must occur. Transfer can take several forms. Positive transfer occurs when job performance is improved due to the training. Zero transfer takes place when there is no change in job performance as a result of training. Negative transfer takes place when job performance is worse as a result of training, which is unfortunately sometimes the outcome of diversity-related training.

There are also issues of "near transfer" versus "far transfer." Near transfer occurs when individuals can apply what has been learned in training directly back to the job with very little modification or adjustment. Far transfer refers to an individual's ability to apply what was learned in training to the work environment, even though the work environment is not identical to that found in the training program. Near transfer can occur when individuals are being trained on equipment; far transfer, however, is the type of transfer that must occur when the work environment is unpredictable and highly variable, such as when one is attending training to increase multicultural awareness, knowledge, and skills. With these types of processes, trainees must learn to generalize the principles learned to many different types of work situations.

Multicultural awareness, knowledge, and skills training is not the only training that faces far transfer challenges. The Baltimore Police Department needed to teach police sergeants the skills necessary to handle hostage situations where lives were at stake, such as negotiation. The first hour of a hostage crisis is critical. The sergeant needs to organize resources quickly to avoid a situation where injuries occur. The police department chose a simulation to provide a model of reality without the inherent danger present in a real hostage situation. Multiple scenarios are incorporated into the simulation, allowing the sergeants the necessary time and situation to practice the exact skills they will need when they are faced with a hostage crisis (Reintzell, 1997).

The process this police department follows can be used as a template for training leaders in multicultural skills. The simulation begins by having the trainee briefed on the hostage situation while being charged with taking control of the situation. An instructor who has been personally involved in similar real-life incidents observes the trainee as he or she works through one difficult and one easy hostage simulation. The design of the simulation emphasizes the importance of clear thinking and decision making under the pressure of time. Trainees must take actions according to a set of priorities that place the greatest value on minimizing risk to the hostage and isolating suspects before communicating with them. The simulation scenarios all include elements of actual hostage situations such as forced entry, taking someone against his or her will, a weapon, and threats. An instructor evaluates the actions of the trainee and can either correct mistakes as they happen or provide feedback to the trainee after the simulation is completed.

Behavior modeling can also be used in situations requiring far transfer. Behavior modeling has been used to teach people interpersonal and cognitive skills. The technique is based on Bandura's social learning theory (1977b, 1986). Social learning theory proposes that outcome and self-efficacy expectations influence trainee performance. Self-efficacy has been defined as

> people's judgments of their capabilities to organize and execute courses of action required to attain designated types of performances. It is concerned not with the skills one has but with judgments of what one can do with whatever skills one possesses. (Bandura, 1986, p. 391)

Self-efficacy can be thought of as a person's judgment of the likelihood that he or she can successfully perform a certain task. A person's self-efficacy beliefs are malleable and can be influenced by the person's accomplishments, observations, verbal persuasion, and physiological states (Bandura, 1977a).

Bandura suggests that people who have high self-efficacy for a certain task will focus their attention on the challenges of the situation and use greater effort in mastering them, which increases the chances of successful task performance. People with low self-efficacy for a certain task will focus on obstacles and shortcomings, which reduces their chances of successful task performance. Thus, leaders' thoughts about their skill level in dealing with others who are multiculturally different from themselves will likely influence how they approach multicultural skill training and what they get out of it.

Social learning theory suggests that most behavior is learned by observing the actions of others and the consequences of those actions. In behavior modeling, the trainees are told the behaviors to be learned and shown a video or DVD of an actor (the model) demonstrating the behavior. The trainees practice the behavior, receiving feedback from others and then receiving social reinforcement for performing the behavior correctly.

Although this level of detail may seem more appropriate for trainers as opposed to leaders, we believe that if leaders understand the reasons behind the design of training programs, they will be more likely to accept the programs.

As shown in Figure 6.1, the transfer process is influenced by trainee characteristics, training design, and work environment (Baldwin & Ford, 1988). Transfer of training refers to trainees effectively and continually applying what they learned in training (awareness, knowledge, skills, cognitive strategies) to their jobs (Broad & Newstrom, 1992). Transfer of training includes both generalization of training to the job, which includes applying the learned capabilities to similar situations found in training, and maintenance of material that has been learned, which refers to the process of using newly acquired capabilities over time. Generalization and maintenance cannot occur if the material has not been learned and retained.

A great deal of work goes into preparing the leaders, their superiors, and all the employees for multicultural training and providing an environment conducive to the awareness, knowledge, and skills to transfer (to generalize and be maintained). Often participants, regardless of their level in the organization, come into diversity or multicultural training with emotional barriers already erected and standing tall. Much of the training time is spent attempting to lower the barriers enough to create an awareness, with little time left for knowledge or skill building.

As shown in Figure 6.1 and discussed by Baldwin and Ford (1988), training design is directly linked to learning and retention. There are several areas related to pre-training, and much of the research has focused on four basic principles that serve as the foundation for understanding the principles of learning: (1) identical elements, (2) teaching of general principles, (3) stimulus variation, and (4) various conditions of pre-practice, practice, and post-practice.

Identical Elements: The theory of identical elements, proposed by Thorndike and Woodworth (1901), suggests that transfer of training is maximized to the

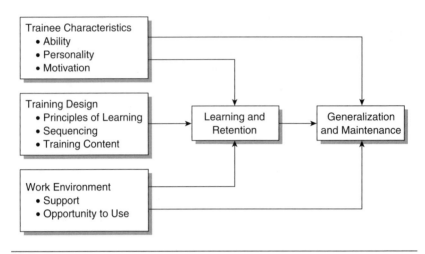

Figure 6.1   A Model of the Transfer Process

SOURCE: Baldwin, T. T., & Ford, J. K. (1988). Transfer of training: A review and discussion for future research. *Personal Psychology, 41,* 65. Reprinted with permission.

extent that the training and performance situations are similar in terms of the stimuli present and the responses required of the participants. For example, if leaders born and raised in the Midwest are expected to interact effectively with employees born and raised in Mexico, practice with individuals from this culture, possibly using role playing, can improve the transfer of training. Of course, the examples used in the role play must contain the range of expected behaviors from the employees from Mexico.

Similarity has two dimensions: Physical fidelity and psychological fidelity. Physical fidelity is the extent to which the conditions of training, such as tasks, equipment, and surroundings, are the same as in the performance situation. Psychological fidelity is the extent to which trainees attach similar meanings to both the training situation and the performance situation (DeSimone, Werner, & Harris, 2002). There is some evidence that psychological fidelity is more important to the transfer process than physical fidelity (Berkowitz & Donnerstein, 1982), and it is likely that transferring multicultural capabilities to the workplace is heavily influenced by psychological fidelity.

The principle of identical elements is particularly relevant in simulation training, a process frequently used to teach multicultural competencies. However, increasing fidelity often means increasing costs and complexity, resulting in tradeoffs between what can actually be achieved in terms of fidelity and identical elements (DeSimone et al., 2002).

General Principles. A second element in creating a learning environment involves general principles. This theory suggests that learning the fundamental elements of a task will enhance transfer of training. The usefulness of the general principles theory to the training of multicultural capabilities is unknown. The theory, in a historical study, was shown to work well with a more physical task (hitting underwater targets by learning the principles of light refraction; Hendrikson & Schroeder, 1941), but it is not clear if training programs that apply the general principles theory to a certain group of tasks will result in better performance on those tasks (Goldstein & Ford, 2002).

Stimulus Variability. The third element in principles of learning is stimulus variability, which suggests that using multiple examples of a concept or using several different practice situations can enhance transfer (Ellis, 1965). Trainees presented with several examples of a concept to be learned are more likely to see the applicability of the concept to enhancing transfer. Recent research has shown that high-variability training may result in lower performance at the end of training, but that for younger adults (age 18–40) retention was slightly better and significantly more transfer occurred on transfer problems that were not practiced compared to those trained with low variability (Sanders, Gonzalez, Murphy, Pesta, & Bucur, 2002). However, for older adults (age 60–80), high-variability training resulted in the same results as low-variability training for younger adults.

Conditions of Practice. "Practice makes perfect" has long been an accepted universal principle of learning. However, all practice may not be considered equal. Many issues have been researched that relate to conditions of pre-practice, practice, and post-practice and how they all relate to learning (Cannon-Bowers, Rhodenizer, Salas, and Bowers, 1998; DeSimone et al., 2002). Cannon-Bowers et al. provided a framework for conceptualizing conditions of practice, focusing on the pre-practice conditions.

Pre-practice conditions include:

Attentional advice is defined as "providing information, independent of performance content, about the process or strategy that can be used to achieve an optimal learning outcome during training" (Cannon-Bowers et al., 1998, p. 294). Providing attentional advice is like giving trainees a problem-solving, task-related strategy or schema to apply across similar tasks (Phye, 1989). It allows the trainees to know where to focus their attention during training. Research has shown that attentional advice contributes to transfer of learning (e.g., Phye & Sanders, 1994). This is likely because the type of learning encouraged by attentional advice leads to general strategies and rules that can be applied across a variety of job situations (Cannon-Bowers et al., 1998). An example of providing attentional advice in training on conflict management in a multicultural setting might be to inform leaders about the different types of conflict that can arise, the different ways that various cultures view conflict, how to recognize the differences, and some general task strategies on how to handle the conflict.

Metacognitive strategies, in contrast to task strategies presented with attentional advice, provide advice on self-regulatory strategies that helps people guide their own performance in complex situations (see Cohen, Freeman, & Wolf, 1996). Metacongitive strategies encourage trainees to take ownership of their learning process. Trainees with metacognitive skills are likely to be more deliberate in training (Smith, Ford, & Kozlowski, 1997). Trainees are more likely to ask themselves, "Why am I doing this?" It also helps trainees understand their thoughts and limitations (Paris & Winograd, 1990). Research has shown that groups using metacognitive strategies made fewer errors during problem-solving tasks and focused more on solving the problem (planning, sub-goaling, strategy development) as opposed to focusing on the problem itself (rules, current state; Berardi-Colette, Dominowski, Buyer, & Rellinger, 1995). An example of how a metagcognitive strategy might be applied to multicultural training would be asking leaders to ask themselves, "Why am I choosing this course of action in dealing with the issue of allowing employees to speak to each other in their native language?" or, "Have I fully considered all of the interrelationships among the elements of communication within my multicultural organization?"

Advance organizers provide trainees with an initial organizing structure or framework that clarifies their expectations and allows them to organize or retain the material to be learned (Mayer, 1975). Advance organizers are useful because they attract attention to important relationships to be learned in training, they provide an organizing framework into which new information can be incorporated, and they assist with the integration of new material into existing information (Mayer, 1989). Research has found that allowing trainees to develop their own advance organizers by creating their own organization of concept examples, led to the greatest adaptive transfer (DiVesta & Peverly, 1984). Advance organizers consisting of a written sentence outlining the primary scenes from a foreign language video were shown to facilitate comprehension (Herron, 1994). Research has also shown that the use of a graphic advance organizer (e.g., a concept tree) was related to an increased level of perceived motivation, satisfaction, confidence, and ability to read the text (Hirumi & Bowers, 1991). An example of using an advance organizer for multicultural training would be laying out the three-step process of awareness, knowledge, and skills, and asking trainees to create their own organization of concepts that they believe falls under each step.

Goal orientation is one of the best-supported theories of work motivation, and one of the best-supported theories in management overall (Miner, 1984;

Pinder, 1984). Goals that are specific, difficult, and accepted by employees have been overwhelmingly shown to lead to higher levels of performance than easy, vague goals or no goals at all (Locke, Shaw, Saari, & Latham, 1981). Research has proposed two types of goals individuals pursue in achievement situations: performance goals and mastery or learning goals. Performance goals are typically normative, with individuals comparing their performance to others' performance. Mastery or learning goals are self-referenced, with individuals focusing on improving their performance on a task over time (Harackiewicz & Elliot, 1993). Setting learning or mastery goals may be made more valuable by focusing the trainees' attention on learning the task rather than on performing well in training (Cannon-Bowers et al., 1998). This is especially true for leaders whose self-efficacy for learning to lead in a multicultural environment is low. An example of using goal orientation as a pre-practice condition for multicultural training would, for a performance goal, be to ask trainees to set goals related to improving their performance evaluation ratings on interpersonal effectiveness with all employees. An example of a learning goal would be to ask trainees to focus on gaining knew knowledge about how to interact effectively with others.

Preparatory information sets trainees' expectations about the events and consequences of actions that are likely to occur in the training environment (Inzana, Driskell, Salas, & Johnston, 1996). Research on the use of preparatory information in pre-practice has focused on training individuals for stressful task conditions (e.g., Inzana et al., 1996) and to prepare individuals entering therapy (e.g., Hilkey, Wilhelm, & Horne, 1982). Preparatory information helps trainees know what will confront them during the task they are going to perform (Harackiewicz & Elliot, 1993) and primes them to learn strategies that will help them cope with stressors that could disrupt performance (Cannon-Bowers et al., 1998). Many leaders entering training to increase their multicultural awareness report that being presented with information suggesting that they have been "unaware" is stressful. Preparatory information could be used before such training to give leaders a heads-up as to what to expect during each step of the training process. This could help lower the barrier that is often raised by trainees entering diversity-related training sessions.

Conditions related to practice include the following:

Active practice, which proposes that learners are more likely to learn the material if they are given the opportunity to repeatedly perform the task or use the knowledge being learned. Although one can easily picture practicing a physical task, research has shown that mental practice, or cognitive rehearsal of a task, can also improve performance (Driskell, Copper, & Moran, 1994). This study also found that as the length of time increased between practicing and performing, the effect of mental rehearsal decreased. Overall, these findings suggest that mentally rehearsing the tasks they have learned to perform in training will enhance trainees' performance on the job.

Massed versus spaced practice sessions deal with whether to conduct training in a single session or divide it into different segments separated by periods of time. If the content to be learned is complicated, breaking up the training sessions can lead to better results.

Overlearning is defined as practice beyond the point at which the material, task, or process is mastered (McGehee & Thayer, 1961). The rationale for over-learning is threefold (DeSimone et al., 2002): First, overlearning can improve performance in a variety of situations because stronger associations are developed between the parts of a task being learned. Therefore it is less likely that situational changes will interfere with learning. Second, when there is little opportunity to use a skill in the performance of a job, overlearning provides additional practice so that the skill will be ready to be used when the time arrives. Third, overlearning makes what is learned more "automatic," thus improving performance in a stressful situation or when the pressure is on. Research has shown that overlearning does increase retention of material that is learned (Schendel & Hagman, 1982), but it can also increase the time and cost of training.

Task sequencing is important enough that Baldwin and Ford (1988) set it out as a separate section of training design in their transfer of training model. Task sequencing is based on the idea that tasks and knowledge can be learned more effectively if what is to be learned is broken down into subtasks that are arranged and taught in an appropriate order or sequence (Gagne, 1962).

The Evolution of Diversity Training

The development of diversity initiatives in organizations and views on multi-culturalism seem to have advanced along two parallel paths, resulting in two distinct camps. It has been suggested that diversity training programs are more likely to have problems when trainers do not distinguish between the definitions of valuing diversity and of managing across cultures (Mobley & Payne, 1992). We are familiar with the definitional differences between diversity and multiculturalism as discussed in Chapter 1, but we also recognize that for leaders, the two areas are inextricably intertwined. *Training's* 2003 "Industry Report" (Galvin, 2003) combines diversity and cultural awareness in reporting that 51% of responding companies offered such training in a year when expenditures on training fell. In comparison, in the 2000 Industry Report, only diversity training was listed and more than 70% of companies reported offering such training.

Early diversity initiatives (early 1980s) were often started as corrective measures addressing racial bias and sexual harassment. Avoidance of lawsuits was often the impetus behind these initiatives. Not surprisingly, these programs did not receive a great deal of support from leaders. The training style was often lecture-based, and participants often left feeling accused of sexual or racial discrimination (Koonce, 2001). Diversity training programs continued and became more interactive, with more exercises, but the focus often remained on compliance instead of commitment to multiculturalism.

More recent research suggests that the effectiveness of diversity training can make a difference, but the focus often starts and stops with generating awareness. For example, one survey of employees who attended diversity training reported that 62% of the participants felt that the training was worthwhile in raising awareness of racial and gender differences; interestingly, however, most of the participants (87% of Whites and 52% of African Americans) reported that race relations did not improve or actually got worse after the training (Lynch, 1997). An organizational evaluation conducted at the Federal Aviation Administration found that training made a significant difference in raising participants' awareness (Tan, Morris, & Romero, 1996). Finally, a custom-designed diversity-training program at Wisconsin Power and Light Company resulted in employees' being more receptive toward each other and reporting that the training had improved how they behaved toward others (Mueller, 1996).

A survey of 785 human resource professionals about diversity training efforts (Rynes & Rosen, 1994, 1995) found the following:

• The most common area addressed through diversity training is the pervasiveness of stereotypes, assumptions, and biases.

• Fewer than one third of companies do any kind of long-term evaluation or follow-up. The most common indicators of success were reduced number of grievances and lawsuits, increased diversity in hiring and promotions, increased self-awareness of biases, and increased consultation of HR specialists on diversity-related issues.

• Most programs lasted one day or less.

• Three fourths of the respondents indicated that they felt that the typical employee leaves diversity training with positive attitudes toward diversity. However, more than 50% reported that the programs did not have an effect over the long term.

Characteristics associated with diversity training programs' long-term success include top management support (provides resources, personally intervenes, and publicly advocates diversity) and a structured program that is strategically linked to other management programs such as performance appraisal, recruiting, and general management training.

Problems With Diversity Training

However, diversity training has plenty of critics with supporting survey results to back up their position. For example, even though diversity programs have evolved, there are still complaints of White male bashing, political correctness, and punishment for insensitivity. Some participants claim that the workshops are a waste of their valuable time (Nemetz & Christensen, 1996). Potential problems with diversity training can occur when trainers have political agendas, are chosen because they represent or advocate for a minority group, force people to reveal their feelings about others, or do not model the philosophy or skills associated with valuing diversity. In addition, problems can occur if the training programs are presented as remedial and trainees as people with problems, if the curriculum does not adapt to trainees' needs or is outdated, or if discussion of certain issues (e.g., reverse discrimination) is not allowed (Mobley & Payne, 1992).

Unfortunately, for every diversity training success story, there is an example of diversity training gone bad. In a widely publicized case, in 1994, the Federal Aviation Administration sponsored a workshop on gender differences and sexual harassment (Gordon, 1995). One of the exercises mirrored the navy's Tailhook scandal: Male air traffic controllers were ordered to walk a gauntlet of female controllers who patted the men's rear ends, grabbed their crotches, made lewd comments, and, at a later time, ridiculed their sexual prowess. This was all done in the name of "sensitivity" and spawned employee lawsuits and a congressional investigation.

Another example of inappropriate diversity training was conducted at Chicago-based R. R. Donnelley & Sons Co. In an effort to make White employees confront their alleged racism, employees, both Black and White, had to sit through a movie showing lynchings in the Old South. Some had to watch the movie four times (Lubove, 1997). Donnelly employees also had to respond to offensive questionnaires with statements about the unpleasant body odor of Black people and the sexual looseness and immorality of Puerto Ricans. Ironically, the diversity training including these egregious acts was established in response to the settlement of a previous discrimination lawsuit. Much to Donnelley's credit, however, they did not let the results of poor diversity training define their company. In 2002 they were selected by *LATINA Style* magazine as one of the best places for Latinas to work, and in 2003 they were chosen by *FORTUNE* magazine as one of "America's Most Admired Companies," based in part on their efforts to establish a corporate culture that values diversity and multiculturalism.

Conclusion

There is much preparatory work that must be done before training begins. The effectiveness of all training programs depends on a thorough needs assessment.

All three levels—organizational, task, and individual—are important either directly or indirectly to the development of leaders' multicultural awareness, knowledge, and skills. Training that does not transfer is wasted. Focusing on trainee characteristics, training design, and the work environment will not ensure the desired training results, but not considering these three facets will almost ensure that multicultural and diversity training fails.

CHAPTER 6 DISCUSSION QUESTIONS

1. Will a leader who has an interest in a culture because it is required in the workplace be able to develop multicultural knowledge and skills to the same extent as a leader who has an innate desire to know about other cultures?

2. Should pre-practice or practice conditions change based on a leaders predisposition toward other cultures?

3. What factors do you think will influence how a company responds to diversity training failure?

Critical Incident: With the Best of Intentions

Sandy came back from her multicultural skills training session very fired up. She entered the training program quite apprehensive, not really knowing what to expect. Since she had been promoted to a leadership position in retail, she knew that she needed to improve her interpersonal skills to be sure she could minimize miscommunications between her and her employees. She hadn't given much consideration to cultural issues in the past, even though several of her employees were from India and she had noticed that her customer base had become much more multicultural over the past 2 years. Sandy decided that she would go to the new Indian restaurant for lunch some time soon, and that she would try to ask all employees more about their culture. Sandy quickly returned to her typical thoughts, which did not include cultural considerations. One week passed, and then two, and then a month went by before she even remembered that she was going to try the Indian restaurant. Her relationships with her employees and customers were no worse for her attendance at the multicultural training program, but she realized that they were no better either.

CRITICAL INCIDENT DISCUSSION QUESTIONS

1. Why didn't Sandy's initial enthusiasm for the multicultural training program continue to grow?

2. What should Sandy do to try to regain her interest in cultural issues?

3. Should her organization do anything to try to encourage the transfer of multicultural training?

Exercise 6: A Self-Assessment of Multicultural Awareness, Knowledge, and Skills

OBJECTIVE

To audit your own abilities to demonstrate multicultural awareness, knowledge, and skill

DESCRIPTION

This inventory of questions allows the participant to self-assess the extent to which multicultural awareness, knowledge, and skill have been achieved. Some participants will overestimate their degree of competence and others will underestimate their competence. This list of questions is similar to a test; participants, however, grade their own answers. Individual participants will assign themselves a grade based on their own self-assessment.

Time required: About an hour

Risk/expertise level: Low

Participants needed: Any number of participants plus one facilitator

PROCEDURE

1. The facilitator will ask each participant to "read the following items and indicate how well you think you would be able to answer the item (using your own criteria) if you were to write out an answer."

2. The facilitator will then say, "If you think you would provide an excellent answer, give yourself an A, if you think your answer would be generally good give yourself a B, if you think your answer would be acceptable but not as good as you would like give yourself a C, and if you feel unable to answer the question give yourself an F."

3. At the end of this self-assessment, participants will be encouraged to compute their grade point average (GPA), with an A counting for 3 points, a B for 2 points, a C for 1 point, and an F for 0 points.

4. Participants will divide the number of points they have awarded themselves by the number of items to find their GPA.

DEBRIEFING

After the participants have given themselves a "grade" on their self-assessment of their own multicultural competencies, the facilitator will lead a general group discussion. Discussion questions might include the following:

1. Is it possible to earn an A grade in the multicultural awareness, knowledge, and skill competencies?

2. Did you underestimate your level of competence before taking this test?

3. Did you overestimate your level of competence before taking this test?

4. What are the consequences of not having multicultural competence?

5. How do you plan to increase your level of multicultural competence?

INSIGHT

We have a long way to go in developing multicultural awareness, knowledge, and skill competencies.

EXHIBIT

A. AWARENESS
   1. Can you construct a genogram of your family for the last three generations on your mother's and father's sides?

   2. What is your "cultural heritage"?

   3. How well do you value and respect and model cultural differences in your life?

   4. Who are the significant people in your lifetime who have influenced your attitudes, values, and biases?

   5. What cultures do you least understand and why?

   6. What do you do to recruit employees who are different from you in race, ethnicity, culture, and beliefs?

   7. What culturally learned assumptions do you have that are different from those of other leaders?

   8. In what ways do issues of oppression, racism, discrimination, and stereotyping influence how you lead or manage?

   9. To what extent would you consider yourself as having "racist attitudes, beliefs and feelings"?

   10. Have you had any social impact during your career as a leader?

   11. Can you lead or manage with a variety of different communication styles?

   12. Do you know how your culturally different subordinates feel about your natural communication style?

   13. In what specific ways have you trained yourself to work with culturally different subordinates?

14. In what specific ways do you evaluate your leadership skills with culturally different subordinates?

15. When have you sought consultation from more qualified resource persons when working with culturally different subordinates?

16. How well do you understand yourself and your own cultural identity?

17. How well are you able to present a nonracist identity as a leader of culturally different subordinates?

18. Do you have a plan for increasing your multicultural awareness in the future?

19. Do you consider yourself to have achieved multicultural awareness?

B. KNOWLEDGE
1. Can you describe the social, political, and economic history of negative emotional reactions toward specific racial and ethnic groups?

2. How well can you lead and manage those whose beliefs and attitudes are profoundly different from your own?

3. Can you be nonjudgmental toward those whose beliefs are profoundly different from your own?

4. Are you aware of stereotypes and preconceived notions in your thoughts or practices?

5. Do you lead and manage individuals without knowing about their cultural attitudes, values, and backgrounds?

6. Are you aware of the life experiences, cultural heritages, and historical backgrounds of your culturally different subordinates?

7. Are you aware of the similarities and differences between yourself and your employees?

8. Are you able to explain how your subordinates' cultural backgrounds affects
   a. personality formation?
   b. vocational choices?
   c. team behavior?
   d. help-seeking behavior?
   e. appropriate leadership styles?

9. Can you intelligently discuss sociopolitical issues that influence the quality of life of your subordinates or peers?

10. Can you discuss immigration issues that influence the quality of life of your subordinates or peers?
    a. poverty?
    b. racism?
    c. stereotyping?
    d. powerlessness?

11. In the past month have you read books and/or articles regarding culture and organizational issues of individuals within your organization?

12. In the past month have you participated in training to increase your knowledge and understanding of cultural contexts where leading occurs?

13. In the past month have you been actively involved with cultural minority groups outside your role as a leader?
    a. community events?
    b. social functions?
    c. political functions?
    d. celebrations?
    e. friendships?
    f. neighborhood gatherings?

C. SKILLS

1. Do you understand how your beliefs and attitudes affect the functioning of your employees?

2. Can you talk with your employees about their indigenous helping practices and respect indigenous help-giving networks?

3. Are you able to defend the positive values of bilingualism or multilingualism?

4. Do you understand the culture-bound features of your leadership style?
   a. class-bound features?
   b. linguistic features?

5. Can you explain why employees from a minority group might be reluctant to seek feedback from you?

6. Can you identify ways that your own cultural background might cause conflict with your minority employees from a different background?

7. Do you compensate for the cultural bias in tests developed in and for one cultural context when those tests are used with a culturally different population?

8. Do you interpret your developmental assessment data differently to culturally different employees who come from significantly different backgrounds?

9. Do you incorporate information about your employees' hierarchies when rating or assessing your relationship?
   a. values?
   b. beliefs?

10. Are you able to change relevant discriminatory practices in the community that affect the psychological welfare of your employees?

11. Do you have a large repertoire of verbal and nonverbal skills to match the cultural contexts of your different employees?

12. Is the verbal message your employee receives the same as the message sent and intended?

13. Is the nonverbal message your employee receives the same as the message sent and intended?

14. Are you skilled in a variety of different helping roles, methods, or approaches?

15. When your helping style is limited or inappropriate, will you realize it and have the skills to change?

16. Are you able to intervene with and change the social institutions in your employees' cultural contexts?

17. Are you able to tell when an employee's problem relates to cultural bias by others from when the problem might be personal to the employee?

18. Are you fluent in the first language of your employees?

19. Do you use a translator when working with employees whose language you do not understand?

20. Do you work actively to eliminate biases, prejudices, and discriminatory practices in your community?

21. Do you take responsibility for educating your employees about your own culturally learned orientation to leadership, outcome goals, and expectations?

SOURCES: Developed from Sue, D. W., Bernier, Y., Durran, A., Feinberg, L., Pedersen, P., Smith E. J., & Vasquez-Nuttal, E. (1982). Position paper: Cross-cultural counseling competencies. *Counseling Psychologist, 19*(2), pp. 45–52. Also developed from Sue, D. W., Arredondo, P., & McDavis, R. J. (1992). Multicultural counseling competencies and standards: A call to the profession. *Journal of Counseling and Development, 70,* 477–486.

7

A Training Program to Lead From Multicultural Awareness to Knowledge and Skills

Major Objective

To describe a training process to move from awareness to knowledge and skill

Secondary Objectives

1. To describe objectives

2. To describe design techniques

3. To discuss specific training approaches

4. To describe an evaluation framework

5. To describe examples of multicultural awareness, knowledge, and skills training

While Chapter 6 focused on assessing leaders' needs for awareness, knowledge, and skills and discussing issues related to pre-practice, practice, and the transfer of training, this chapter progresses to specifics related to moving from awareness to knowledge and skill. We fully acknowledge that these are not easy steps for leaders to take. According to a survey conducted by the World Economic Forum (1997), the United States ranked 46th of the 53 countries on the survey item, "Managers in your country generally speak some foreign language and have good international experience" (p. 292). Luxembourg, Sweden, Belgium, Switzerland, and the Netherlands topped the list, while Russia, Slovakia, China, Ukraine, and Zimbabwe rounded out the bottom five countries. While we are not suggesting that speaking a foreign language and having international experience are necessary to be multiculturally aware, knowledgeable, and skillful, they certainly help.

In the United States, organizations appear to acknowledge the need for training international assignees. A 1997 survey conducted jointly by Arthur Andersen and Cendant Intercultural found that more than 60% of U.S. companies provide cross-cultural training for expatriates (Bennett & O'Gorman, 1998). Unfortunately, less attention is given to the type of training offered leaders who are not going on an international assignment, but have multicultural experiences every day due to a diverse workforce and customer base.

Establishing the Objectives for
Multicultural Awareness, Knowledge, and Skills

Training's objective should not be mastery of all of the skills, but to equip leaders with the insight that shows that awareness is important, the knowledge to recognize cues, and the skill to act on it. No training program can possibly teach all skills needed in every possible culturally different situation, but developing multicultural awareness, knowledge, and skills is a great place to start, and if done correctly can give leaders the confidence that they will be able to interact effectively in a wide variety of cultural situations.

Once the training needs of participants have been analyzed, the next step is to design appropriate objectives for a training plan. The relative emphasis on awareness, knowledge, or skills will depend on the results of the needs assessment. An awareness objective will change leaders' attitudes, opinions, and personal perspectives about a topic. The primary need may be to help a group discover their own stereotypical attitudes and opinions. Usually, the awareness objectives focus on people's unstated assumptions about another culture or about themselves in relation to the other culture.

Once training objectives are identified and clearly stated, it is useful to look at the awareness aspect, the knowledge aspect, and the skill aspect of each objective. We may, therefore, look at a matrix in which each objective has an awareness aspect, a knowledge aspect, and a skill aspect.

The awareness objectives in multicultural training focus on changing leaders' attitudes, opinions, and personal perspectives about themselves and the other culture so that these elements will be in harmony with one another. Specific objectives for multicultural training might be based on several important elements of awareness.

- Is the leader aware of differences in cultural institutions and systems?
- Is the leader aware of the stress resulting from functioning in a multicultural situation?
- Does the leader know how rights or responsibilities are defined differently in different cultures?
- Is the leader aware of differences in verbal and nonverbal communication styles?
- Is the leader aware of significant differences and similarities of practices across different cultures?

When identifying the training objectives for a particular group, it is useful to proceed from an analysis of their awareness needs to their knowledge or information needs and finally to their skill needs. It is important to identify the needs from the group's viewpoint rather than that of outsiders.

The knowledge component for developing multicultural objectives focuses on increasing the amount of accurate information available to the leader. After developing a correct and accurate awareness of the other culture, leaders enrich that awareness by testing attitudes, opinions, and assumptions against the body of factual information they now control. The leaders' level of awareness is certain to increase in direct proportion to the extent of their knowledge about the other culture. However, it is also important to note that "A distinguishing trait of experts, even outside their domain of specialization, is knowledge of what not to do" (Patel & Groen, 1991, p. 121). Specific objectives for multicultural training might be based on several knowledge perspectives.

- Does the leader know the other culture's historical background?
- Does the leader know about the theory of culture shock and the stages of cultural adaptation as they relate to the other culture?
- Does the leader know how the other culture interprets its own rules, customs, and laws?
- Does the leader know patterns of nonverbal communication and language usage within the other culture?
- Does the leader know how differences and similarities are patterned in the other culture and how priorities are set in different critical situations?

The skill objective for developing multicultural objectives focuses on what the leaders can now do. If any of the previous training about awareness and knowledge is missing or inadequate, the leaders will have difficulty making the right decisions in multicultural communication. If awareness has been neglected, they will build their plan on wrong assumptions. If knowledge has been neglected, they will describe the cultural situation inaccurately. If skill has been neglected, they may well send a situation in counterproductive directions. Developing multicultural objectives for skills might be based on several important perspectives.

- Is the leader able to cope with the stress and manage difficulties working with a new culture?
- Is the leader able to understand the consequences of his or her behavior and choose wisely among several options that the other culture presents?
- Is the leader able to use the culture's language to react appropriately to others from that culture?
- Is the leader able to function comfortably in the new environment without losing her or his own cultural identity in the home culture?

These are a few examples of skills objectives that must be assessed to make sure that the leader has been taught to communicate with individuals from other cultures. Many additional skills will be developed for each specific situation.

The importance for leaders to develop awareness, knowledge, and skills cannot be overstated. The order in which they are learned is also important. If skills are taught without the awareness, leaders may do more harm than good in trying to guess which contexts or situations call for which set of skills.

Design Techniques

Developing a training program that shows how the identified objectives will meet the identified needs is imperative. There are many different ways to match techniques with awareness, knowledge, or skill objectives. Some examples follow.

DESIGN TECHNIQUES TO STIMULATE AWARENESS

Experiential exercises such as:

- Role plays
- Role reversals
- Simulations
- Field trips to other cultures in the community
- Critical incidents about the problems that come up across cultures

- Observation of the experiences of culturally different people
- Questions/answers/discussions with resource persons from the community

Teaching increased awareness frequently relies on experiential exercises such as role plays, role reversals, or simulations of multicultural interaction. Other approaches include field trips to areas where the culture is lived daily. Sometimes critical incidents or brief case studies from the culture can be analyzed to increase a leader's awareness of the culture. A resource person or informant from the culture enables effective bicultural observation whereby both individuals and groups may exchange questions and answers in a thorough discussion. Almost any approach that challenges the leader's basic assumptions, tests the leader's prevailing attitudes, and elicits the leader's implicit opinions about the culture will serve to increase the leader's awareness.

DESIGN TECHNIQUES TO IMPART KNOWLEDGE

- Guided self-study with reading list
- Lecture and discussion
- Panel discussion
- Audiovisual presentations
- Interviews with consultants and experts
- Observations

Increasing multicultural knowledge frequently depends on books, lectures, and classroom techniques. Guided self-study with a reading list also is an effective way to help leaders increase their knowledge. Panel discussions about the other cultures help students absorb more information relevant to their particular situation. Audiovisual presentations, when available, provide valuable knowledge. Interviews with consultants or resource persons and experts knowledgeable about the other culture help leaders fill in gaps with accurate information that might otherwise be impossible to secure. Simply observing persons from the other culture in their daily activities is an important means for learning about the culture, providing the leader knows what to look for.

An increase in knowledge about multicultural skills takes many forms. Modeling and demonstrating a skill is an effective means of developing the skill in leaders. When available, audiovisual resources provide important feedback to leaders both about how the skill is performed in the other culture and how they are doing in modeling that skill. Although leaders may be under the impression that they are expected to be in charge, supervising leaders' work in the other culture provides a valuable ongoing means of assessing developing levels of skill. The opportunity to practice new skills and behaviors enables leaders to improve their skill in a variety of different situations.

DESIGN TECHNIQUES TO DEVELOP SKILLS

- Modeling and demonstration of effective leadership skills
- Using video and media resources for feedback to and from other cultures
- Supervising and/or being supervised by someone from another culture
- Practicing a new behavior pattern to target intentional change
- Practicing writing skills to describe other cultures as they see themselves

Increasing multicultural skills is premature if the leader has not yet acquired competence in awareness and knowledge. The standard leadership skills are very relevant when they are based on a foundation of multicultural awareness and knowledge learned in sequence. It is important to realize that "one size does not fit all" and that each skill must be adapted and adjusted to each cultural context.

Training Approaches

Most training workshops begin in more or less the same way. There is an introduction with some attempt to break the ice. This might include a formal welcome from an official host or an informal welcome by the workshop leader. This is a particularly important step for multicultural training because it achieves buy-in from participants early in the process. A discussion of the group's objectives and expectations as well as sharing of the trainer's objectives and expectations ensues. Then the agenda is reviewed so that all participants know what is likely to happen in sequence; this helps them to review the materials in their workshop packet for any necessary clarification. The better participants are prepared to work with one another, the more positively they are likely to view the training experience.

Once these general group-building tasks have been completed, the workshop may begin by emphasizing a balance of appropriate objectives focused on awareness and planning data. Each of these three components (awareness, knowledge, and skill) suggests a different training format.

- In training for awareness, the leaders should be made aware of the contrast and conflict between their background and that of multiculturally different employees.
- In training for knowledge, the leaders should be helped to gain knowledge of culturally different employees.
- In training for skill, leaders should be helped to bring about appropriate change by working with interpreters and/or cultural informants.

EXAMPLES OF MULTICULTURAL AWARENESS TRAINING

Training is an attempt to increase a person's alternatives for being accurately understood in a wide variety of cultures. Multicultural training of leaders must be responsive to the variety of cultures within both the leader and those being led. The benefits of multicultural training are measured by their relevance to real-life situations. Counselors and leaders share many similar circumstances related to multicultural awareness. For example, for both groups, the more culturally defined alternatives or strategies they possess, the more likely they will identify the right choice in culturally different settings (Pedersen & Ivey, 1993). A variety of multicultural training approaches have been used to prepare leaders to work in other cultures. These various approaches can be classified according to their emphasis on awareness, knowledge, or skill as the primary focus. An examination of examples for training will help clarify the specific emphasis at each developmental level.

Awareness requires the ability to see a situation accurately from both your own and the other person's perspective. Several multicultural leadership training approaches emphasize awareness through experiential learning, cultural awareness, and specific cultural values clarification.

Experiential learning allows participants to "experience" the effect of cultural similarities and differences through their own involvement with others. The assumption is that increased involvement in the lifestyle of culturally different people through field trips and direct or simulated contact will increase the trainee's accuracy of judgments, attitudes, and assumptions about other cultures. A trainer facilitates this involvement by providing a "safe" setting in which the trainee can/will take risks. Having a significant intercultural experience through immersion, field trips, or role plays is not, by itself, enough. The trainee needs to analyze the effect of that experience to "capture" the resulting insights for future reference.

Cultural immersion requires the trainee to live and work in another culture and learn by experience alongside culturally different persons. The example from United Parcel Service given earlier provides a perfect example of cultural immersion. Any contact with culturally different persons or groups can provide the opportunity for learning through immersion. Some leaders have become highly skilled without any formal training, by learning through their own mistakes and triumphs. Unguided immersion is an effective training approach, although learning from experience without any preparation tends to be expensive in time, money, and emotional stress for the leader.

AT&T uses cultural immersion as part of its diversity training efforts (Brown, 2000). Teams of managers are sent into areas in the United States where they have to learn to interact with people from a specific culture. In one cultural immersion experience, six AT&T managers went to Harlem in New York City where they were sent on a scavenger hunt requiring them to learn about the people, community, and culture. Harlem is an eclectic community representing Africans, Asians, African Americans, Hispanics, and Puerto Ricans. During the scavenger hunt, the managers had to find a Harlem bilingual community directory and a Jamaican meat patty. As part of their experience, they also had to eat soul food. Although the scavenger hunt was a game, it required the managers to leave their comfort zones and interact with others in an unfamiliar environment.

Another example of a type of cultural immersion can be found at the Union Bank of Switzerland (UBS). Managers are exposed to the subcultures of less privileged members of their community to further mutual understanding between both parties. Managers of UBS are assigned for a short period of time (usually about 2 weeks) to social welfare programs that require them to take care of homeless people, work with youthful offenders, look after HIV patients who were terminally ill, or live with immigrants who were seeking asylum. Both parties benefit from the program—the citizens receive much needed support and the managers learn how the world looks through the eyes of people very different from themselves. Managers claim that the program helps them reduce subjective barriers and prejudices, helps them learn more about themselves, broadens their horizons, and enhances their interpersonal skills. All of these competencies are part of global leadership (Mendenhall, Jensen, Black, & Gregersen, 2003). Participation in the program also motivates managers to take more responsibility for others who need help.

> By exposing employees to subcultures within their own country, a foreign assignment can be simulated—they are immersed in a foreign culture at a relatively deep level, and they have to integrate into a different social system, function effectively in a strange environment, and deal with cultural diversity. (Mendenhall et al., 2003, p. 271)

Field trips provide a less traumatic example of experiential training through brief visits to other cultures on their home turf. Many aspects of a host culture can be learned by observation but cannot be "taught" through abstract principles. Leaders visiting a host culture can become participant observers in that host culture in its own home context. By observing host-culture people cope with problems and make decisions, the leader is able to recognize culturally distinctive patterns of activity. To be effective, field trips require skilled debriefing to help the leader articulate what was learned. There are two types of field trips possible. The first is organized around a detailed agenda. These field trips need to be organized around an explicit focus to illustrate or challenge specific attitudes, opinions, and assumptions from one or both cultures. The second type deliberately avoids any agenda preconception or expectation before the experience and lets the insights grow out of the interaction itself.

Role-playing is another frequently used experiential training approach in which an individual learns about other cultures by taking on the role of a person from that culture. The experience of becoming someone from the other culture—to the extent that is possible—often changes a participant's level of awareness. This approach usually relies on articulate and authentic resource persons from the host culture to guide the leader. It is easy to find resource persons who are authentic but not articulate or who are articulate but not authentic. It is more difficult to find resource persons who are both articulate and authentic. When asked how they manage to do such a good job, skilled but untrained resource persons frequently respond, "I can't tell you or teach you how to do it but I can demonstrate for you what I would do if you give me a problem situation." In any case, careful structures must be provided to guide the learning through role-playing, both to provide a safe context in which the role player might take risks and to generate insights about the other culture.

Experiential approaches to awareness training are expensive and require highly skilled trainers as well as cooperative host culture resource persons. Experiential training works when participants feel safe enough to take risks. If the experience becomes unsafe, the leader will experience high levels of stress that might be counterproductive to training and potentially dangerous to the participants. Sometimes awareness is focused on several insights and at other times it is focused on a specific culture.

Culture-general approaches help people articulate their own implicit cultural attitudes, opinions, and assumptions about themselves. Self-awareness emphasizes the values of a person's home culture as contrasted with the values of other cultures. The emphasis is usually on areas of general similarity and difference. Our own cultural values are frequently so familiar that we are not explicitly aware of them. In some cultures, for example, the importance of individualism is not seen as "cultural" but simply "the way things naturally are." Brislin, Cushner, Cherrie, and Young (1998) describe 18 culture-general themes for training illustrating where each person assumes his or her perspective is in the normal and universal perspective: culture-general experiences (1–5), knowledge areas (6–13), and ways of organizing information (14–18). These themes include: (1) anxiety, (2) disconfirmed expectancies, (3) belonging, (4) ambiguity, (5) confronting one's prejudices, (6) work, (7) time and space, (8) language, (9) roles, (10) importance of the group and importance of the individual, (11) rituals and superstitions, (12) hierarchies of class and status, (13) values, (14) categorization, (15) differentiation, (16) ingroup-outgroup distinction, (17) learning style, and (18) attribution.

Culture-specific approaches require training in the specific values of a particular target culture. Culture-specific training is usually limited to the particular target group and has a very specific focus. Learning the language of a host culture, for example, is an important culture-specific way of learning about the attitudes, opinions, and assumptions in that particular culture. Other examples include learning the behaviors, expectations, and values of a particular culture.

A variety of other awareness training approaches focus on the leader's self-awareness and awareness of his or her home culture. This awareness emphasizes both similarities and differences by contrasting the home culture with one or more other cultures. The emphasis of awareness training is always on reevaluating leaders' attitudes, opinions, and assumptions about their own culture and other cultures.

EXAMPLES OF MULTICULTURAL KNOWLEDGE TRAINING

Increasing leaders' knowledge about other cultures is another popular focus for multicultural training. Knowledge training means having correct and sufficient information about their own as well as target cultures. The most frequently used knowledge training approaches are through publications and reading materials, and audio and visual media presenting the other cultures to the leader in terms of facts and information.

Classroom training emphasizes lectures, group discussions, written materials, and media presentations to help leaders increase their information about other cultures. Leaders are provided with factual information about the host culture to understand their own role as outsiders. These facts might relate to socioeconomic, political, or social structures; the climate and physical setting; the culture's decision-making styles and habits; or the values underlying daily behavior. Classroom training provides models and structures for organizing, classifying, and analyzing other cultures.

The facts themselves will be most useful if leaders are highly motivated to learn the new information and see an immediate relevancy of these facts for their own situation. It is essential that the factual data be based on an awareness of why the data are important to leaders. Unless the leaders have adequate awareness, they are not likely to be motivated to learn information about other cultures. Leaders who have achieved awareness of the target culture in relation to themselves will be prepared to document that awareness in the facts and information describing similarities and differences. With appropriate preparation, leaders can become highly motivated to increase their knowledge through learning facts and information-oriented training.

Attribution training is a second form of knowledge-based training that has proven to be successful. Attribution training methods guide leaders to explain behavior from the host culture's viewpoint rather than from their own self-reference criteria. Presented with a critical incident or paragraph-length description of an event, the leader chooses between several alternative explanations "attributed" to the incident. One of the attributed explanations offered to the leader is more accurate than the others for specific reasons. Leaders are coached to select the most accurate and appropriate attribution through practice in analyzing a series of critical incidents. This method assumes that leaders will learn a culture's implicit patterns of decision making through attribution training where they can generalize from the critical incidents to unfamiliar cultures and situations. Brislin et al. (1998) provide 100 critical incidents using attribution training methods in a culture-general approach.

The best-known application of attribution training is the culture assimilator developed by Harry Triandis and others (Triandis, 1975). Many different culture assimilators have been designed for specific cultures and social groups, resulting in a great deal of research and evaluation data. There is probably more data on the culture assimilator than any other cross-cultural training approach. Culture assimilators provide a structured series of incidents and alternative responses in a specific cultural context with a series of explanations or attributions. One of the alternative attributions is more accurate and appropriate than the others. Each alternative is matched with explanations to clarify the rightness, wrongness, and consequences of each choice. To the extent that culturally accurate and appropriate attributions can be determined for each situation, culture-specific culture assimilators have been extremely successful.

In addition to the formal knowledge-training approaches, there is also an informal alternative where the individuals who have achieved a high level of awareness look for their own answers. One sign of having achieved awareness is increased sensitivity to the implicit cultural learning in all reported facts and information. We are accumulating cultural facts and information whether we are aware of doing so or not, as we are socialized by the media and sources of facts or information. Self-guided training will provide purpose to the accumulation of facts and information through reading, observation, and reflective experiences. These facts may be about a specific culture, one's self, or cultures that generally contrast with one's own. A purposive program for self-guided learning about other cultures can be an inexpensive and very effective approach. If "awareness" training articulates the questions we ought to be asking, then "knowledge" training guides us toward comprehensive answers to those questions.

EXAMPLES OF MULTICULTURAL SKILL TRAINING

Multicultural skill goes beyond "knowing" what needs to be done toward actually being able to do it. Skill training provides the multicultural leader with the strategies to match the right method to the right situation in the right way at the right time. Because multicultural skills are based on awareness and knowledge, they require cognitive comprehension and affective sensitivity as well as behavioral facility to interact with others' complex and dynamic cultural contexts. There are many different examples of these more comprehensive and "general" multicultural skill training approaches.

Cognitive or behavioral modification training depends on identifying what members of the other culture would consider rewarding. When others move to an unfamiliar culture, the strategies that used to work might not work as well, and new or unfamiliar ways of thinking or acting need to be learned to feel respected, earn trust and give it, be successful, or form friendships. If the new ways of thinking and acting can be matched with the organization's agenda and can be shown to work better than the old ways, the leader can be persuaded to try them. For this training to work, the leader needs to know the organization's agenda, the problems and opportunities in the other's cultural context, and ways of thinking or acting that would be appropriate and effective.

Training approaches focused on affective or "feeling" goals also depend on structured interaction among the individuals in the organization, the culture, and the method. This training can occur in either a real-life or simulated setting where skills can be practiced and rehearsed with feedback. In the safety of a simulated encounter, the leader can learn to deal with risky or dangerous feelings but avoid the consequences of hurting people. As leaders become more skilled in dealing with dangerous feelings in the new cultural context, they become more confident of trying their skills out in real-world settings.

Microskills training has also proven effective in multicultural settings (Ivey, 1988; Pedersen & Ivey, 1993). When the more general skills are divided into smaller "micro" units, leaders learn step-by-step how to increase their skills. These skills build on "attending behaviors" through "influencing skills" toward "integrative skills." The leader-trainee "builds" or "constructs" a hierarchy of skills toward the ultimate goal of becoming a skilled leader. As the micro-skills become progressively more difficult and complicated, the leader builds on basic foundation skills toward more advanced skills. There are more empirical research data supporting the effectiveness of microskills training than any other skill building-method.

Structured learning is another social behavioral method used in building multicultural skills (Goldstein, 1981). This method focuses on practical skills and the abilities to do a necessary function or achieve a valued goal in the leader's home culture. Structured learning proceeds through a sequence of steps. First, the skill is presented and discussed; second, the skill is demonstrated with an opportunity for clarification; third, the skill is rehearsed and practiced in role-playing with feedback; and fourth, the skill is transferred to the real-world setting.

Culture-general skill training assumes a foundation of international or multicultural attitudes, opinions, and assumptions that apply to several cultures. The previously mentioned and other popular methods of leader training can be applied to the multicultural setting providing they are based on appropriate multicultural awareness and accurate multicultural knowledge. These culture-general methods document the ways in which different groups share some of the same values and expectations even though they display very different behaviors.

Culture-specific skill training also provides strategies that target a specific group, problem, identity, or role. Large amounts of specific factual knowledge and information help document the ways in which each group's behavior is different and distinct even though it shares some values and expectations with other groups. There are many examples in the literature of culture-specific skill training for groups defined by nationality, ethnicity, religion, language, age, gender, region, socioeconomic status, educational background, and an almost unlimited number of formal or informal affiliations. The culture-specific focus may be on the group's identity, a specific problem, or any other carefully defined context. Culture-general and culture-specific skill training approaches complement one another. In any multicultural setting there are both cultural similarities and cultural differences on which to focus.

Evaluation

The last step of a training sequence is evaluating whether the persons trained have met the objectives in awareness, knowledge, and skill. This is called "formative" evaluation. Another kind of evaluation is a long-term and much more complicated evaluation to verify whether or not the objectives were appropriate and met the long-term needs of the participants. This second type of evaluation is called "summative" evaluation.

There are several models or frameworks for evaluating training criteria (e.g., Brinkerhoff, 1987; Bushnell, 1990; Galvin, 1983; Holton, 1996; Kaufman & Keller, 1994; Kirkpatrick, 1967, 1987, 1998; Kraiger, Ford, & Salas, 1993; Phillips, 1996; Warr, Bird, & Rackham, 1970). Kirkpatrick's four-level model introduced in 1959 has become a classic that is used by many trainers. Kirkpatrick (1998) describes his four levels as follows:

Level 1: Reaction is a measure of how participants feel about various aspects of a training program. Reaction is really a measure of customer satisfaction. Did they like it and did they find the training useful? This is important information to have, especially for diversity and multicultural training, since positive reactions encourage participants to attend future programs. However, at this level of measurement, whether or not the program met its objectives, beyond participant satisfaction, remains unknown.

Level 2: Learning is a measure of the knowledge obtained, skills improved, or attitudes changed as a result of the training. Did the trainees learn the objectives? Measuring whether trainees learned the objectives may require giving some sort of test as opposed to a survey that might have been used to measure reactions during level one.

Level 3: Behavior is a measure of the extent to which the trainees actually use what was learned back on the job. This is often termed transfer of training and is measured by observing the trainee's on-the-job behavior or checking organizational records (e.g., reduction in waste, reduced customer complaints).

Level 4: Results can be considered a measure of the improvement in organizational effectiveness (e.g., increased sales, higher productivity, larger profits, lower employee turnover) attributable to the training. This is the most difficult level to assess.

Kirkpatrick says that although evaluation becomes more meaningful as you progress from level 1 to level 4, it also becomes more difficult, complicated, and expensive. However, all levels are important and none should be skipped.

Evaluation methods range from informal discussions over wine and cheese to formal written evaluations of long-term changes in productivity determined by random work samples. However you proceed, room should be allowed for evaluation in training activities. These data will be valuable to leaders in providing feedback on their accomplishment, valuable to demonstrate the strength or weakness of the training design, and valuable to those sponsoring the training activity as a basis for making decisions.

Some criteria for evaluating multicultural training are as follows:

Leaders are trained to increase their awareness so they will
- Appropriately recognize the value of the priority they give to basic attitudes, opinions, and assumptions
- Accurately compare their own cultural perspective with that of a person from the other culture
- Sensitively articulate their own professional role in relation to the other culture
- Appropriately estimate constraints of time, setting, and resources in the other culture
- Realistically estimate the limit of their own resources in the other culture

Leaders are trained to increase their knowledge so they will
- Understand the process of institutional change in the other culture at local, national, and regional levels
- Cite the relevant literature of the other culture
- Identify similarities and differences of their own home culture and the other cultures
- Identify referral resources in the other culture
- Select key resource persons from the other culture for more information

Leaders are trained to increase their skill so they will
- Efficiently plan, conduct, and evaluate training about the other culture
- Accurately assess the needs of people from the other culture
- Utilize the talents of interpreters and cultural informants from the other culture

- Observe, understand, and accurately report about culturally learned behaviors in the other culture
- Interact, advise, and appropriately manage their assigned task in the setting of the other culture

Multicultural development is presumed to proceed from an awareness of attitudes, opinions, and assumptions to knowledge of facts and information to skill in taking the appropriate action. Most persons being trained, however, are at different stages of development. Some trainees will require more emphasis on awareness, some on knowledge, and others can proceed directly to skill development.

In considering different types of training for different levels of awareness, knowledge, and skill development, Black and Mendenhall (1989) present eight scenarios for cross-cultural training varying on rigor, duration, technique, and content. The highest amount of rigor required 60 to 180 hours of training consisting of lecture, factual briefing, books, culture assimilator, role plays, cases, field experiences, and simulations. The content of this training included equal emphasis on job and culture—job demands, constraints, choices, country economics, history, and religion. The lowest amount of rigor was reported for the training scenario that lasted only 4 to 8 hours and used only lecture, film, and books. The content involved little treatment of either job or culture.

Implications of Cultural Differences for Training

As training sessions are designed, consideration should be given to cultural dimensions (Filipczak, 1997). Trainees from cultures high in individualism will expect participation in exercises and discussion to be determined by status in the organization or culture. Trainees from cultures high in uncertainty avoidance will expect a formal instructional style; impromptu trainer styles will not be appreciated. Trainees from cultures low in masculinity will be more accepting of female trainers and will value relationships with other trainees. Trainees from cultures high in power distance will expect the trainers to be authoritarian and in control of the training session. Trainers will also be expected to be experts on the subject matter being taught. Finally, trainees from cultures with a long-term time orientation will be more accepting of developmental plans and assignments compared to those from cultures with short-term time orientations.

Conclusion

Just as culture is complex but not chaotic, so should multicultural training be guided by a sequence of learning objectives that reflect the needs of both the leader and the multicultural context. Teaching multicultural leadership and communication should include any and all methods relevant to the multicultural context from the viewpoint of the culture that is being taught. Training designs need to be comprehensive enough to include both culture-general and culture-specific perspectives. The developmental sequence from awareness to knowledge to skill provides an eclectic framework for organizing the content of multicultural training and a rationale for leader development in multicultural settings.

CHAPTER 7 DISCUSSION QUESTIONS

1. State an objective for a leader who is about to enter his or her first multicultural training and describe the matrix in which the objective has an awareness aspect, a knowledge aspect, and a skill aspect.

2. What is the best way to handle a leader who does not feel comfortable with experiential learning?

3. Design your own comprehensive multicultural training program. Which types of training designs compliment each other best?

Critical Incident: Flavor-of-the-Month Diversity Training

"I can't believe it!" Jim, a Hispanic manager said angrily. "My phone is ringing off the hook, I'm two days behind in processing the special order purchase orders that can't be shipped without my approval, I have to finish my benchmarking report by tomorrow, and I have to spend three hours this afternoon in a diversity workshop." "Why don't you tell her that you don't have time?" Sara, Jim's recently hired colleague asked. "I can't," Jim explained. "This one, like so many other wastes of my time, is coming down from the top." "Well, I figure that means it promises to be a decent program, right?" Sara said. "Oh Sara, your naiveté would be refreshing if I wasn't so busy," Jim laughed. "We've had a diversity-related training program every year for the past four years and nothing has ever changed because of them." "Could it be your attitude that is getting in the way of your taking something from the training?" Sara asked a little sheepishly, hoping she wasn't offending Jim. "Talk to me after this afternoon and we will see how Pollyanna you are then." Jim said.

CRITICAL INCIDENT DISCUSSION QUESTIONS

1. Whose fault is it that Jim has not seen any changes based on past diversity training programs?

2. Should Jim be required to attend the training program?

3. What should the trainers be told about the history of diversity training and the attitudes of some of the participants?

Exercise 7: Predicting the Decisions of a Resource Person

OBJECTIVE

To learn how persons from other cultures make decisions

DESCRIPTION

The facilitator will bring a resource person into the class from a culture or population with which the group members are not likely to have had previous contact. It is important to find a resource person who is both articulate and authentic. It is easy to find people who are authentic to a population but not articulate, or who are articulate but not authentic. Ask the resource person to describe difficult decisions he or she has had to make. Have that person describe the situation up to *but not including* the actual decision that was made. Stop the resource person at that point and have each group member predict what decision the resource person would have made and why. When everyone has made a prediction, have the resource person explain what decision was made and why it was made.

Time required: 30 minutes or less

Risk/expertise level: Higher

Participants needed: Any number of participants plus one facilitator and one culturally different community resource person

PROCEDURE

1. Select an articulate and authentic resource person from the community and bring that resource person into the classroom.

2. Ask the resource person to describe events leading up to a decision but not disclosing the decision that was made.

3. Ask each participant to say what he or she thinks the resource person decided and why.

4. When all participants have guessed what the resource person decided, the resource person will explain what decision was made and why.

5. The facilitator will lead the group and the resource person in a debriefing discussion.

6. Allow the group members to ask their questions directly of the resource person and back off as a leader as much as you can.

7. Be open to the possibility that the resource person's style might be quite different from your own.

DEBRIEFING

In debriefing this exercise it is a good idea to have worked with the resource person ahead of time and coached that person to help you teach the concepts of logical consequences or reflection of meaning, because they are different in each cultural context. Questions for discussion may include the following:

1. Did you agree with the resource person's decision? If so, why?

2. Did you disagree with the resource person's decision? If so, why?

3. Did the resource person represent the perspective of others in his or her group in the community?

4. Was the resource person able to convince you of what an appropriate decision would be?

5. What would have been the consequences of your working with this resource person before understanding how he or she made decisions?

INSIGHT

The "self-reference criterion" that reflects our own view may not apply to others.

SOURCE: Pedersen, P. B. (2004). *110 experiences for multicultural learning.* Washington, DC: American Psychological Association Press.

8

Constructive Conflict Management in a Cultural Context

Major Objective

To demonstrate the importance of making cultural issues central for leaders in constructive conflict management

Secondary Objectives

1. To discuss the causes of cross-cultural conflict

2. To describe a culture-centered approach to conflict management

3. To contrast Westernized with non-Westernized approaches to conflict management

4. To describe an Interpersonal Grid for constructive conflict management

5. To examine the consequences of a culture-centered conflict management model for the future

M anaging conflict is an important part of every leader's job. Organizational behavior textbooks often define conflict as any situation where incompatible goals, attitudes, emotions, or behaviors lead to disagreement or opposition between two or more individuals or groups. A dated survey shows that managers used to spend about 21% of their time dealing with conflict in the workplace (Thomas & Schmidt, 1976). However, as multicultural organizations have grown in number, the varying cultures representing differences among employees also increases the potential for conflict, likely increasing the time leaders and managers deal with conflict.

It is important to note that not all conflict is bad. Conflict can lead to both positive and negative outcomes. Some of the often overlooked positive consequences of conflict include generating new ideas, stimulating creativity, motivating change, promoting organizational vitality, helping individuals and groups establish identities, and serving as an indicator of problems. The more familiar negative consequences include diverting energy from work, threatening the psychological well-being of those involved and those familiar with the conflict, wasting resources, creating a negative climate, breaking down group cohesion, and potentially leading to increased hostility and aggressive behaviors (Nelson & Campbell Quick, 2003).

A General Model for Handling Conflict

Regardless of whether conflict is the result of personal factors or organizational factors, and whether it results in positive or negative outcomes, it must be managed or it will likely lead to unintended consequences. The handling of conflict has been part of the management literature for more than 60 years. Follet (1940) discussed five ways of dealing with conflict: domination, compromise, integration, avoidance, and suppression. Blake and Mouton (1964) presented a framework for classifying styles for handling interpersonal conflicts into five types: forcing, withdrawing, smoothing, compromising, and problem solving. Thomas (1976) reinterpreted Blake and Mouton's framework considering the intentions and assertiveness in handling conflict. Figure 8.1 shows Thomas's five conflict-handling orientations according to each party's desire to satisfy their own or other's concerns.

Avoiding is a style low on both cooperativeness and assertiveness. It is a decision to take no action or to stay out of a conflict. This style is often considered to be withdrawal or indifference.

The *Accommodating* style reflects concern for the other party in meeting its goals, but a relative lack of concern about your own goals. The result is a cooperative but unassertive style.

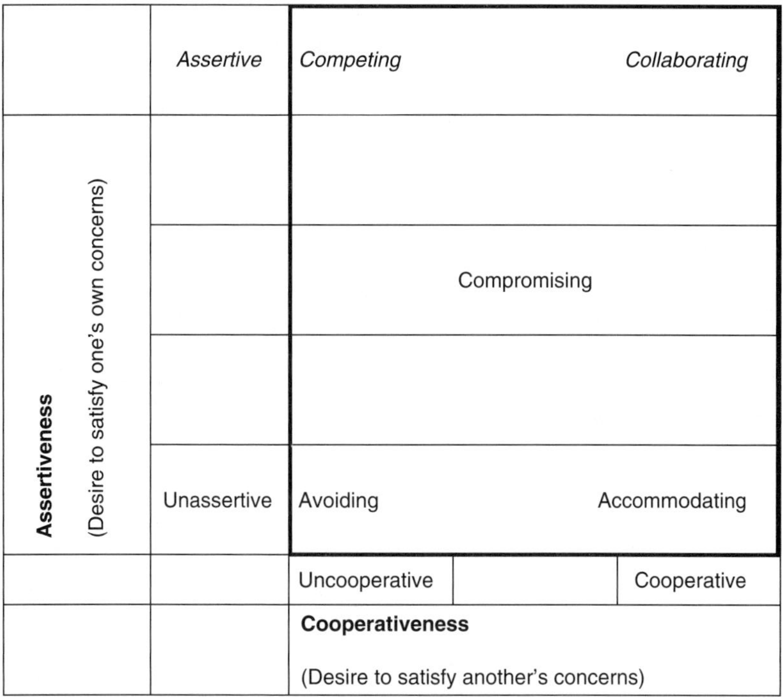

		Assertive	Competing		Collaborating
Assertiveness	(Desire to satisfy one's own concerns)			Compromising	
		Unassertive	Avoiding		Accommodating
			Uncooperative		Cooperative
			Cooperativeness		
			(Desire to satisfy another's concerns)		

Figure 8.1   Conflict Management Styles

SOURCE: K. W. Thomas, "Conflict and Conflict Management," in M. D. Dunnette, *Handbook of Industrial and Organizational Psychology* (Chicago: Rand McNally, 1976), 900. Used with permission of M. D. Dunnette.

The *Competing* style is characterized by assertive and uncooperative behavior. Your own concerns take precedence over the other party's concerns.

Compromising is a style that is intermediate in both cooperativeness and assertiveness because each party must give something up to resolve the conflict. This is not seen as the optimal solution to conflict due to each party surrendering part of its position for the sake of agreement.

Collaborating is seen as a win-win situation that is high on both cooperativeness and assertiveness. This solution to conflict is satisfactory to both parties and is usually obtained after much discussion.

Understanding conflict management styles provides a foundation for understanding conflict. As we have discussed, however, all behaviors are both learned and displayed in cultural context, and conflict is no exception. In a multicultural environment, the competencies necessary to manage conflict effectively include an awareness of one's own cultural values, behaviors, and expectations, as well as the cultural values, behaviors, and expectations of those involved in the conflict. Research has shown that cultural differences can influence the use of different styles of conflict management. For example, Kozan (1989) found that Turkish, Jordanian, and U.S. managers all preferred the collaborating style. Differences were found for preference for the competing style, which Turkish managers reported using frequently, while U.S. and Jordanian managers reported that it was one of their least frequently used styles. It has also been found that Asians prefer the avoiding and accommodating styles, while expatriates from the United States and Canada preferred the competing, collaborating, and compromising styles (McKenna, 1995).

Acknowledging that these differences were adversely affecting the organization, workshops were conducted where Asian participants shared that they felt that Americans would often "shout first and ask questions later," which, from their perspective, reflected an arrogant attitude. Interestingly, while culture did not play a part in their description of others' styles, the Asian participants attributed their conflict managing styles to their cultural backgrounds. Americans, on the other hand, stereotypically attributed the results to their view that Asians were timid and unassertive while their own results reflected their desire to "get things out in the open." The workshops and the discussions that ensued allowed both groups to discard stereotypes in favor of shared meanings and mutual understanding.

Additional research has found cultural differences in the way conflict is handled. Trubinsky, Ting-Toomey, and Lin (1991) found that individuals from Taiwan were more likely to use accommodating, avoiding, collaborating, and sharing styles of conflict management compared to respondents from the United States. Research has also found that individuals from collectivistic cultures, such as Japan, are more likely to avoid conflicts in the interest of preserving the relationship (Ohbuchi & Takahashi, 1994). Gabrielidis, Stephan, Ybarra, Dos Santos-Pearson, and Villareal (1997) found that respondents from Mexico (a collectivist culture) were more likely to show more concern for others by using accommodation and collaboration than Americans (an individualist culture). Finally, Pearson and Stephan (1998) found that respondents from Brazil were more likely to show concern for the outcomes of others compared to American respondents, who were more concerned with their own outcomes. Obviously, taken together, the results from these studies show that culture influences individuals' attitudes, expectations, and behaviors regarding conflict.

Next, two Cultural Grids are presented to demonstrate the importance of common ground and shared positive expectations in constructive conflict management. The danger of interpreting behaviors outside one's own cultural context is demonstrated. A culture-centered perspective will identify shared positive expectations among persons in conflict and help to understand all parties' behavior in the context of those shared positive expectations. The same behavior might have different meanings, and different behaviors might have the same meaning, when those behaviors are understood in context.

A Culture-Centered Perspective

There are many opportunities for conflict as culturally defined special interest groups, both within and outside of organizations, compete for limited resources. The increase in conflict due to cultural differences has profoundly changed the way conflict is successfully managed.

> Dramatically changing demographics in the United States increase the likelihood that community disputes, often involving a public policy issue, will have race, ethnicity and national origin as a factor. No longer can anyone who intervenes in an intergroup conflict assume that she or he has the tools necessary to understand and assist in properly resolving the dispute. (Kruger, 1992, p. 1)

Conflict is a normal aspect of any relationship. As stated earlier, conflict may be positive (functional) or negative (dysfunctional). Negative conflict threatens to erode the consensus needed for growth and development. Positive conflict, when it is managed appropriately, is usually about less central or fundamental issues and takes place within the context of a general consensus. Positive conflict can actually strengthen group relationships, especially if different members of the conflicting groups share common values across cultures. The importance of culture and cultural symbols in facilitating or hindering cross-cultural communications drives the need to incorporate cultural attitudes and perceptions into models and theories of conflict analysis and conflict resolution. Models produced by Western specialists continue to lack the proper tools to deal with individuals from non-Western nations, and thus they have remained largely irrelevant to those people (Rabie, 1994).

The ways that conflicts are perceived and managed reflect culturally shared patterns of attitudes and beliefs. These typical ways of perceiving and responding to conflict are so natural to the in-group members of a culture that their assumptions typically go unquestioned and innovative alternatives are neglected. Many anthropological investigations of conflict resolution have examined particular cultures and have emphasized the culturally specific nature of conflict resolution processes. However, many nonanthropological conflict-resolution sources have tended to focus on the modern, complex Western societies, yet they sometimes convey an implicit assumption that conflict-resolution models and techniques are very generally applicable to all, regardless of culture (Fry & Bjorkqvist, 1997).

The impact of culture on conflict has important implications for leaders and organizations. First, groups in conflict might be limiting their alternatives to those within their specific culture. Second, given an appreciation of cultural complexity, they are less likely to accept or give quick and easy answers or force one cultural perspective on others. Third, by understanding a range of culturally different approaches to conflict management, their practical and theoretical options for managing conflict are increased. "Only when people learn to understand and respect each other can peaceful coexistence begin" (Bjorkqvist & Fry, 1997, p. 252).

Cultural systems are not abstract models of reality but are primarily guidelines for action through patterned activity that creates reality (Geertz, 1973). The cultural systems of two conflicting groups present fundamentally different interpretations of what is happening. Each group uses its own cultural standards to evaluate the actions of the other, rather than the standards by which the others guide themselves. The job of the analyst is twofold. First, a cultural interpretation must present both of the contrasting native cultural systems so that they are both comprehensible and compelling as worldviews in themselves. Then the contrasting native interpretations of each group by the other must be shown to reveal how these patterns contribute to the generation of conflict (Dubinskas, 1992). By understanding each conflict according to culturally constructed differences, we discover a unified platform for understanding the persistence and intensity of the conflict.

A culture-centered model of conflict management interprets the conflict in a cultural context that makes that conflict meaningful in terms of causes, processes, and effects. The cultural context provides data that the antagonists themselves might take for granted but that can now be understood in a joint meaning-construction process.

> In a failing, conflictual process, two groups are blocked in their efforts to achieve agreement by a fundamental inability (or unwillingness) to interpret each other's position or perspective. In moving toward resolution, however, conflicting groups are actively seeking meaning in the other's actions as well as proactively trying to make their own actions understandable to that other. (Dubinskas, 1992, p. 205)

By jointly constructing cultural meaning, the cultural differences are not erased, the cultural integrity of all parties is preserved, and a new basis for intercultural cooperation and coordination is constructed as a metaphoric bridge to an island of common ground for both sides in the dispute.

The Intrapersonal Cultural Grid

As shown in Figure 8.2, the categories of the inside-the-person or Intrapersonal Cultural Grid provides a conceptual framework for demonstrating how cultural

Social System Variables	Behavior	Expectation	Values
Ethnographic Nationality Ethnicity Religion Language			
Demographic Age Gender Affectional orientation Physical abilities			
Status Social Economic Political Educational			
Affiliation Formal (e.g., family or career) Informal (e.g., shared idea or belief)			

Figure 8.2   The Intrapersonal Cultural Grid

and personal factors combine to interact in a relationship. The Cultural Grid links each behavior or action to an expectation or reason behind that action, and each expectation to a value learned from the cultural teachers.

Each cultural context is complicated and dynamic, influenced by many cultural teachers from the individual's cultural context who take turns being salient according to the time and place. An awareness of one's cultural identity requires being able to recognize how each action is the expression of specific expectations, how each expectation developed from specific values, and how each value was learned from one or more cultural teachers in the cultural context. Cultural teachers might come from family relationships such as relatives, or from business associates, fellow countrypersons, ancestors, or those with shared beliefs. Power relationships based on social friendships, sponsors and mentors, subordinates, and supervisors or superiors may provide cultural teachers. Memberships shared with coworkers or in organizations, gender or age groups, and workplace colleagues may contribute cultural teachers. A wide range of nonfamily relationships, friendships, classmates, neighbors, or just people like yourself may also have contributed teachers.

The Interpersonal Cultural Grid

The Intrapersonal Cultural Grid is intended to show the complex relationships among what you did (behavior), why you did it (expectation), and where you learned to do it. Judging other people's behavior out of context, or without regard to why the person did it and where the person learned it, is likely to be misleading at best and totally wrong at worst. It is not easy to discover why people do what they do. Many if not most of us often do not know why we do what we do, not to mention where we learned to do it. The Cultural Grid is not a quick and easy solution for understanding behaviors in their cultural context. Yet unless a behavior is understood in context, it is very likely to be misunderstood. For example, assume a meeting was occurring with a leader from Taiwan and as some key points were being made, and papers were being passed around the room, the leader from Taiwan abruptly stood up and left the room. It may be assumed that one of the key points offended the Taiwanese leader, when in fact it was the papers being passed around the room and that were passed over his head by two participants who were standing up to get coffee. Being unfamiliar with the culture of Taiwan, which includes the belief that the head is sacred, could cause a serious business problem and potential conflict.

The Interpersonal Cultural Grid (see Figure 8.3), on the other hand, is an attempt to describe the relationship between people or groups by separating what they do (behaviors) from why they do it (expectations). The Interpersonal Cultural Grid has four quadrants. Each quadrant explains a large or small part of any relationship between two individuals or groups. There will be some data in all four cells for any relationship, but the salience may change from one cell to another over time as the relationship changes.

I. In the first quadrant, two individuals have similar (perceived positive) behavior and similar (perceived positive) reasons for doing that behavior. The relationship is congruent and harmonious. There is a high level of accuracy in both individuals' interpretation of the other's behavior and the positive shared expectations or reasons behind that behavior. Both persons are smiling (behavior), for example, and both persons expect friendship. There is little conflict in this quadrant and few surprises.

		Behavior	
		Same	Different
Expectation	Same or Positive	I (Harmony)	II (Cross-cultural conflict)
	Different or Negative	III (Personal conflict)	IV (War)

Figure 8.3   The Interpersonal Cultural Grid

II. In the second quadrant, two individuals act differently or perceive the other's action in negative terms, but they still share the same positive expectations or reason for doing what they did. There is a high level of agreement in that both persons expect trust, friendliness, and safety, for example, but there is a low level of accuracy because each person perceives the other's behavior or action as negative, wrong, or inappropriate, and probably hostile. This quadrant is characteristic of cultural conflict in which each person applies a self-reference criterion to interpret the other person's behavior. The conditions described in the second quadrant are very unstable and, unless the shared positive expectations are quickly found and made explicit, the salience is likely to change toward the third quadrant, favoring the more powerful of the two. It is important for at least one of the two people to discover and identify the presence of shared positive expectations for trust, respect, safety, and fairness in their different cultural contexts, despite the apparent differences in their behaviors as they express those reasons.

III. In the third quadrant, the two persons have the same behaviors but now they have different or negative expectations or reasons. The similar behaviors give the "appearance" of harmony and agreement by displaying the desired behavior or action, but the hidden different or negative expectations and reasons for acting will ultimately destroy the relationship. Although both persons are now in disagreement, this might not be obvious or apparent. One person may continue to expect trust and friendliness, whereas the other person is now distrustful and unfriendly, even though they both present the same smiling and glad-handing behaviors. If these two people discover that at an earlier time they shared positive expectations or reasons for working together, they might be able to salvage the relationship and return to the second quadrant, reversing the escalating conflict between them. If the difference in expectations or reasons is ignored or undiscovered, the conflict will ultimately move to the fourth quadrant.

IV. The fourth quadrant is where two people have different and/or negative expectations, and they stop pretending to be congruent. The two persons are now "at war" with one another and may no longer even want to increase harmony in their relationship. They may just want to hurt one another. Both persons are in disagreement, and that disagreement is now obvious and apparent. This relationship is likely to result in hostile disengagement. It is very difficult to retrieve conflict from the fourth quadrant because one or both parties have stopped trying to find shared positive expectations. Unfortunately, most conflicts between people and groups remain undiscovered until they reach the fourth quadrant. An appropriate prevention strategy would be to identify the conflict in behaviors—as indicated in the second quadrant—early in the process, when those differences in behaviors might be positive because there are still shared positive reasons or expectations for behaving, thus allowing the parties to build on their common ground without losing integrity.

Therefore two leaders or groups may both share the same positive expectations or reasons for what they do but continue to act differently. They may both want trust, but one may be loud and the other quiet. They may share respect, but one may be open and the other closed. They can both believe in fairness, but one may be direct and the other indirect. They may value efficiency, but one may be formal and the other informal. They can seek effectiveness, but one may be close and the other distant. They may want safety, but one may be task oriented and the other relationship oriented. Only when each behavior is assessed and understood in its own cultural context does that behavior become meaningful. Only when positive shared expectations can be identified will two individuals or groups be able to find and build on common ground without sacrificing integrity.

Western and Non-Western Alternative Models

As stated in Chapter 3, non-Western cultures have typically been associated with "collectivistic" perspectives while Western cultures have typically been associated with "individualistic" value systems (Kim, Triandis, Kagitçibasi, Choi, & Yoon, 1994). Individualism describes societies in which the connections between individuals are loose and each individual is expected to look after him- or herself, while collectivism describes cultures where people are part of strong cohesive in-groups that protect them in exchange for unquestioned lifetime loyalty (Hofstede, 1991).

The conflict between individuals in finite time, typical of a westernized conflict, is quite different in both theory and practice from collectivized conflict in an infinite time context. In many non-Western cultural conflicts, the ways to manage differences are found in quoted proverbs or stories and historical examples that instruct all parties about managing power differentials, handling disputes, locating mediators or go-betweens, and achieving mutually satisfactory settlements (Augsburger, 1992).

Watson-Gegeo and White (1990) prefer the term *disentangling* to conflict resolution or dispute management for describing solutions to conflict in Pacific Island cultures. Disentangling is more process oriented than an outcome, and the image of a tangled net or line blocking purposeful activity has a practical emphasis as well as implying the ideal state where the lines of people's lives are "straight." Katz (1993) likewise talks about "the straight path" as a healing tradition in Fiji, with spiritual dimensions of health for the individual and for society. In contrasting collectivistic with individualistic cultures, the nature of the self becomes important.

> The self in most collectivistic cultures is maintained and defined through active negotiation of facework. By contrast, in Western societies the self is grounded intrapsychically in self-love, self-definition, and self-direction. In the solidarity of a collectivistic setting, the self is not free. It is bound by mutual role obligations and duties as it is structured and nurtured in an ongoing process of give-and-take in facework negotiations. In the West, there must be high consistency between public face and private self-image. In the East, the self is not an individual but a relational construct. (Augsburger, 1992, p. 86)

Another distinction between Western and non-Western models identifies the more complex, technologically advanced, and multi-institutional cultures as "low context," with some notable exceptions. Hall (1976) contrasts the American (low context) with the Japanese (high context) perspective regarding justice, for example. The Japanese trial puts the accused, the court, the public, and the injured parties together to work toward settling the dispute, in contrast with the protagonist-antagonist conflict model in an American court. The function of the trial in Japan is to locate the crime in context so that the criminal and society can see the consequence. In high-context systems, persons in authority are responsible for subordinates, whereas in low-context systems responsibility is diffused, making it difficult to fix blame. Low-context cultures are also usually characterized by individualism, overt communication, and heterogeneity. The United States, Canada, and Central and Northern Europe are described as areas where low-context cultural practices are most prevalent. On the other hand, high-context cultures feature collective identity-focus, covert communication, and homogeneity. This approach is most evident in Asian countries, including Japan, China, and Korea, as well as Latin American countries (Hall, 1976).

Gudykunst and Ting-Toomey (1988) associate high and low context with individualism and collectivism:

- Low-context persons view indirect conflict management as weak, cowardly, or evasive; members of high-context cultures view direct conflict management as impolite and clumsy.
- Low-context persons separate the conflict issue from the person; high-context cultures see the issue and person as interrelated.
- Low-context persons seek to manage conflict to reach an objective and fair solution; high-context cultures focus on the affective, relational, personal, and subjective aspects that preclude open conflict.
- Low-context cultures have a linear and logical worldview that is problem oriented and sensitive to individuals; high-context cultures see the conflict, event, and all actors in a unified context.
- Low-context cultures value independence focused on autonomy, freedom, and personal rights; high-context cultures value inclusion, approval, and association.

With data from a 1994 conference on "Conflict Resolution in the Asia Pacific Region," Jandt and Pedersen (1996) developed a series of 17 hypotheses about how high- and low-context cultures experience conflict differently.

1. In low-context cultures, individual participants must first accept and acknowledge that there is a conflict before resolution/mediation can begin.

2. In high-context cultures, traditional groups must first accept and acknowledge that there is a conflict before resolution/mediation can begin.

3. In low-context cultures, conflict and the resolution/mediation process must often be kept private.

4. In high-context cultures, conflict is not private and must be made public before the resolution/mediation process can begin.

5. In low-context cultures, societal conflict management is most effective in preparing an individual's skill for teaching individuals how to negotiate/mediate or resolve conflict reactively.

6. In high-context cultures, social conflict management emphasizes preventive measures by monitoring or mediating stress in a more proactive manner.

7. In low-context cultures, resolution and mediation are individually defined by the individuals involved in conflict.

8. In high-context cultures, conflict and its resolution/mediation are defined by the group or culture.

9. The role of internationals and the media in low-context cultures is not to intervene in conflicts in high-context cultures but to call public attention to the situation so that resolution/mediation can take place on its own.

10. In low-context cultures, settlements are usually devoid of ritual and spirituality.

11. In high-context cultures, settlements are most often accompanied by ritual and spirituality.

12. New arrivals from high-context cultures will not be served best by conflict resolution/mediation strategies developed in low-context cultures.

13. In groups combining high- and low-context cultures, the most powerful group's style of dispute resolution/mediation will predominate.

14. Low-context organizations in high-context cultures will avoid "traditional" alternative dispute resolution strategies and prefer court settlements.

15. Relying on courts to resolve/mediate conflict is regarded as a failure in high-context cultures.

16. Low-context cultures prefer dispute resolution/mediation to be face-to-face.

17. High-context cultures prefer to do dispute resolution/mediation through intermediaries.

Conflict in an Asian-Pacific Context

Barnes's (1991) writing about conflict management in the Asia-Pacific region describes the four goals of traditional conflict as making rights effective, diverting the dispute from the court system, preserving social solidarity against change, and resisting the centralized legal bureaucracy. The Asia-Pacific perspective of these functions is unique in several ways, as described by a Chinese mediator.

> We who engage in mediation work should use our mouths, legs and eyes more often. This means we should constantly explain the importance of living in harmony and dispense legal education. We should also pay frequent visits to people's houses and when we hear or see any symptoms of disputes we should attempt to settle them before they become too serious. (Barnes, 1991, p. 26)

Conflict management in the Asian context has been described as face maintenance, face saving, face restoration, and face loss (Duryea, 1992). The concept of "face" is Chinese in origin and is a literal translation of the Chinese term *lian*, indicating the confidence of society in the integrity of moral character. Without moral character, the individuals cannot function in their community, so *lian* is both a social sanction for enforcing moral standards and an internalized sanction (Hu, 1945, p. 45). Face is lost when an individual or group or someone representing the group fails to meet the requirements of their socially defined role or position. Face can become more important than life itself, as the evaluation of the self by the community is essential to identity.

What one thinks of self is less important than what one thinks others think. Ting-Toomey and Cole (1990) define the concept of face in conflict management as important in all communications but especially in ambiguous conflict situations as defined by each cultural context and face-management strategies.

The traditional Chinese approach to conflict resolution is based on saving face for all parties through the choices made regarding personal goals and interpersonal harmony, following the Confucian tradition (Hwang, 1998). First, giving up personal goals for the sake of interpersonal harmony requires endurance. Second, giving up interpersonal harmony for the sake of personal goals requires confrontation. Third, simultaneously maintaining interpersonal harmony and personal goals requires public obedience and private disobedience. Fourth, focusing on maintaining interpersonal harmony more than personal goals requires compromise. Fifth, disregard for both interpersonal harmony and personal goals results in quarreling and the destruction of the relationship. These choices become more complicated in actual situations.

A subordinate in conflict with a superior must protect the superior's face to maintain interpersonal harmony, requiring "endurance." Opinions are expressed indirectly, and any personal goal must be achieved privately while pretending to obey the superior. When the conflict involves horizontal relationships among in-group members, the members may communicate directly, and to protect harmony they may give face to each other through compromise. If, however, one insists on his or her personal goal in spite of the feelings of the other, the fight may continue for a long time. If both parties insist on their conflicting personal goals, they may treat the other as an "out-group" member and confront that person directly, disregarding harmony and protecting their own face. A third party might be required to mediate this conflict, and if it is not resolved it may result in destroying the relationship.

Hwang (1998) describes the Confucian relationships of father/son, husband/wife, senior/junior brother and superior/subordinate in a vertical structure emphasizing the value of harmony. "When one is conflicting with someone else within his or her social network, the first thing one has to learn is forbearance. . . . In its broadest sense, forbearance means to control and to suppress one's emotion, desire and psychological impulse" (p. 28). Therefore a subordinate must obey and endure the superior's demands, relying on indirect communication from some third party in their social network to communicate with the superior. Direct confrontation is described as when both parties "tear off their faces" and confront each other openly. When Chinese people are in direct conflict, third parties from their social network tend to intervene between them to reduce the escalation of violence. Confucian rules of politeness require both sides to "care about the other's face" at least superficially, so conflict among family members may not be evident to outsiders. Members of the family take care of each other's face in front of outsiders to maintain superficial harmony by obeying publicly and defying privately.

Rubin, Pruitt, and Kim (1994) describe conflict in Western cultures in terms of general strategies that vary in terms of outcomes and feasibility.

> The strategies include contending (high concern for one's own outcomes and low concern for other's outcomes), problem solving (high concern for both one's own and the other's outcomes), yielding (low concern for one's own outcomes and high concern for other's outcomes), and avoiding (low concern for both one's own and other's outcomes). (p. 11)

Integrative solutions were judged the most desirable, longer lasting, and most likely to contribute to the relationship of parties and the welfare of the broader community than compromises or arbitration. It would seem that the science of conflict management is moving toward Asian models.

A Pacific Islands model for maintaining conflict and managing conflict is through *ho'oponopono,* which means "setting to right" in the Hawaiian language. This traditional system is based on family systems, and variations of this model occur throughout the Pacific region. The traditional Hawaiian cultural context emphasizes working together, cooperation, and harmony (Shook, 1985). The extended family or *ohana* is the foundation of traditional Hawaiian society, with child-rearing practices fostering interdependence and contributions to the family's welfare emphasizing the value of affiliation. "The successful maturation of a person in the Hawaiian culture thus requires that an individual cultivate an accurate ability to perceive and attend to other people's needs, often without being asked. These are attitudes and behaviors that help cement the relationship of the *ohana* and the community" (Shook, 1985, p. 6).

Unregulated conflict disrupts balance and harmony, and requires self-scrutiny, admission of wrongdoing, asking forgiveness, and restitution to restore harmony. Negative sanctions of illness and social pressure result from negative actions or feelings toward others. The traditional *ho'oponopono* approach to problem solving and conflict management was revived in the early 1970s by Pukui, Hartig, and Lee (1972) who, along with Panglinawan (1972), increased an awareness of this traditional strategy. LeResche (1993) describes this relationship-centered and agreement-centered process of peacemaking as "sacred" justice. Meyer (1994) describes how peacemaking is unique:

> Peacemaking and mediation have two distinct vocabularies. Mediation terms like dispute and conflict become, in a peacemaking context: stubborn disagreement, having differences and, for Hawaiians, entanglement. Words like "punishment," "revenge," and "rights" in mediation become "restitution," "forgiveness," and "truth" in peacemaking. Clearly, in a philosophical way, mediation and peacemaking differ in both process and product. Peacemaking is not concerned with distributing justice, finding who is right, dispensing punishment, but rather strives for the maintenance of harmony between individuals and the exhibition of spiritual efficacy. Both peacemaking and mediation, however, strive for the ending of conflict. (p. 2)

Attempts to adapt *ho'oponopono* to Westernized contexts have applied those aspects of (a) recognizing the importance of conflict management in a spiritual context, (b) channeling the discussion, with sanctions of silence should disruption occur; and (c) bringing the wrongdoer back into the community as a full member with complete restitution and forgiveness.

Constructive Conflict Management in the 21st Century

Cultural backgrounds shape leaders' ways of thinking, believing, and behaving by influencing their perceptions of themselves and others. The more cultural differences there are between people, the more difficulty they have communicating or understanding why they fail to communicate. Each culture expresses the same core values in different behaviors, increasing the likelihood of misunderstanding. Increased intercultural understanding introduces new ideas, identifies new values, and constructs new sociopolitical structures at the macro and micro levels to increase the quality of interpersonal and institutional interaction.

> Diverse human interests and needs, largely incompatible religious social beliefs and competing individual and group goals cause conflict to arise and prevail. Moreover, different loyalties, cultural values, ideologies and geopolitical considerations provide a fertile ground for the planting and nurturing of conflict within and between states. Disparities in wealth, natural resources, technology and power among social classes and ethnic groups within and between states have also been a cause of increased grievances and conflict. (Rabie, 1994, p. 2)

Sunoo (1990, p. 388) provides seven guidelines for mediators of intercultural disputes: (1) Expect different expectations; (2) do not assume that what you say is being understood; (3) listen carefully; (4) seek ways of getting both parties to validate the concerns of the other; (5) be patient, be humble, and be willing to learn; (6) apply win-win negotiating principles to the negotiation rather than traditional adversarial bargaining techniques; and (7) dare to do things differently. These recommendations parallel eight guidelines for the negotiator by Cohen (1991): Study the opponent's culture and history, try to establish a warm personal relationship, do not assume that others understand what you mean, be alert to indirect communication, be sensitive to face/status issues, adapt your strategy to your opponent's cultural needs, be appropriately flexible and patient, and recognize that outward appearances are important.

Lund, Morris, and LeBaron-Duryea (1994) concluded their review of research on disputes and culture beyond the "taxonomy trap" of lists and guidelines for each cultural group. Culture is complicated and dynamic with considerable diversity within each cultural group. "The challenge is to develop a view of culture that delineates differences among individuals and subgroups within a culture and encompasses commonalities within that group without simplification, overgeneralization and stereotyping" (p. 24). The findings of that project provide guidelines for managing problems in intercultural understanding in the 21st century.

Dominant-culture methods of conflict resolution incorporate values and attitudes not shared by members of minority groups, but based on culture-bound assumptions. These culture-bound assumptions are implicit or explicit in the staged models of mediation and negotiation taught by the dominant culture.

First, "Conflicts are in essence communication problems. If effective communication can be facilitated, then the problem can be solved." In fact, the cultural context mediates all communications between groups so that good communication is only one of many factors in conflict management.

Second, "There is a middle ground in which both parties can get some of what they want in any given conflict." In fact, the conflict may not fit a win-lose model, and compromising may be less effective than reframing the conflict so both parties can get what they want without losing integrity.

Third, "The optimal way to address conflict is to get the parties in the same room to facilitate an open, forthright discussion of the issues." In fact, in many cultural contexts, open conflict may be destructive.

Fourth, "Parties in conflict emphasize their individual interests over collective values of family, community, or society." In fact, collective interests may be more important than individual interests in the context of long-term solutions.

Fifth, "A third-party intervener must be a neutral person with no connections to any of the parties." In fact, neutrality may be impossible or even undesirable when it requires going outside the group to find a third party.

Sixth, "Good intact procedures for conflict resolution should be standardized according to fair, reasonable, and rational formats and policies." In fact, the expectation of fairness, reasonableness, and rationality may be expressed quite differently by each culture.

Culture-based conflict between ethnocultural groups has become a serious problem in recent times and promises to be a major problem of the 21st century. By better understanding the positive contribution that a culture-centered approach to intercultural understanding provides, we might be better prepared to survive the problems of intercultural understanding in the coming years.

Conclusion

By reframing conflict between people into cultural categories, it becomes possible for two persons to disagree without either of them being wrong based on their different culturally learned assumptions. This chapter has described the advantages of reframing conflict into cultural categories for constructive conflict management. Until recently the influence of cultural similarities and differences has been typically overlooked in the published literature about conflict management, applying a dominant-culture, white, middle-class, urban, male, Euro-American model to the management of conflict across cultures and countries. With the increased influence of non-Western cultures and countries, a variety of different styles of conflict management have become more visible.

It is necessary for leaders to understand how conflict is understood and managed in non-Western cultures, not only because individuals from those countries are increasingly employed in organizations in the United States, but also because Western cultures can learn a great deal from non-Western cultures about constructive conflict management. Conflict is managed quite differently in a high-context culture compared to a low-context culture, and each perspective has its advantages and disadvantages. The skilled conflict manager will need to understand both perspectives and know when either may be more appropriate.

Asian and Pacific cultures in particular offer a perspective for managing conflict in harmony, where conflict between people is often described in a cosmic context with spiritual implications. The goal in Asian and Pacific cultures is often to prevent overt conflict from occurring at all, while the Western perspective is more often about resolving conflict once it has occurred.

Constructive conflict management may become the first priority of leaders in the 21st century, especially when conflict is between culturally different people. Leaders need to find common ground without losing their integrity and without forcing others to lose their integrity. It will become important for leaders to understand interpersonal and intrapersonal conflict in the cultural context in which those behaviors are learned and displayed.

Parts of this chapter were adapted from Pedersen's "Intercultural Understanding: Finding Common Ground Without Losing Integrity," in D. Christie, D. Wagner, and D. Winter, *Peace, Conflict and Violence: Peace Psychology for the 21st Century.* Prentice Hall, 2001.

CHAPTER 8 DISCUSSION QUESTIONS

1. What important aspects of handling conflict differ between Western and non-Western cultures?

2. Should leaders encourage conflict as a motivation tool? Would this technique be expected to work better in certain cultures?

3. Which conflict management style (competing, collaborating, compromising, avoiding, or accommodating) is likely to gain the best results for a conflict in a non-Western culture? For a Western culture? Why?

Critical Incident: What Type of Conflict Is This?

Young Kyu was one of Don's best software developers. He always did more than was expected of him and never missed a deadline. His expertise was essential for two of the company's major projects last year, and his individual contributions really made him shine. The only problem seems to center around the team projects in which Young Kyu participates. His teammates always complain about his lack of contribution, and they claim they have to work harder since Young Kyu doesn't pull his weight. This confuses Don since he knows that Young Kyu emigrated from Korea to the United States 10 years earlier, and that Korea is a collectivist culture. Don figured this meant that Young Kyu would actually work harder on the team projects than on his individual projects due to what Don assumed was Young Kyu's more collectivist nature. Don asked Young Kyu about his perceptions of team processes for all of the groups he had been on, and Young Kyu said that he felt that they had all gone well. Because a problem has been reported on two different projects, Don decided he needed to figure out why.

CRITICAL INCIDENT DISCUSSION QUESTIONS

1. How can Don determine if there is a personal conflict or a cross-cultural conflict?

2. Because Young Kyu's individual performance has been outstanding, should Don try to give him more individual projects?

Exercise 8: The Cultural Grid

OBJECTIVE

To separate expectations from behaviors when analyzing multicultural case examples

DESCRIPTION

The Cultural Grid provides a framework with cultural factors in one dimension and personal factors in the other, resulting in a "personal-cultural orientation." The Cultural Grid provides a convenient framework for interpreting each behavior in the cultural context where that behavior was learned and is displayed.

Time required: Several hours

Risk/expertise level: High

Participants needed: Any number of participants plus a facilitator

PROCEDURE

Participants will be presented with an Interpersonal Cultural Grid visual figure to help them understand the importance of matching culturally learned behaviors with the culture teachers from whom the behaviors were learned.

1. Identify one or more significant behavior.

2. What is the expectation behind the behavior?

3. Who are the culture teachers behind the expectation?

4. The facilitator can read about the Interpersonal Cultural Grid in this chapter, or for a more detailed explanation, he or she can read Pedersen (2000), *A Handbook for Developing Multicultural Awareness*. It will be important for the facilitator to understand the Interpersonal Cultural Grid before introducing it to the group.

5. Participants are encouraged to analyze their relationship with their "best friend" to see if their best friend thinks differently, acts differently, and behaves differently from themselves in other ways. However, since the best friends share their positive expectation for "best friend-ness," the differences actually enrich the relationship.

6. Participants are encouraged to give examples of successful conflict management from their own experience to test the usefulness of the Interpersonal Cultural Grid. In debriefing, the facilitator might want to point out the following insights:

   a. Changing behavior is easy. You hold a gun to the other person's head and they do what you ask. You will, however, lose any positive shared expectations in the process.
   b. Accepting and tolerating different and seemingly negative behavior is difficult. It may nevertheless be necessary to manage conflict constructively and to preserve the importance of shared positive expectations.
   c. Conflict moves quickly from the second cell (different behavior, same expectation) to the third cell (same behavior, different expectation) because we are intolerant of different behaviors. This conflict will finally move to the fourth cell (different expectation, different behavior) and war will be declared.

7. Participants may role-play conflict between coworkers or between boss and employee to provide feedback to the persons in conflict to help them maintain positive shared expectations as their common-ground foundation for a win-win outcome.

INSIGHT

Separating culturally learned behaviors from expectations in constructive conflict management helps create win-win outcomes.

SOURCE: Pedersen, P. B. (2004). *110 experiences for multicultural learning.* Washington, DC: American Psychological Association Press.

9

Redefining Leadership
Through Multiculturalism

◆

Major Objective

To describe the importance of aligning leadership with the goals of multi-culturalism

Secondary Objectives

1. To discuss the problems with culture-bound leadership theory

2. To examine mentoring through a multicultural lens

3. To examine ethical dimensions of multicultural leadership

4. To determine the influence that culture has on negotiation styles

◆

Multiculturally skilled leaders provide an environment for their employ-ees that allows for each employee's unique culture to be respected while still allowing for the work of the organization to be completed. Most of us have been raised to "do unto others as we would have them do unto us," regardless of what they want. We are captured by our own self-reference criteria in all of our evaluations of others.

Leadership Styles and Multiculturalism

Research over the past 40 years suggests that leadership style should be situational (Freeman, Knott, & Schwartz, 1994). In other words, leadership should be appropriate to the people, time, place, and cultural context. It is also important to point out that recent research suggests that women and non-Whites tend to have more positive attitudes (tolerance) toward those who are different from them than men and Whites (e.g., Fuertes, Miville, Mohr, Sedlacek, & Gretchen, 2000; Miville et al., 1999; Strauss & Connerley, 2003; Strauss, Connerley, & Ammermann, 2003). This is not to lay the path for what some would call "White male bashing," but to raise awareness. In all diversity-related statistics, one should never make judgments or decisions for an individual based on group means. We know multiculturally competent people of all races, ethnicities, genders, and religions. The above-cited research suggests, however, that as a group, White males may need to work harder than others to break down preconceived notions in their quest to become multiculturally competent leaders.

Several extensive reviews on the importance of leadership in international business have been written. Bass (1990) included a chapter on cross-cultural leadership themes in research through the 1980s. Several other researchers have written reviews covering research through much of the 1990s (Dorfman, 1996; House, Wright, & Aditya, 1997; Peterson & Hunt, 1997). Dorfman (2004) and Smith and Peterson (2002) have written two recent reviews that build nicely on previous reviews.

Much has been written about theories of leadership. Many theories are American-based, such as Douglas McGregor's Theory X versus Theory Y manager (McGregor, 1960) and Rensis Likert's System 4 management (Likert, 1961). In general, these theories suggest that a participative style of leadership is more effective than an authoritarian style. Nevertheless, countries may differ on important characteristics, such as power distance (Hofstede, 1980), which would lead to different preferences for leadership styles. For example, the United States and Denmark, two low power distance countries, may prefer a participative style, whereas in high power distance countries such as France, Spain, and Mexico, employees may expect and respond much better to an authoritative leadership style (Rodrigues, 2001). Of course, an alternative would be to train the employees on how to work effectively with a participative leader.

Blake and Mouton (1964) proposed a relationship-oriented versus a task-oriented leadership emphasis. Task-oriented leaders place more emphasis on the performance of tasks, while relationship-oriented leaders place more importance on maintaining a good relationship with their subordinates. Culture has also been found to play a role in this type of leadership style preference (Westwood, 1997). A strong task orientation has been found in North American leaders and in leaders from most Western European countries, whereas a strong relationship-orientation has been found in leaders in African, Arab, and Latin American countries (Cellich, 1997). Interestingly, when Blake and Mouton surveyed 2,500 managers from four countries, in addition to participants from the Middle East and South America, the majority stated that a combination of task and relationship orientations was ideal, but when their actual style was assessed, they were more task oriented than relationship oriented (Bass, 1990).

Research has also shown that no one leadership style is universally effective, but that the situation dictates the most appropriate leadership style (Aldag & Kuzuhara, 2002, p. 331). The situational leadership model of Paul Hersey and Ken Blanchard states that the most appropriate style of leadership depends on the readiness of the group members being led (Hersey, Blanchard, & Johnson, 2001, pp. 175–191). Readiness is the extent to which the members have both the ability and willingness to accomplish a specific task. The situational leadership model shows that followers may be able and willing, able but unwilling, unable but willing, or unable and unwilling. The leader behavior will be delegating, participating, selling, or telling, respectively, depending on the readiness of the followers. This research was conducted on an American sample, however, leaving the question open as to whether the results generalize to other cultures.

Similar to the lists presented for global leadership competencies, many lists have been developed addressing the factors that make a great leader. In their book, *The Leadership Challenge*, Kouzes and Posner (2002) define the five practices of exemplary leadership:

- Model the way
- Inspire a shared vision
- Challenge the process
- Enable others to act
- Encourage the heart

All five of these practices should be easier for leaders who have an enhanced level of multicultural awareness, knowledge, and skills. Leaders who are developing their multicultural competencies must realize that, as in all new learning, they will make mistakes and errors will occur. Yet if a culture of openness and forgiveness is prevalent, it should encourage an environment in which new skills for both the leader and his or her constituents can be practiced. Learning requires letting people try things they have not tried before, which pushes people out of their comfort zones. It is important for leaders to show that it is acceptable to try new things, even if one is not polished at what is being attempted.

One way leaders can determine what they are modeling is by conducting a personal cultural audit. Kouzes and Posner (2002) suggest that in addition to watching your own actions, you should also have your audit conducted by someone else. They also go farther and state that leaders should make their results public, explaining what is working and what needs to be fixed. In dealing with multicultural issues, this would certainly be perceived as making the leaders vulnerable, but it would also set the stage for a more open environment. It is of course critical for leaders to develop an action plan to address their shortcomings, and they should be sure to follow through. Whether or not the cultural audit results are made public, it would still be a very useful exercise for leaders to go through to help them determine how they perceive their own multicultural competencies, and also how others perceive them.

Examining Mentoring Through a Multicultural Lens

To be successful in organizations, individuals need more than a basic knowledge of the employee handbook and job description. All organizations are full of subtleties that rule day-to-day interactions and operations. The unwritten rules that everyone "in the know" plays by can determine success or failure for a career. An important role that leaders can play, for both individuals and the organization, is mentoring.

First, we must establish that the term *mentoring* can mean different things in different cultures. In North America, the learner tends to be a younger, less powerful, and naïve junior member of the organization, who is guided by a more senior and more powerful individual. In Europe, instead of being older and more powerful, a mentor traditionally has more experience relevant to the protégé's needs, and the focus of the relationship is on mutual learning as opposed to sponsorship (Klasen & Clutterbuck, 2002). Even though the term may have different connotations in Europe and in North America, the roles taken on by the mentor should be based on the needs of the protégé.

Kram (1983, 1985) described four distinct phases of mentorship. The first is the Initiation phase, the time period when the mentoring relationship forms. This stage is characterized by the first 6 to 12 months of a potential mentor-protégé relationship. If the relationship matures into a mentorship, then Cultivation, the second stage, occurs. Kram (1983) states that the mentorship functions are maximized during this stage, which typically lasts from 2 to 5 years. It is during this stage that the mentor develops the protégé's performance, potential, and visibility throughout the organization. The third phase, Separation, involves both structural and psychological separation between the mentor and protégé as the protégé asserts more independence. This stage may last between 6 and 24 months and may be emotionally stressful, as both the mentor and the protégé embark on new roles, which can be characterized by anxiety or defiance. Finally, the Redefinition stage ends the mentorship, and both the mentor and former protégé, now acting as partners, evolve their relationship to one of informal contact and mutual support. Kram (1985) found that career functions were most important during the Initiation stage of the mentor-protégé relationship, with psychosocial functions becoming more important during the Cultivation stage. Career functions include providing activities that influence the protégé's career advancement, such as sponsorship, exposure, visibility, protection, coaching, and assignments that are challenging. Psychosocial functions include activities that influence the protégé's self-image and competence, such as role modeling, acceptance, counseling, confirmation, and friendship.

The jury is still out on how the mentoring relationship, especially a multicultural relationship, should be established. Some state that protégés should take the responsibility for finding a mentor (Brinson & Kottler, 1993). In a multicultural context, however, the protégé needs to understand that some potential mentors may be reluctant to serve. This may or not be related to cultural issues. Some potential mentors are just not comfortable serving in that role regardless of the demographic makeup of the pair. Protégés may need to select several different mentors for different purposes and develop varying levels of intimacy with them (Bowman, Kite, Branscombe, & Williams, 1999).

Research on mentoring has shown that when mentors do the choosing, they tend to choose protégés who are seen as being similar to themselves (Allen, Poteet, & Burroughs, 1997) and that satisfaction with the mentor-protégé relationship increases with similarity (Ensher & Murphy, 1997). This could be due in part to the easier time mentors and protégés from like cultures have in recognizing emotions. Recent research has found that individuals were more accurate in recognizing emotions expressed by others that were from their own cultural group (Elfenbein & Ambady, 2002). The findings held true across several channels of communication, including facial expressions, tone of voice, and body language. Cultural differences in understanding emotion can have real consequences for the mentor-protégé relationship. The fact is that we tend to mentor those we are most comfortable with, often those who share our cultural background. In addition, protégés are also likely to choose mentors based on how well they identify with the characteristics of the mentor. In other words, there is a mutual identification process underlying the development of the mentor-protégé relationship that provides a clear challenge for diversity or multiculturalism (Ragins, 2002).

Regardless of how the relationship is established, mentors, especially White mentors, need to develop a genuine interest in multicultural issues. They need to understand that adjustment issues for those who are culturally different will likely be exacerbated compared to those who are members of the cultural majority in a company. Both mentors and protégés will be entering the relationship with stereotypes that need to be acknowledged, at least internally, and actions that support the individual developmental needs of the protégé. As Crosby (1999) notes, multicultural mentoring benefits both the individuals and the organizations by encouraging everyone involved to bring more of themselves to work, which facilitates more productive questioning and problem solving (Thomas & Ely, 1996).

Ethical Dimensions of Multiculturalism

Different cultures have developed different values. For example, as cited in Carroll and Gannon (1997), after Japan imported the practice of rice farming from China around the seventh century, in order for each village to survive, each member had to work very hard toward the common good of the village. Compare this to Americans in the 17th and 18th centuries, when their culture was being established on the principles of individual rights and plentiful resources. These different histories have led to differences in many areas, including views on ethical behavior.

Carroll and Gannon (1997) propose a model of culture and ethical behavior for managers. Their model starts with the origins of culture itself, which includes history, geography, and natural resources. The next element in their model is the culture of a nation. This consists of two elements: management practices and basic values that lead to differences in the practices. Next, the model incorporates both primary and secondary influences on values and behaviors. Primary influences include parenting and socialization, education, and religion and directly influence managers' values and beliefs. Secondary influences, which are not as direct as primary influences, consist of laws, human resource management systems, and organizational culture. Secondary influences can also directly impact managers' ethical behavior along with their values and beliefs. For example, tight management controls will reduce unethical behavior.

Most of the research on culture and ethics focuses on values and beliefs as opposed to actual behaviors and decisions. Of course, there is overlap between these attitudes and behaviors, but they are not the same thing. The theory of reasoned action indicates that attitudes, beliefs, and values often do affect behavioral intentions and subsequent behaviors (Ajzen & Fishbein, 1980; Fishbein & Ajzen, 1975). Part of the problem of attempting to predict behavior from individual characteristics, however, is that situational factors not just influence, but may overwhelm individual propensities or actions in a given situation (Carroll & Gannon, 1997).

It has been stated that the four moral goals of leadership are the following (Gardner, 1990):

- Releasing human potential
- Balancing the needs of the individual and the community
- Defending the fundamental values of the community
- Instilling in individuals a sense of initiative and responsibility

All of these goals are consistent with a multicultural leadership focus. It has been suggested that global leaders must have uncompromising integrity along with unbridled inquisitiveness, personal character traits of emotionally connecting with people from diverse backgrounds, the ability to handle the duality between the need for additional information and the need to act under uncertainty, and that they have both business and organizational savvy (Gregersen, Morrison, & Black, 1998).

Most organizations have codes of ethics by which their employees are expected to act. However, there is usually plenty of gray area for personal codes of ethics and uncertainty to play into decision making. Sometimes leaders make decisions in multicultural settings that call into question the ethics involved. For example, in 1995, IBM offered $10 million to officials of Argentina's state-owned Banco Nacion to secure a $350 million contract to computerize the bank's 525 branches. The media attention generated by this incident went on for years. However, before readers pass judgment on Argentina, consider results from a recent study that found that incumbents from the United States scored lower on an integrity test than incumbents or applicants from Argentina, Mexico, and South Africa (Fortmann, Leslie, & Cunningham, 2002).

Donaldson and Dunfee (1994, 1999) developed integrative social contracts theory (ISCT) to apply to situations involving two or more conflicting sets of ethical norms. Fundamental to ISCT are the concepts of hypernorms and moral free space. Hypernorms are universal principles considered to be so basic that they serve as higher-order norms by which lower-order norms can be judged. These higher-order norms "include, for example, fundamental human rights or basic prescriptions common to most major religions. The values they represent are by definition acceptable to all cultures and organizations" (Donaldson & Dunfee, 1999, p. 221). Hypernorms present key limits to moral free space. Moral free space is defined as the "freedom of individuals to form or join communities and to act jointly to establish moral rules applicable to the members of the community" (1999, p. 38). ISCT is a useful theory for analyzing situations in which the norms of two cultures conflict. Donaldson and Dunfee caution, however, against simply copying one culture's values or ethics onto another culture. It can be disrespectful of the second culture and violates the concept of moral free space. A solution in one culture may need to take into account the moral rules of the other culture. The trick is to stick to one's own sense of right and wrong while respecting the right of the other culture to shape its own cultural and economic values (Donaldson & Dunfee, 1999).

One might think that dealing with ethical issues within a single company that has specific ethical guidelines would be clearer than using an "ethical algorithm" (developed by Donaldson to aid decision making concerning ethical or unethical behavior on the part of multinational corporations in host countries). Yet even within a single company within the United States, when individuals from different cultures interpret the same ethical codes of conduct, different understandings can result.

Times are changing. In 1998, Congress passed the International Anti-Bribery and Fair Competition Act. In January 2003, Turkey implemented anti-bribery legislation, becoming the last of 35 signatories to put laws in place to criminalize the bribery of foreign public officials in international business transactions (U.S. Department of Commerce, 2003). There are still a lot of gray areas for leaders to wade through, however. McFarlin and Sweeney (2003), in their international management textbook, gathered many excellent examples of practices that are not illegal under the Foreign Corrupt Practices Act, but that are still questionable. For example, many companies use donations and other "philanthropic" activities to influence decisions. In 1995, when IBM chairman Louis Gerstner visited Beijing, IBM donated $25 million in hardware and software to 20 Chinese universities. Another common practice is to offer trips to foreign officials. These trips usually involve visiting the business, but side trips to Disney World, Las Vegas, and Atlantic City also appear to be common. Often the U.S. company gives allowances to its visitors. One electronics company operating in China pays each of their Chinese visitors $125 a day while they are visiting the California headquarters. This is not illegal, but considering that some of these officials make the equivalent of $25 a week, the influence on his (the visitors from China are almost always men) decision making could be substantial. As long as the culture of bribery exists in other countries, however, U.S. companies will continue to be "creative" in developing strategies that help secure new contracts.

Leaders must be realistic about the situation in which they find themselves. For example, a recent discussion with a U.S. businessman revealed that he had recently worked for 2 months in an African country, checking out its potential for outsourced work. On a Monday, he arrived several hours early at the only airport within hundreds of miles to ensure that he did not miss his flight, because the next flight he could take would not leave until Thursday. When he went to give his ticket to the agent, the agent looked at him, grinned, and said, "sorry, no flight for you today." This businessman, a staunch supporter of ethics and anti-bribery policies, knew what was expected of him. He could slip the agent $10 and get on his flight, or he could stand by his principles, miss this flight, and hope that he would be allowed to take the flight on Thursday. In the meantime, he would have to sit idle for at least 3 days. Meetings set up back in the States would have to be rescheduled, not to mention his having to break promises he made to his children. Should he perpetuate the problem by paying the bribe, or should he stand by his values at a large price? Well, this business-man paid the $10, felt guilty about it, but realized that he wouldn't be solving any problems by staying in the African country for another 3 days or more.

Culture's Influence on Negotiation Styles

In Chapter 8 we discussed the influence of culture on conflict management. A related yet distinct concept is negotiation across cultures. Culture provides schemas or templates for interpreting both the situation and the behavior of others (Fiske & Taylor, 1991) and scripts that are sequences of appropriate social action (Shank & Abelson, 1977). Culture plays a large role in the outcomes of negotiation processes because negotiators tend to create less value when they have a lower understanding of the other party's priorities (Thompson, 1991). It might be assumed that negotiators from different cultures would be less willing to share information. However, research has found that U.S. and Japanese nego-tiators both ascribed to a schema for information sharing, but were less able to enact information-sharing scripts in intercultural negotiations compared to intracultural ones (Brett & Okumura, 1998). "Schemas and scripts appropriate for intracultural negotiations but inappropriate for intercultural negotiations may be impossible to turn on and off at will. If effective intercultural negotia-tions require a common negotiation script, how should negotiators determine whose script should prevail?" (Brett & Okumura, 1998, p. 508).

In addition, leaders who find themselves as negotiators should not rely solely on predetermined images they may have about a culture. For example, we frequently hear that the Chinese value harmony, good relationships, and respect (Blackman, 1997), and that they are cooperative and pursue "win-win" outcomes when relationships have been properly established (Adler, Brahm, & Graham, 1992). However, when foreign negotiators arrive in China, they are often met with fierce adversarial bargaining (Blackman, 1997) and Chinese negotiators who are "inscrutable, skillful, tough, shrewd, and tenacious" (Fang, 1999, p. 46). Interestingly, it has been suggested that the Chinese rely on a for-eigner's ignorance of the Chinese bureaucratic system to make claims of regu-lations or policies to their advantage that may or may not exist (Miles, 2003).

Of course, it is not only the Japanese and Chinese cultures that differ from U.S. culture in terms of negotiation style. Negotiators from Russia generally do not expect to develop long-term relationships with their bargaining partners and therefore do not spend much time on relationship building. They also make few concessions and view concession by others as signs of weakness. They also often start out with extreme positions, ignore established deadlines, and need to check back frequently with headquarters due to their limited authority (Adler, 2002). In contrast, individuals from Arab cultures use emotional appeals because they use subjective feelings as a basis for their arguments. They often want to build long-term relationships with their bargaining partners and therefore are willing to make concessions throughout the negotiating process. They often approach deadlines casually because time does not rule as it usually does in the American culture. Finally, in Arab cultures, those doing the negotiating are usually individuals with broad enough authority to make all decisions related to the deal being negotiated (Adler, 2002).

Negotiators from Latin American cultures are often emotionally expressive and passionate. As in the Japanese culture, face-saving to preserve honor and dignity is crucial in negotiations. Decision making may seem spontaneous or impulsive and special interests of the decision maker are expected and condoned. Finally, good personal relationships are necessary for good negotiations (Casse, 1982). As has been mentioned many times in this book, the skills leaders need in international cross-cultural situations are the same skills they need in a multicultural and diverse domestic situations.

Conclusion

As mentioned in Chapter 2, cultural encapsulation is defining reality according to one set of cultural assumptions and stereotypes. Culturally encapsulated leaders assume that their view is the only real or legitimate one. A leader who uses a self-reference criterion can make assumptions that influence tangible outcomes for culturally different others. Some examples of encapsulation of leaders of multicultural workforces include using a hypothetical normal standard, disregarding the cultural context, and ignorance of their own cultural bias. Having a culture-centered leadership style can help explain some of the differences in views on ethical behavior, mentoring relationships, and negotiation.

CHAPTER 9 DISCUSSION QUESTIONS

1. When leaders find themselves in a situation that goes against what they believe is right, what factors, if any, should be considered before they make a decision concerning that situation?

2. Should organizations assign leaders to mentoring relationships or should individual leaders be allowed to choose their protégées? Do the demographic characteristics of either party influence your decision?

3. What cultural dimensions lead to what you would describe as the "best" negotiation style?

Critical Incident: Ethics Across Cultures

"I don't know how we can compete," Jenny, a vice president at a large aircraft manufacturer, said to Eric. "The Foreign Corrupt Practices Act (FCPA) has so many holes in it that there's not an even playing field out there." "Yeah, tell me about it," Eric said. "Even though getting caught violating the act can cost a company big time, I bet only one percent of violators gets caught." "I remember a few years ago when one of our competitors got caught paying $1.5 million to an Egyptian official who was instrumental in helping them get an airline contract," Jenny stated. "Even though they were fined $24 million, how many times have they, or some other competitor, cheated?" "Do you think it's worth it?" Eric asked Jenny. "There're a lot of places around the world where bribes are business as usual, and if we aren't willing to play their game, we aren't going to be competitive. We'd be doing our shareholders and passengers a favor."

CRITICAL INCIDENT DISCUSSION QUESTIONS

1. What types of considerations should Jenny and Eric contemplate as they think about the advantages and disadvantages of bribing officials to gain contracts?

2. What should Jenny and Eric's employer do to ensure that the company continues to be competitive while remaining ethical?

Exercise 9: Four Contrasting Ethical Orientations

OBJECTIVE

To better understand your own culturally learned patterns of determining what is right and what is wrong

DESCRIPTION

The four classical positions of judgments in ethical thinking are "Consequentialists," who judge according to consequences; "Intentionalists," who judge according to the person's intention; "Absolutists," who judge according to a set of absolute standards; and "Relativists," who judge the person in context. The following 24-item rating sheet will help participants better understand the extent to which they follow one or another of these positions.

Time required: About an hour

Risk/expertise level: Moderate

Participants needed: Any number of participants plus one facilitator

PROCEDURE

1. The facilitator will distribute the 24-item rating sheet below to each participant.

2. The facilitator will ask each participant to rate his or her reaction to each item as indicated.

3. When the participants have completed their ratings, they will be asked to compute their score as indicated.

4. The facilitator will post all the scores to determine which ethical tradition is most popular and which is least popular among the participants.

5. The facilitator will then organize a general discussion.

DEBRIEFING

If you were surprised by your ethical position, you may want to go back and examine the items themselves to make sure you scored each item correctly. You may want to discuss in dyads or small groups the similarities and differences in your ethical position compared to the ethical positions of others. There are no right or wrong ethical positions among the four indicated above; however, it is important that you be intentional in deliberately defining your position if you expect to "do the right thing." Some discussion questions are given below:

1. What are the good and bad consequences of following each of the four traditions?

2. Are you comfortable with your own preferred style of ethical thinking?

3. Are you able to work with others who may believe in a different tradition than yours?

4. Would you be able to change your own style of ethical thinking?

5. Which countries or cultures do you associate with each of these classical traditions?

INSIGHT

There is more than one way of deciding what is right and wrong across cultures.

EXHIBIT

The facilitator will ask that participants respond to the following statements by indicating whether they agree very much, somewhat, very little, are uncertain, disagree very little, somewhat, or very much.

1 = disagree very much	5 = agree very little
2 = disagree somewhat	6 = agree somewhat
3 = disagree very little	7 = agree very much
4 = uncertain	

1. Actions are judged according to their good or bad consequences.

2. There is an appropriate behavior for every situation.

3. Some decisions must be in the best interest of the group at the expense of the individual.

4. The consequences of rules and regulations will change from one situation to another.

5. Decisions are made by balancing good and bad consequences.

6. Public leaders make decisions according to the consequences of their actions.

7. There are basic moral principles to guide us in all our decisions.

8. It is essential to know a person's good or bad intention to judge that person's behavior.

9. Individuals or groups acting in good faith are not responsible for the consequences of their actions.

10. Teaching the rules of morality will lead to higher levels of ethical behavior.

11. Moral decisions depend on encouraging people to be well intentioned.

12. Public actions are typically defended by the high moral intention of the promoters.

13. Biological factors are likely to determine a person's behavior.

14. Culture has a limited role in justifying variations in behavior.

15. Similarities are more important than differences across populations.

16. Cultural differences are not important.

17. It is possible to compare measured levels of moral development across cultures.

18. A good test will be valid in different cultural settings.

19. Variations in behavior are usually the result of cultural differences.

20. Apparent similarities across cultures are misleading.

21. Each culture influences its members to behave in unique ways.

22. Each culture must be understood from its own indigenous cultural perspective.

23. It is usually not possible to judge a person's behavior outside that person's cultural context.

24. Measures always need to be generated or modified to fit each cultural context.

SCORING AND DEBRIEFING GUIDELINES

1. Derive a score for Items 1 through 6 by adding up their scores. A high score will demonstrate your affiliation with the "consequentialist" approach to ethical judgment.

2. Derive a score for Items 7 through 12 by adding up their scores. A high score will demonstrate your affiliation with the "nonconsequentialist" but intention-based approach to ethical judgment.

3. Derive a score for Items 13 through 18 by adding up their scores. A high score will demonstrate your affiliation with an "absolutist" approach to ethical judgment.

4. Derive a score for Items 19 through 24 by adding up their scores. A high score will demonstrate your affiliation with a "relativist" approach to ethical judgment.

SOURCE: Adapted with permission from Pedersen, P. (1997b). Doing the right thing: A question of ethics. In K. Cushner & R. Brislin (Eds.), *Improving intercultural interactions: Vol. 2. Models for cross cultural training programs* (pp. 149–165) Thousand Oaks, CA: Sage.

Appendix

A Synthetic Culture Training Laboratory

OBJECTIVES

To simulate the interaction of four contrasting groups discussing problems caused by outsiders, who attempt to find common ground without sacrificing their integrity

DESCRIPTION

This activity provides a structured interaction for participants to rehearse the dangers and opportunities of interacting with other cultures around the world. A teacher/trainer who has experienced the Synthetic Culture Laboratory as a participant and who is familiar with Geert Hofstede's 55-country database will be well prepared to run this laboratory. The cultures are described as "synthetic" because they are each derived from one end of four dimensions in Hofstede's data, and as extreme examples they do not exist in the real world. This Synthetic Culture Lab includes only 4 types of culture; an expanded version of Synthetic Cultures describing all 10 types is available in Hofstede, Pedersen, and Hofstede (2002).

> *Time required:* A half day
>
> *Risk/expertise level:* Moderate
>
> *Participants needed:* Any number of participants and a facilitator acquainted with the Synthetic Culture Lab and/or Geert Hofstede's research

PROCEDURES

1. Activities will occur according to the following approximate time schedule.

1 hour	Introduction to four synthetic cultures: Alpha (high power distance), Beta (strong uncertainty avoidance), Gamma (strong individualism), and Delta (high masculine). Participants will be divided into four corresponding groups to do the following:
	1. Learn the assumptions and rules of their synthetic culture
	2. Discuss the problems created by the "outsiders" in each synthetic culture
	3. Select a team of two consultants from each synthetic home culture who will visit the other three host cultures to help them deal with the problem of "outsiders"
30 minutes	By this time each of the four small groups should have completed the above three tasks and be ready to do the following activities:
	The first rotation will require sending teams of consultants from each synthetic home culture to each synthetic host culture for a 10-minute consultation in role, followed by a 10-minute debriefing out of role and 10 minutes to report back to their home synthetic culture on what they learned.
30 minutes	The second rotation will follow the same pattern with the next synthetic host culture.
30 minutes	The third rotation will follow the same pattern with the final synthetic host culture.
30 minutes	Each synthetic culture group will report back to the assembled participants on how to find common ground and agreement between their own culture and persons from different cultural backgrounds.
	Synthesis of learning for the day and completion of evaluation forms.

2. Role-play four contrasting synthetic cultures in a simulation, demonstrating the importance of identifying cultural similarities and differences.

3. Listen to the four synthetic cultures as they are introduced.

4. Select one synthetic culture identity for yourself, either because it fits with your own viewpoint or because it contrasts with your own viewpoint or for any other reason you choose.

5. Assemble in a small group with your synthetic culture comembers to social-ize one another into the new synthetic culture identity.

6. As you discuss the written rules for your synthetic culture, incorporate them into your communication with other group members.

7. Take on your new synthetic culture identity in everything you say and do.

8. Review the list of problems created in your synthetic culture because of "outsiders."

9. Write a list of two or three specific problems that have resulted from interacting with outsiders.

10. Select a team of two consultants who will be sent to another synthetic culture to help them work with the problems caused by outsiders.

11. Send the team of two consultants to the next synthetic host culture and receive a team of two consultants from another, different synthetic culture.

12. Complete the three rotations so that each home culture has sent a team to each of the three other host cultures in turn.

13. Each synthetic culture community is having a problem with "outsiders" from the other three synthetic culture communities; outsiders are coming into the community as refugees, visitors, tourists, students, and immigrants.

14. These outsiders have caused serious problems in your schools, institutions, and community because they disregard your way of doing things. They do not believe the same things you and your people believe.

15. Outsiders cause problems in Alpha culture by emphasizing the equality of all persons, demanding accountability to the community of powerful people, encouraging shared responsibility in the family, promoting shared authority in classrooms, and advocating the decentralization of power.

16. Outsiders cause problems in Beta culture by emphasizing the importance of uncertainty, dangers of stress and assertiveness, leniency of rules, interest in things that are different, open-ended learning situations, taking time off, flexibility of time, moderation, and the value of human rights.

17. Outsiders cause problems in Gamma culture by emphasizing the importance of the group, welfare guarantees, the dominant role of government, harmony and consensus, avoidance of confrontations, diplomas as measures of credibility, and relationships prevailing over task goals.

18. Outsiders cause problems in Delta culture by emphasizing caring for others, warm relationships, modesty, equal rights for men and women, tenderness in relationships, sympathy for the weak, promoting androgyny of gender roles, compromise, negotiation, permissiveness, preservation of the environment, and helping the less fortunate.

DEBRIEFING

In debriefing the Synthetic Culture Laboratory it is useful to have each group discuss and present a report to the larger group on their advice to persons coming to their culture and their feedback to the other three synthetic cultures. Some discussion questions follow:

1. Were you able to discover elements of all four synthetic cultures in your own culture?

2. Were you able to find common ground without sacrificing integrity?

3. Which synthetic cultures did you work with most constructively?

4. Which synthetic cultures were most difficult?

5. How will you use what you learned from this activity?

INSIGHT

If the training context is safe and if you take some risks you can learn to find common ground across cultures without sacrificing integrity.

Exhibit: Guidelines for the Four Synthetic Cultures

ALPHA CULTURE (HIGH POWER DISTANCE)

Power distance indicates the extent to which a culture accepts that power is unequally distributed in institutions and organizations.

Alpha Behaviors

1. Language
   1.1. Alphas will use the following words with a *positive* meaning: *respect, father* (as a title), *master, servant, older brother, younger brother, wisdom, favor, protect, obey, orders,* and *pleasing.*
   1.2 Alphas will use the following words with a *negative* meaning: *rights, complain, negotiate, fairness, task, necessity, co-determination, objectives, question,* and *criticize.*

2. The Cultural Grid
   2.1. The following behaviors by Alphas will express the following expectations.

Behavior	Expectation
Soft-spoken, polite, listening	Friendly
Quiet, polite, and not listening	Unfriendly
Asks for help and direction	Trust
Does not ask for help and direction	Distrust
Positive and animated, but no eye contact	Interest
Expressionless, unanimated, but with eye contact	Boredom

3. Barriers
   3.1. Language: Alphas are very verbal but usually soft-spoken and polite.
   3.2. Nonverbals: Alphas are usually restrained and formal.
   3.3 Stereotypes: Alphas are hierarchical and seek to please.

3.4. Evaluation: Alphas tend to blame themselves for any problems that come up.

3.5. Stress: Alphas internalize stress and express stress indirectly.

4. Gender Roles

4.1. Role of gender: Leadership roles may be held by either male or female. If the society is matriarchal, the visible power of women in decision making is likely to be more obvious than in patriarchal societies, where the visible power of males would be more obvious.

4.2. Role of women: In home and family affairs, women are likely to be very powerful even though that power might be less visible than the more visible male roles. While women may seem subservient, that may not in fact be true.

4.3. Role of men: Males in leadership roles are often held accountable for the consequences of their decisions. If they lose the support of the women, new leaders will emerge. While males may be the visible traditional leaders, the men may be much more subservient in less visible and more private social roles in a balance of power.

BETA CULTURE (STRONG UNCERTAINTY AVOIDANCE)

Uncertainty avoidance indicates the lack of tolerance in a culture for uncertainty and ambiguity.

Beta Behaviors

1. Language

1.1. Betas will use the following words with a *positive* meaning: *structure, duty, truth, law, order, certain, clear, clean, secure, safe, predictable,* and *tight.*

1.2. Betas will use the following words with a *negative* meaning: *maybe, creative conflict, tolerant, experiment, spontaneous, relativity, insight, unstructured, loose,* and *flexible.*

2. The Cultural Grid

2.1. The following behaviors by Betas will indicate the following expectations.

Behavior	Expectation
Detailed responses, formal and unambiguous, specific	Friendly
Generalized, ambiguous responses; anxious to end the interview	Unfriendly
Polarized structures in response separate right from wrong unambiguously	Trust
Openly critical and challenging the other person's credentials	Distrust
Verbal and active questioning with direct eye contact, task oriented	Interest
Passive and quiet with no direct eye contact	Boredom

3. Barriers
   3.1. Language: Betas are very verbal and well organized, somewhat loud.
   3.2. Nonverbal: Betas are animated in using hands but with little or no physical contact.
   3.3. Stereotypes: Betas have rigid beliefs that don't change easily.
   3.4. Evaluation: Betas quickly evaluate a situation to establish right and wrong, sometimes prematurely.
   3.5. Stress: Betas externalize stress and usually make the other person feel the stress rather than themselves.

4. Gender Roles
   4.1. Role of gender: The right and appropriate roles of men and women are rigidly defined and without ambiguity. The dress, behavior, and functions of men and women are defined by rules, traditions, and carefully guarded boundaries.
   4.2. Role of women: Women tend to be in charge of home, family, children, and religious or traditional spiritual rituals, as guardians of society through the romantic and idealized role of what a woman should be. Society can be very unforgiving to women who rebel or violate those rules, although elderly women may take on traditional power roles otherwise reserved for males.
   4.3. Role of men: Men are expected to take care of the woman and protect the home and family by providing for material needs and demonstrating strength in their public posture. Men are expected to be more visible in their public posture. Men are expected to be more visible in their public roles than women and women—especially younger women—might have difficulty sharing power with men in public or work roles.

GAMMA CULTURE (HIGH INDIVIDUALISM)

Individualism indicates the extent to which a culture believes that people are supposed to take care of themselves and remain emotionally independent from groups, organizations, and other collectivities.

Gamma Behaviors

1. Language
   1.1. Gammas will use the following words with a *positive* meaning: *self, friendship, do-your-own-thing, contract, litigation, self-respect, self-interest, self-actualizing, individual, dignity, I/me, pleasure, adventurous,* and *guilt.*
   1.2. Gammas will use the following words with a *negative* meaning: *harmony, face, we, obligation, sacrifice, family, tradition, decency, honor, duty, loyalty,* and *shame.*

2. The Cultural Grid
   2.1. The following behaviors by Gammas will indicate the following expectations.

Behavior	Expectation
Verbal and self-disclosing	Friendly
Criticizes others behind their back, sabotages enemies	Unfriendly
Aggressively debate issues and control the interview actively	Trust
Noncommittal on issues and more passive, ambiguous, or defensive	Distrust
Loudly verbal with lots of questions, touching, and close physical contact	Interest
Maintains physical distance with no questions or eye contact	Boredom

3. Barriers
   3.1. Language: Gammas are verbal and self-centered, using *I* and *me* often.
   3.2. Nonverbal: Gammas touch a lot and are somewhat seductive.
   3.3. Stereotypes: Gammas are defensive and tend to be loners who see others as potential enemies.
   3.4. Evaluation: Gammas use other people and measure the importance of others in terms of how useful they are.
   3.5. Stress: Gammas like to take risks and like the challenge of danger to continually test their own ability.

4. Gender Roles
   4.1. Role of gender: Power might as easily be held by females as by males, especially in urban and modernized areas. Gender roles are less rigidly defined, with each gender taking on the roles of the other—to serve individual self-interests—in public and/or private activities.
   4.2. Role of women: Women are free as long as they have the power to protect themselves. Attractive women can gain power by being manipulative and taking advantage of their beauty. *Less* assertive—and particularly older—women are likely to become victims of exploitation by both younger men and women.
   4.3. Role of men: Men excel in areas requiring physical strength. Younger, taller, and physically attractive men can be expected to be aggressive in asserting their power over others. Men who are uncomfortable being competitive—especially older men—are likely to be ridiculed as weak and losers.

DELTA CULTURE (HIGH MASCULINITY)

Masculinity indicates the extent to which traditional masculine values of assertiveness, money, and things prevail in a culture as contrasted to traditional feminine values of nurturance, quality of life, and people.

Delta Behaviors

1. Language
   1.1. Deltas will use the following words with a *positive* meaning: *career, competition, fight, aggressive, assertive, success, winner, deserve, merit, balls, excel, force, big, hard, fast,* and *quantity.*
   1.2. Deltas will use the following words with a *negative* meaning: *quality, caring, solidarity, modesty, compromise, help, love, grow, small, soft, slow,* and *tender.*

2. The Cultural Grid
   2.1. The following behaviors by Deltas will indicate the following expectations.

Behavior	Expectation
Physical contact; seductive and loud	Friendliness
Physical distance; sarcastic and sadistic	Unfriendly
Tend to dominate discussion and be competitive	Trust
Openly critical, disparaging; and attempts to end the discussion	Distrust
Sports oriented and eager to debate every issue from all points of view	Interest
No eye contact; discourteous and drowsy	Boredom

3. Barriers
   3.1. Language: Deltas are loud and verbal, with a tendency to criticize and argue with others.
   3.2. Nonverbal: Deltas like physical contact, direct eye contact, and animated gestures.
   3.3. Stereotypes: Deltas are macho, hero and status oriented, and like winners.
   3.4. Evaluation: Deltas are hard to please, tend to be overachievers, are defensive, and blame others for their mistakes.
   3.5. Stress: Deltas are Type A personalities, generating stress through fast-paced lifestyles.

4. Gender Roles
   4.1. Role of gender: Men and more masculine women are typically more powerful and are highly favored in leadership roles. Passive and facilitating behaviors are tolerated in women but not in men. Men are stereotyped as strong and women as weak.
   4.2. Role of women: Women tend to be either masculine in their personal style as "one of the guys" or completely subservient and docile, with few women between these extremes. Young and attractive women can use their beauty to win, but without romantic illusions. Older or less attractive women are at a great disadvantage.

4.3. Role of men: Young, strong, tall, and attractive men are idealized as heroes and are admired or envied by others. Men see life as a game played by men with women as cheerleaders.

SYNTHETIC CULTURE: EXPECTATIONS AND BEHAVIORS

Expectations by Behaviors of Synthetic Cultures				
Expectation	*Behaviors*			
	Alpha	**Beta**	**Gamma**	**Delta**
Friendly	Polite and listening	Formal and specific	Verbal and disclosing	Physical and loud
Unfriendly	Polite and not listening	General and ambiguous	Critical and attacking	Sarcastic and distant
Trust	Asks for help	Actively listens	Debates all topics	Challenges and competes
Distrust	Does not ask for help	Attacks and challenges	Noncommittal and passive	Critical and insulting
Interest	Positive, no eye contact	Active with eye contact	Loud and physical	Playful
Boredom	Passive and direct	Passive, no eye contact	Distant, with eye contact	Detached, quiet, and distant

Barriers by Behaviors of Synthetic Cultures				
Barrier	*Synthetic Cultures*			
	Alpha	**Beta**	**Gamma**	**Delta**
Language	Verbal and soft-spoken	Loud and verbal	Verbal and self-centered	Critical and arguing
Nonverbals	Restrained and formal	Animated and non-physical	Seductive and physical	Physical and direct
Stereotypes	Hierarchical and pleasing	Promotes rigid beliefs	Defensive and paranoid	Macho and hero oriented
Evaluation	Self-blaming in evaluations	Premature and selfish	Utilitarian	Over-achieving
Stress	Internalizes stress	Externalizes stress	Risk taking	Generates stress
Organizational constraint	Follows formal rules	Highly structured	Disorganized and chaotic	Competes to win

MEDIATING CONFLICT BETWEEN SYNTHETIC CULTURES

Examine examples of conflict between the following synthetic cultures and identify examples of common ground in positive expectations and/or values that persons from both synthetic cultures share.

1. Conflict between an Alpha and a Beta

Alphas emphasize a hierarchy of power where each person has her or his place, showing respect to those above and expecting obedience from those below that level. Betas dislike uncertainty and do not tolerate ambiguity, so there is a structure of laws that must be obeyed that goes beyond the needs of individuals or society. A possible conflict between Alpha and Beta might be a high power level group of Alphas who do whatever they like and disregard the rules in spite of objections by Betas in that society.

2. Conflict between an Alpha and a Gamma

Alphas emphasize a hierarchy of power where each person has her or his place, showing respect to those above and expecting obedience from those below that level. Gammas are individualistic and believe everyone should take care of themselves and remain emotionally independent from groups, organizations, or society. A possible conflict between Alphas and Gammas might be a group of Gammas who fail to show proper respect to Alpha leaders.

3. Conflict between an Alpha and a Delta

Alphas emphasize a hierarchy of power where each person has her or his place, showing respect to those above and expecting obedience from those below that level. Deltas are assertive, materialistic, and success oriented, seeking rapid progress and ultimate domination in their relationships with others. A possible conflict would be a group of Deltas who attack the Alpha hierarchy as uneconomic and inefficient and attempt to remove the Alphas from power.

4. Conflict between a Beta and a Gamma

Betas avoid uncertainty whenever possible and prefer a structure of clear, unambiguous rules to define truth and duty in their relationships. Gammas are individualistic and believe everyone should take care of themselves and remain emotionally independent from groups, organizations, or society. A possible conflict between Betas and Gammas might be the increased power of Gammas who promote individual freedom where anybody can do whatever they want and where nobody has a right to control their behavior.

5. Conflict between a Beta and a Delta

Betas avoid uncertainty whenever possible and prefer a structure of clear, unambiguous rules to define truth and duty in their relationships. Deltas are assertive, materialistic, and success oriented, seeking rapid progress and ultimate domination in their relationships with others. A possible conflict between Betas and Deltas might be the increased power of a small clique of Deltas who interpret the rules to their own advantage or find ways around the rules to increase their own power in society.

6. Conflict between a Gamma and a Delta

Gammas are individualistic and believe everyone should take care of themselves and remain emotionally independent from groups, organizations, or society. Deltas are assertive, materialistic, and success oriented, seeking rapid progress and ultimate domination in their relationships with others. A possible conflict between Gammas and Deltas might be a power struggle where the Deltas use teamwork in their organization to destroy individualistic Gammas and take over power in society.

SOURCE: Adapted from Pedersen, P., & Ivey A. E. (1993). *Culture-centered counseling and interviewing skills* (pp. 67–75). Reproduced with permission of Greenwood Publishing Group, Inc., Westport, CT.

References

Abe-Kim, J., Okazaki, S., & Goto, S. (2001). Unidimensional versus multidimensional approaches to the assessment of acculturation for Asian America populations. *Cultural Diversity and Ethnic Minority Psychology, 7,* 232–246.

Aboud, F. (1988). *Children and prejudice.* Oxford, UK: Blackwell.

Abraham, R. (2000). The role of job control as a moderator of emotional dissonance and emotional intelligence-outcome relationships. *Journal of Psychology, 134,* 169–184.

Adler, N. J. (1986). Cultural synergy: Managing the impact of cultural diversity. In *1986 annual: Developing human resources.* San Diego, CA: University Associates.

Adler, N. J. (1999). Global leadership: Women leaders. In W. H. Mobely (Ed.), *Advances in global leadership* (Vol. 1, pp. 49–73). Stamford, CT: JAI.

Adler, N. J. (2002). *International dimensions of organizational behavior* (4th ed.). Cincinnati, OH: South-Western College Publishing.

Adler, N. J., & Bartholomew, S. (1992). Managing globally competent people. *Academy of Management Executive, 6*(3), 52–65.

Adler, N. J., Brahm, R., & Graham, R. L. (1992). Strategy implementation: A comparison of face-to-face negotiations in the People's Republic of China and the United States. *Strategic Management Journal, 13*(6), 449–466.

Ahmed, N. R. (2002). Leading by example (in a diverse world). *LIMRA's MarketFacts Quarterly, 21*(4), 46–49.

Ajzen, I., & Fishbein, M. (1980). *Understanding attitudes and predicting social behavior.* Englewood Cliffs, NJ: Prentice Hall.

Aldag, R. J., & Kuzuhara, L. W. (2002). *Organizational behavior and management.* Cincinnati, OH: South-Western College Publishing.

Allen, T. D., Poteet, M. L., & Burroughs, S. M. (1997). The mentor's perspective: A qualitative inquiry and future research agenda. *Journal of Vocational Behavior, 51,* 70–89.

Allport, G. W. (1954). *The nature of prejudice.* Reading, MA: Addison-Wesley.

Allport, G. W., & Kramer, B. M. (1946). Some roots of prejudice. *Journal of Psychology, 22,* 9–39.

Arce, C. A. (1981). A reconsideration of Chicano culture and identity. *Daedalus, 10,* 177–192.

Arredondo, P., & Arciniega, G. M. (2001). Strategies and techniques for counselor training based on the multicultural counseling competencies. *Journal of Multicultural Counseling and Development, 29*(4), 263–273.

Arvey, R. D., Bhagat, R. S., & Salas, E. (1991). Cross-cultural and cross-national issues in personnel and human resource management: Where do we go from here? In

G. R. Ferris & K. M. Rowland (Eds.), *Research in personnel and human resources management* (Vol. 9, pp. 367–407). Greenwich, CT: JAI.

Ashkanasy, N. M., Hartel, C. E. J., & Daus, C. S. (2002). Diversity and emotion: The new frontiers in organizational behavior research. *Journal of Management, 28,* 307–338.

Atkinson, D. R., Morten, G., & Sue, D. W. (1983). *Counseling American minorities: A cross cultural perspective* (2nd ed.). Dubuque, IA: William C. Brown.

Atkinson, D. R., Morten, G., & Sue, D. W. (1998). *Counseling American minorities* (5th ed.). Boston: McGraw-Hill.

Augsburger, D. W. (1992). *Conflict mediation across cultures.* Louisville, KY: Westminster/ John Knox Press.

Australian Bureau of Statistics. (2001). Retrieved March 16, 2003, from http://www.abs .gov.au/ausstats

Aycan, Z. (1997). *Expatriate management: Theory and research.* Greenwich, CT: JAI.

Baldwin, T. T., & Ford, J. K. (1988). Transfer of training: A review and directions for future research. *Personnel Psychology, 41,* 63–105.

Bandura, A. (1977a). Self-efficacy: Toward a unifying theory of behavior change. *Psychological Bulletin, 84,* 122–147.

Bandura, A. (1977b). *Social learning theory.* Englewood Cliffs, NJ: Prentice Hall.

Bandura, A. (1986). *Social foundations of thought and action.* Englewood Cliffs, NJ: Prentice Hall.

Barnes, B. (1991). *Mediation in the Pacific pentangle (PCR)* (Working Paper). Honolulu: University of Hawaii Press.

Barr, D. J., & Strong, L. J. (1987, May). Embracing multiculturalism: The existing contradictions. *ACU-I Bulletin,* pp. 20–23.

Bass, B. M. (1990). *Bass & Stogdill's handbook of leadership: Theory, research, & managerial applications* (3rd ed.). New York: Free Press.

Bass, B. M., & Avolio, B. J. (1990). The implications of transactional and transformational leadership for individual, team, and organizational development. In R. W. Woodman & W. A. Pasmore (Eds.), *Research in organizational change and development* (Vol. 4, pp. 231–272). Greenwich, CT: JAI.

Bennett, M. J. (1986). Towards ethnorelativism: A developmental model of intercultural sensitivity. In R. M. Paige (Ed.), *Cross-cultural orientation: New conceptualizations and applications* (pp. 27–70). New York: University Press of America.

Bennett, M. J. (1993a). Cultural marginality: Identity issues in intercultural training. In R. M. Paige (Ed.), *Education for the intercultural experience* (pp. 109–136). Yarmouth, ME: Intercultural Press.

Bennett, M. J. (1993b). Towards ethnorelativism: A developmental model of intercultural sensitivity. In R. M. Paige (Ed.), *Education for the intercultural experience* (pp. 21–71). Yarmouth, ME: Intercultural Press.

Bennett, R., & O'Gorman, H. (1998). Benchmark with the best. *HR Magazine, 43*(5), 19–22.

Bennis, W. (1984). The 4 competencies of leadership. *Training and Development, 38*(8), 14–19.

Berardi-Colette, B., Dominowski, R. L., Buyer, L. S., & Rellinger, E. R. (1995). Metacognition and problem-solving: A process-oriented approach. *Journal of Experimental Psychology: Learning, Memory, and Cognition, 21,* 205–223.

Berkowitz, D., & Donnerstein, E. (1982). External validity is more than skin deep: Some answers to criticisms of laboratory experiments. *American Psychologist, 37,* 245–257.

Berman, M. A. (1997). CEOs assess their globalization efforts [Abstract]. *Across the Board, 34 (8)*, 55.

Bernstein, A. (2001, July 30). Racism in the workplace: In an increasingly multicultural U.S., harassment of minorities on the rise. *BusinessWeek*, p. 64.

Berry, J. (1990). Psychology of acculturation: Understanding individuals moving between cultures. In R. W. Brislin (Ed.), *Applied cross-cultural psychology* (pp. 232–253). Newbury Park, CA: Sage.

Berry, J. W., & Kim, U. (1988). Acculturation and mental health. In P. Dasen, J. W. Berry, & N. Sartorius (Eds.), *Cross-cultural psychology and health: Towards applications* (pp. 207–236). London: Sage.

Bhawuk, D. P. S., & Brislin, R. (1992). The measurement of intercultural sensitivity using the concepts of individualism and collectivism. *International Journal of Intercultural Relations, 16*(4), 413–436.

Birchall, D., Hee, J. T., & Gay, K. (1996). Competencies for international management. *Singapore Management Review, 18*(1), 1–13.

Bjorkqvist, K., & Fry, D. P. (1997). Conclusions: Alternatives to violence. In D. P. Fry & K. Bjorkqvist (Eds.), *Cultural variation in conflict resolution* (pp. 243–254). Mahwah, NJ: Lawrence Erlbaum.

Black, J. S., & Mendenhall, M. (1989). A practical but theory-based framework for selecting cross-cultural training methods. *Human Resource Management, 28*(4), 511–539.

Blackman, C. (1997). *Negotiating China: Case studies and strategies*. St. Leonards, Australia: Allan & Unwin.

Blake, R. R., & Mouton, J. S. (1964). *The managerial grid*. Houston, TX: Gulf.

Blanchard, P. N., & Thacker, J. W. (1999). *Effective training: Systems, strategies, and practices*. Upper Saddle River, NJ: Prentice Hall.

Bohr, N. (1950, January 20). On the notion of causality and complementarily. *Science, 111*(2873), 51–54.

Bowman, S. R., Kite, M. E., Branscombe, N. R., & Williams, S. (1999). Developmental relationships of Black Americans in the academy. In A. J. Murrell, F. J. Crosby, & R. J. Ely (Eds.), *Mentoring dilemmas: Developmental relationships within multicultural organizations* (pp. 21–46). Mahwah, NJ: Lawrence Erlbaum.

Brake, T. (1997). *The global leader: Critical factors for creating the world class organization*. Chicago: Irwin Professional.

Brett, J. M., & Okumura, T. (1998). Inter- and intracultural negotiation: U.S. and Japanese negotiations. *Academy of Management Journal, 41*, 495–510.

Brief, A. P., Dietz, J., Reizenstein Cohen, R., Pugh, S. D., & Vaslow, J. B. (2000). Just doing business: Modern racism and obedience to authority as explanations for employment discrimination. *Organizational Behavior and Human Decision Processes, 81*, 72–97.

Brief, A. P., & Hayes, E. L. (1997). The continuing "American dilemma": Studying racism in organizations. In C. L. Cooper & D. M. Rousseau (Eds.), *Trends in organizational behavior* (Vol. 4, pp. 89–106). Chichester, UK: Wiley.

Brinkerhoff, R. O. (1987). *Achieving results from training*. San Francisco: Jossey-Bass.

Brinson, J., & Kottler, J. (1993). Cross-cultural mentoring in counselor education: A strategy for retaining minority faculty. *Counselor Education and Supervision, 32*, 241–253.

Brislin, R. S., Cushner, K., Cherrie, C., & Young, M. (1998). *Intercultural interactions: A practical guide*. Thousand Oaks, CA: Sage.

Broad, M. L., & Newstrom, J. W. (1992). *Transfer of training.* Reading, MA: Addison-Wesley.

Brown, A. (2000, January 17). Cultural immersion part of diversity exercise. *Columbus Dispatch,* Business Today section, p. 3.

Burke, M. J., & Day, R. R. (1986). A cumulative study of the effectiveness of management training. *Journal of Applied Psychology, 71,* 232–245.

Bushnell, D. S. (1990). Input, process, output: A model for evaluating training. *Training and Development Journal, 44*(3), 31–43.

Cannon-Bowers, J. A., Rhodenizer, L., Salas, E., & Bowers, C. A. (1998). A framework for understanding pre-practice conditions and their impact on learning. *Personnel Psychology, 51,* 291–320.

Carr-Ruffino, N. (1996). *Managing diversity: People skills for a multicultural workplace.* Cincinnati, OH: International Thompson.

Carroll, S. J., & Gannon, M. J. (1997). *Ethical dimensions of international management.* Thousand Oaks, CA: Sage.

Carter, R. T. (1995). *The influence of race and racial identity in psychotherapy.* New York: John Wiley.

Carter, R. T., & Qureshi, A. (1995). A typology of philosophical assumptions in multicultural counseling and training. In J. G. Ponterotto, J. M. Casas, L. A. Suzuki, & C. M. Alexander (Eds.), *Handbook of multicultural counseling* (pp. 239–262). Thousand Oaks, CA: Sage.

Casse, P. (1982). *Training for the multicultural manager.* Yarmouth, ME: Intercultural Press.

Cellich, C. (1997). When cultures collide: Managing successfully across cultures. *International Journal of Conflict Management, 8*(2), 176.

Chemers, M. M. (1994). *A theoretical overview of the role of culture in the leadership processes.* Paper presented at the 23rd International Congress of Applied Psychology, Madrid, Spain.

Chongde, L., & Tsingan, L. (2003). Multiple intelligence and the structure of thinking. *Theory & Psychology, 13,* 829–834.

Cohen, M. S., Freeman, J. T., & Wolf, S. (1996). Metacognition in time-stressed decision making: Recognizing, critiquing, and correcting. *Human Factors, 38,* 206–219.

Cohen, R. (1991). *Negotiating across cultures.* Washington, DC: U.S. Institute of Peace.

Cokley, K. O. (2002). Testing Cross's revised racial identity model: An examination of the relationship between racial identity and internalized racialism. *Journal of Counseling Psychology, 49,* 476–483.

Conejo, C. (2002). Managers must become multicultural. *Nonprofit World, 20*(6), 23–24.

Cox, T., & Finley-Nickerson, J. (1991). Models of acculturation for intraorganizational cultural diversity. *Canadian Journal of Administrative Sciences, 8*(2), 90–100.

Cox, T. H., Jr. (1994). *Cultural diversity in organizations: Theory, research & practice.* San Francisco: Berrett-Koehler.

Cox, T. H., Jr., & Blake, S. (1991). Managing cultural diversity: Implications for organizational competitiveness. *Academy of Management Executive, 5*(3), 45–56.

Crosby, F. (1984). Relative deprivation in organizational settings. *Research in Organizational Behavior, 6,* 51–93.

Crosby, F. J. (1999). The developing literature on developmental relationships. In A. J. Murrell, F. J. Crosby, & R. J. Ely (Eds.), *Mentoring dilemmas: Developmental relationships within multicultural organizations* (pp. 3–20). Mahwah, NJ: Lawrence Erlbaum.

Cross, W. E. (1971). The Negro to Black conversion experience: Towards a psychology of Black liberation. *Black World, 20,* 13–27.

Cross, W. E. (1991). *Shades of Black: Diversity in African-American identity.* Philadelphia: Temple University Press.

Csoka, L. S. (1998). *Bridging the leadership gap* (The Conference Board, Report Number 1190–98-RR). New York: Conference Board.

Dalton, M. A. (1998). Developing leaders for global roles. In C. D. McCauley, R. S. Moxley, & E. Van Velsor (Eds.), *The Center for Creative Leadership handbook of leadership development* (pp. 379–402). San Francisco: Jossey-Bass.

D'Andrea, M., & Daniels, J. (1991). Exploring the different levels of multicultural counseling training in counselor education. *Journal of Counseling and Development, 70,* 78–85.

Darden, C. (2003, June/July). Delivering on diversity leadership: A walk in the other guy's shoes. *Executive Speeches, 17*(6), 20.

Day, D. V., Cross, W. E., Jr., Ringseis, E. L., & Williams, T. L. (1999). Self-categorization and identity construction associated with managing diversity. *Journal of Vocational Behavior, 54,* 188–195.

de Merode, J. (1997). *Readings on global leadership: Synthesis.* Unpublished manuscript, Center for Creative Leadership, Greensboro, N.C.

Deming, W. E. (1986). *Out of the crisis* (2nd ed.). Cambridge: MIT Center for Advanced Engineering Study.

DeSimone, R. L., Werner, J. M., & Harris, D. M. (2002). *Human resource development* (3rd ed.). Mason, OH: Thomson South-Western.

Dickson, M. W., Hanges, P. J., & Lord, R. G. (2001). Trends, developments and gaps in cross-cultural research on leadership. In W. H. Mobley & M. W. Morgan, Jr. (Eds.), *Advances in global leadership* (Vol. 2, pp. 75–100). Oxford, UK: Elsevier Science.

DiVesta, F. J., & Peverly, S. T. (1984). The effects of encoding variability, processing activity, and rule-example sequence on the transfer of conceptual rules. *Journal of Educational Psychology, 76,* 108–119.

Donaldson, T., & Dunfee, T. W. (1994). Towards a unified conception of business ethics: Integrative social contacts theory. *Academy of Management Review, 19,* 252–284.

Donaldson, T., & Dunfee, T. W. (1999). *Ties that bind: A social contracts approach to business ethics.* Boston: Harvard Business School Press.

Dorfman, P. W. (1996). International and cross-cultural leadership research. In B. J. Punnett & O. Shenkar (Eds.), *Handbook for international management research* (pp. 267–349). Oxford, UK: Blackwell.

Dorfman, P. W. (2004). International and cross-cultural leadership. In B. J. Punnett & O. Shenkar (Eds.), *Handbook for international management research* (2nd ed., pp. 265–355). Ann Arbor: University of Michigan Press.

Dovidio, J. (1997, September 30). *Understanding contemporary racism: Causes, consequences, challenges.* Presentation to President Clinton's Race Advisory Board, Washington, DC. Available online at http://clinton4.nara.gov/Initiatives/One America/Dovidio.html

Dovidio, J., & Gaertner, S. L. (1999). Reducing prejudice: Combating intergroup biases. *Current Directions in Psychological Science, 8,* 101–106.

Dowling, P. J., Welch, D. E., & Schuler, R. S. (1999). *International human resource management: Managing people in a multicultural context* (3rd ed.). Cincinnati, OH: South-Western College Publishing.

Driskell, J. E., Copper, C., & Moran, A. (1994). Does mental practice enhance performance? *Journal of Applied Psychology, 79,* 481–492.

Dubinskas, F. A. (1992). Culture and conflict: The cultural roots of discord. In D. M. Kolb & J. M. Bartuneck (Eds.), *Hidden conflict in organizations* (pp. 187–207). Newbury Park, CA: Sage.

Dulewicz, V. (2000). Emotional intelligence: The key to future successful corporate leadership? *Journal of General Management, 25,* 1–14.

Dunham, R. B., Grube, J. A., Gardner, D. G., Cummings, L. L., & Pierce, J. L. (1989). *The development of an attitude toward change instrument.* Paper presented at the Academy of Management Meeting, Washington, D.C.

Dunlap, A. J. (1996). *Mean business: How I save bad companies and make good companies great.* New York: Times Books/Random House.

Dunnette, M. (1976). Aptitudes, abilities and skills. In M. Dunnette (Ed.), *The handbook of industrial and organizational psychology.* Chicago: Rand McNally.

Duryea, M. L. B. (1992). *Conflict and culture: A literature review and bibliography.* Victoria, BC: University of Victoria, Institute for Dispute Resolution.

Duval, S., & Wickland, R. (1972). *A theory of objective self-awareness.* San Diego, CA: Academic Press.

Earley, P. C., & Mosakowski, E. M. (2000). Creating hybrid team cultures: An empirical test of international team functioning. *Academy of Management Journal, 43,* 26–49.

EEOC. (2002). The U.S. Equal Employment Opportunity Commission's 2002 annual report. Retrieved on November 25, 2004. from http://www.eeoc.gov/abouteeoc/annual_reports/annrep02.html

Elfenbein, H. A., & Ambady, N. (2002). On the universality and cultural specificity of emotion recognition: A meta-analysis. *Psychological Bulletin, 128,* 203–235.

Ellis, H. C. (1965). *The transfer of learning.* New York: Macmillan.

Elron, E. (1997). Top management teams within multinational corporations: Effects of cultural heterogeneity. *Leadership Quarterly, 8,* 393–412.

Ensher, E. A., & Murphy, S. E. (1997). Effects of race, gender, perceived similarity, and contact on mentor relationships. *Journal of Vocational Behavior, 50,* 460–481.

Erikson, E. H. (1968). *Identity: Youth and crisis.* New York: W. W. Norton.

Fang, T. (1999). *Chinese business negotiating style.* Thousand Oaks, CA: Sage.

Filipczak, B. (1997, January). Think locally, act globally. *Training,* pp. 41–48.

Fine, M., Weiss, L., Powell, L. C., & Wong, L. M. (1997). *OffWhite: Readings on race, power, and society.* New York: Routledge.

Fishbein, M., & Ajzen, I. (1975). *Belief, attitude, intention, and behavior: An introduction to theory and research.* Reading, MA: Addison-Wesley.

Fishman, C. (2001, November). Leader: Bob Moffat. *Fast Company,* pp. 96–104.

Fiske, A. P. (2002). Using individualism and collectivism to compare cultures—A critique of the validity of measurement of the constructs: Comment on Oyserman et al. (2002). *Psychological Bulletin, 128,* 78–88.

Fiske, S. T., & Taylor, S. E. (1991). *Social cognition* (2nd ed.). New York: Random House.

Follet, M. P. (1940). Constructive conflict. In H. C. Metcalf & L. Urwick (Eds.), *Dynamic administration: The collected papers of Mary Parker Follet* (pp. 30–49). New York: Harper & Row. (Original work published 1926)

Fortmann, K., Leslie, C., & Cunningham, M. (2002). Cross-cultural comparisons of the Reid Integrity Scale in Latin America and South Africa. *International Journal of Selection and Assessment, 10*(1/2), 98–108.

Foster, B. G., Cross, W. E., Jackson, B., & Hardiman, R. (1988). *Workforce diversity and business.* Alexandria, VA: American Society for Training and Development.

Franchi, J. (2003). Comparison of learning and performance styles of cross-cultural populations in a global corporate organization (Puerto Rico, Columbia, United States). *Dissertation Abstracts International, 63*(12-A), 4220, US: University Microfilms International.

Freeman, F. H., Knott, K. B., & Schwartz, F. H. (1994). *Leadership education sourcebook* (5th ed.). Greensboro, NC: Center for Creative Leadership.

Fry, D., & Bjorkqvist, K. (1997). Culture and conflict-resolution models: Exploring alternatives to violence. In D. P. Fry & K. Bjorkqvist (Eds.), *Cultural variation in conflict resolution* (pp. 9–23). Mahwah, NJ: Lawrence Erlbaum.

Fuertes, J. N., Miville, M. L., Mohr, J. J., Sedlacek, W. E., & Gretchen, D. (2000). Factor structure and short form of the Miville-Guzman Universality-Diversity Scale. *Measurement and Evaluation in Counseling and Development, 33*(3), 157–170.

Fujimoto, Y., Hartel, C. E. J., Hartel, G. F., & Baker, N. (2000). Openness to dissimilarity moderates the consequences of diversity in well-established groups. *Asia Pacific Journal of Human Resources, 38*(3), 46–61.

Fukuyama, M. A. (1990). Taking a universal approach to multicultural counseling. *Counselor Education and Supervision, 30,* 6–17.

Gabrieldis, C., Stephan, W., Ybarra, O., Dos Santos-Pearson, V., & Villareal, L. (1997). Preferred styles of conflict resolution. *Journal of Cross-Cultural Psychology, 28,* 661–672.

Gagne, R. M. (1962). Military training and principles of learning. *American Psychologist, 17,* 83–91.

Gagne, R. M. (1972). Domains of learning. *Interchange, 3*(1), 1–8.

Gagne, R. M. (1984). Learning outcomes and their effects: Useful categories of human performance. *American Psychologist, 39,* 377–385.

Gagne, R. M., Briggs, L. J., & Wager, W. W. (1992). *Principles of instructional design* (4th ed.). Fort Worth, TX: Harcourt Brace College.

Galvin, J. C. (1983). What trainers can learn from educators about evaluating management training. *Training and Development Journal, 37*(8), 52–57.

Galvin, T. (2003). Industry report. *Training, 40*(10), 21–36.

Gardner, H. (1983). *Frames of minds: The theory of multiple intelligences.* New York: Basic Books.

Gardner, H. (1999). *Intelligence reframed: Multiple intelligences for the 21st century.* New York: Basic Books.

Gardener, J. W. (1990). The moral dimension. *On Leadership* (pp. 67–80). New York: Free Press.

Gardner, L., & Stough, C. (2002). Examining the relationship between leadership and emotional intelligence in senior level managers. *Leadership & Organization Development Journal, 23,* 68–78.

Gardenswartz, L., Rowe, A., Digh, P., & Bennett, M. F. (2003). *The global diversity desk reference: Managing an international workforce.* San Francisco: Pfeiffer.

Geertz, C. (1973). *The interpretation of cultures: Selected essays.* New York: Basic Books.

George, J. M. (2000). Emotions and leadership: The role of emotional intelligence. *Human Relations, 53,* 1027–1041.

Gessner, M. J., Arnold, V., & Mobley, W. H. (1999). Introduction. In W. H. Mobley, M. J. Gessner, & V. Arnold (Eds.), *Advances in global leadership* (Vol. 1, pp. xiii-xviii). Stamford, CT: JAI.

Glastra, F., Meerman, M., Schedler, P., & De Vries, S. (2000). Broadening the scope of diversity management: Strategic implications in the case of The Netherlands. *Relations Industrielles, 55,* 698–721.

Golden, D. (2003, December 30). Not Black and White: Colleges cut back minority programs after court rulings; they're wary of scholarships based on race in wake of the Michigan cases; new ways to define diversity. *Wall Street Journal,* p. A1.

Goldstein, A., (1981). *Psychological skill training: The structural learning technique.* Elmsford, NY: Pergamon.

Goldstein, I. L., & Ford, J. K. (2002). *Training in organizations: Needs assessment, development, and evaluations* (4th ed.). Belmont, CA: Wadsworth/Thompson Learning.

Goleman, D. (1998). *Working with emotional intelligence.* New York: Bantam.

Goleman, D. (2000). Intelligent leadership. *Executive Excellence, 3,* 17.

Gordon, J. (1995). Different from what? Diversity as a performance issue. *Training, 32*(5), 25–33.

Gratz v. Bollinger. 123 S. Ct. 2411 (2003).

Gregersen, H. B., Morrison, A. J., & Black, J. S. (1998). Developing leaders for the global frontier. *Sloan Management Review, 40,* 21–32.

Grossman, R. J. (2000). Is diversity working? *HR Magazine, 45*(3), 46–50.

Grutter v. Bollinger. 123 S. Ct. 2325 (2003).

Gudykunst, W. B., & Ting-Toomey, S. (1988). *Culture and interpersonal communication.* Newbury Park, CA: Sage.

Gudykunst, W. B., Ting-Toomey, S., & Wiseman, R. L. (1991). Taming the beast: Designing a course in intercultural communication. *Communication Education, 40,* 271–285.

Haight, G. (1990). Managing diversity. *Across the Board, 27*(3), 22–29.

Hall, E. T. (1976). *Beyond culture.* Garden City, NY: Anchor.

Hammer, M. R., Bennett, M. J., & Wiseman, R. (2003). Measuring intercultural sensitivity: The intercultural development inventory. *International Journal of Intercultural Relations, 27,* 421–443.

Harackiewicz, J. M., & Elliot, A. J. (1993). Achievement goals and intrinsic motivation. *Journal of Personality and Social Psychology, 65,* 904–915.

Hardiman, R. (1982). *White identity development: A process oriented model for describing the racial consciousness of White Americans.* Unpublished doctoral dissertation, University of Massachusetts, Amherst.

Hartel, C. E. J., & Fujimoto, Y. (2000). Diversity is not the problem: Openness to perceived dissimilarity is. *Journal of the Australian and New Zealand Academy of Management, 5*(2), 14–27.

Hebert, R. (2001, May/June). "U Mich affirmative action": A case for psychological science. *APS Observer, 14*(5), 1, 13–17.

Heilman, M. E., Battle, W. S., Keller, C. E., & Lee, R. A. (1998). Type of affirmative action policy: A determinant of reactions to sex-based preferential selection? *Journal of Applied Psychology, 83,* 190–205.

Helms, J. E. (1984). Toward a theoretical explanation of the effects of race on counseling: A Black and White model. *Journal of Counseling Psychologist, 12,* 153–165.

Helms, J. E. (1985). Cultural identity in the treatment process. In P. Pedersen (Ed.), *Handbook of cross-cultural counseling and therapy* (pp. 239–245). Westport, CT: Greenwood.

Helms, J. E. (1990). *In Black and White racial identity theory.* Westport, CT: Praeger.

Helms, J. E. (1995). An update of Helms' White and people of color racial identity models. In J. G. Ponterotto, J. M. Casas, L. A. Suzuki, & C. M. Alexander (Eds.), *Handbook of multicultural counseling* (pp. 181–198). Thousand Oaks, CA: Sage.

Helms, J. E., & Richardson, T. Q. (1997). How "multiculturalism" obscures race and culture as differential aspects of counseling competence. In D. B. Pope-Davis & H. L. K. Coleman (Eds.), *Multicultural counseling competencies: Assessment, education and training, & supervision* (pp. 60–79). Thousand Oaks, CA: Sage.

Hendrikson, G., & Schroeder, W. (1941). Transfer of training to hit a submerged target. *Journal of Educational Psychology, 32,* 206–213.

Herron, C. (1994). An investigation of the effectiveness of using an advance organizer to introduce video in a foreign language classroom. *Modern Language Journal, 78,* 190–198.

Hersey, P. K., Blanchard, K. H., & Johnson, D. E. (2001). *Management of organizational behavior: Leading human resources* (8th ed.). Upper Saddle River, NJ: Prentice Hall.

Herskovits, M. J. (1955). *Cultural anthropology.* New York: Knopf.

Hickman, J., Tkaczyk, C., Florian, E., & Stemple, J. (2003, July 7). 50 best companies for minorities. *Fortune, 148*(1), 103.

Hilkey, J. H., Wilhelm, C. L., & Horne, A. M. (1982). Comparative effectiveness of videotape pretraining versus no pretraining on selected process and outcome variables in group therapy. *Psychological Reports, 50,* 1151–1159.

Hirumi, A., & Bowers, D. R. (1991). Enhancing motivation and acquisition of coordinate concepts by using concept trees. *Journal of Educational Research, 84,* 273–279.

Hofstede, G. (1980). *Culture's consequences: International differences in work related values.* Beverly Hills, CA: Sage.

Hofstede, G. (1984). The cultural relativity of the quality of life concept. *Academy of Management Review, 9,* 389–398.

Hofstede, G. (1985). The interaction between national and organizational value systems. *Journal of Management Studies, 22,* 347–357.

Hofstede, G. (1991). *Cultures and organizations: Software of the mind.* London: McGraw-Hill.

Hofstede, G. (1993). Cultural constraints in management theories. *Academy of Management Executive, 7,* 81–94.

Hofstede, G. (2001). *Culture's consequences: Comparing values, behaviors, institutions, and organizations across nations* (2nd ed.). Thousand Oaks, CA: Sage.

Hofstede, G. J., Pedersen, P. B., & Hofstede, G. (2002). *Exploring culture: Exercises, stories and synthetic cultures.* Yarmouth, ME: Intercultural Press.

Holden, N. (2002a). *Cross-cultural management: A knowledge management perspective.* London: Financial Times/Prentice Hall.

Holden, N. (2002b). The cross-cultural transfer of best practices: Learning from European and American experiences of knowledge management. In G. F. Simons (Ed.), *Eurodiversity: A business guide to managing difference* (pp. 171–194). Boston: Butterworth Heinemann.

Hollenbeck, G. P. (2001). A serendipitous sojourn through the global leadership literature. In W. H. Mobley & M. W. Morgan, Jr. (Eds.), *Advances in global leadership* (Vol. 2, pp. 15–47). Oxford, UK: Elsevier Science.

Holton, E. F., III. (1996). The flawed four-level evaluation model. *Human Resource Development Quarterly, 7,* 5–21.

Horney, K. (1967). *Feminine psychology.* New York: W. W. Norton.

House, R. J., Wright, N. S., & Aditya, R. N. (1997). Cross-cultural research on organizational leadership: A critical analysis and a proposed theory. In P. C. Earley & M. Erez (Eds.), *New perspectives on international industrial/organizational psychology* (pp. 535–625). San Francisco: New Lexington.

Howard, G. R. (2000). Ways of being White. *Diversity Factor, 8*(3), 20–24.

Hu, H. C. (1945). The Chinese concepts of face. *American Anthropologist, 46,* 45–64.

Hwang, K. K. (1998). Guanxi and Mientze: Conflict resolution in Chinese society. *Intercultural Communication Studies, 7*(1), 17–42.

Inzana, C. M., Driskell, J. E., Salas, E., & Johnston, J. H. (1996). The effects of preparatory information on enhancing performance under stress. *Journal of Applied Psychology, 81,* 429–435.

Ivey, A. E. (1988). *Intentional interviewing and counseling: Facilitating client development.* Pacific Grove, CA: Brooks/Cole.

Jackson, B. (1975). Black identity development. In L. Golubschick & B. Persky (Eds.), *Urban social and educational issues* (pp. 158–164), Dubuque, IA: Kendall-Hall.

Jackson, S. E., & Joshi, A. (2003). *Diversity in social context: A multi-attribute, multi-level analysis of team diversity and performance in a sales organization.* Unpublished manuscript, Rutgers University.

Jackson, S. E., Joshi, A., & Erhardt, N. L. (2003). Recent research on team and organizational diversity: SWOT analysis and implications. *Journal of Management, 29,* 801–830.

Jandt, F. E., & Pedersen, P. B. (1996). *Constructive conflict management: Asia-Pacific cases.* Thousand Oaks, CA: Sage.

Javidan, M., & House, R. J. (2001). Cultural acumen for the global manager: Lessons from Project GLOBE. *Organizational Dynamics, 29*(4), 289–305.

Jehn, K. A., & Bezrukova, K. (2003). *A field study of group diversity, group context, and performance.* Unpublished manuscript, The Wharton School, University of Pennsylvania.

Johnson, A. D. (2004, January 12). The truth about marketing urban legends: Got milk?, Gerber baby food, Chevy Nova. *DiversityInc.* Retrieved February 25, 2004, from http://www.diversityinc.com

Jones, J. M. (1997). *Prejudice and racism* (2nd ed.). New York: McGraw-Hill.

Kanter, R. M. (1995). Thriving locally in the global economy. *Harvard Business Review, 73*(5), 151–161.

Katz, R. H. (1993). *The straight path: A story of healing and transformation in Fiji.* Reading, MA: Addison-Wesley.

Katz, R. L. (1974, September-October). Skills of an effective administrator. *Harvard Business Review,* pp. 90–102.

Kaufman, R., & Keller, J. M. (1994). Levels of evaluation: Beyond Kirkpatrick. *Human Resource Development Quarterly, 5,* 371–380.

Kelly, G. A. (1955). *The psychology of personal construct.* New York: W. W. Norton.

Kets de Vries, M. F., & Mead, C. (1992). The development of the global leader within the multinational corporation. In V. Pucik, N. M. Tichy, & C. K. Barnett (Eds.), *Globalizing management: Creating and leading the competitive organization* (pp. 187–205). New York: John Wiley.

Kim, B. C. (1981). *New urban immigrants: The Korean community in New York.* Princeton, NJ: Princeton University Press.

Kim, U., Triandis, H. C., Kagitçibasi, C., Choi, S. C., & Yoon, G. (1994). *Individualism and collectivism.* Thousand Oaks, CA: Sage.

Kim-Ju, G. M., & Liem, R. (2003). Ethnic self-awareness as a function of ethnic group status, group composition, and ethnic identity orientation. *Cultural Diversity and Ethnic Minority Psychology, 9*(3), 289–302.

Kirkman, B. L., Tesluk, P. E., & Rosen, B. (2001). *The impact of race heterogeneity and team leader–team member demographic fit on team empowerment and effectiveness.* Paper presented at the 15th annual meeting of the Society for Industrial and Organizational Psychology, New Orleans.

Kirkpatrick, D. L. (1967). Evaluation. In R. L. Craig & L. R. Bittel (Eds.), *Training and development handbook* (pp. 87–112). New York: McGraw-Hill.

Kirkpatrick, D. L. (1987). Evaluation. In R. L. Craig (Ed.), *Training and development handbook* (3rd ed., pp. 303–319). New York: McGraw-Hill.

Kirkpatrick, D. L. (1998). *Evaluating training programs: The four levels* (2nd ed.). San Francisco: Berrett-Koehler.

Kirkpatrick, D., Phillips, J. J., & Phillips, P. P. (2003). Getting results from diversity training—in dollars and cents. *HR Focus, 80*(10), 3.

Kitano, H. H. L. (1989). A model for counseling Asian Americans. In P. Pedersen, J. Draguns, W. Lonner, & J. Trimble (Eds.), *Counseling across cultures* (3rd ed., pp. 139–152). Honolulu: University of Hawaii Press.

Klasen, N., & Clutterbuck, D. (2002). *Implementing mentoring schemes: A practical guide to successful mentoring programs.* Oxford, UK: Butterworth-Heinemann.

Kluckhohn, F., & Strodtbeck, F. K. (1961). *Variations in value orientation.* Evanston, IL: Row, Petersen.

Kochanski, J. (1997, October). Competency-based management. *Training and Development,* 41–44.

Kolb, D. A. (1984). *Experiential learning.* Englewood Cliffs, NJ: Prentice Hall.

Kolb, D. A. (1999). *Learning Style Inventory* (Version 3). Boston: Hay/McBer Training Resources Group.

Koonce, R. (2001). Redefining diversity. *Training and Development, 55*(12), 22–32.

Kouzes, J. M., & Posner, B. Z. (2002). *The leadership challenge* (3rd ed.). San Francisco: Jossey-Bass.

Kozan, M. K. (1989). Cultural influence on styles of handling interpersonal conflicts: Comparisons among Jordanian, Turkish, and U.S. managers. *Human Relations, 42,* 787–799.

Kraiger, K., Ford, J., & Salas, E. (1993). Application of cognitive, skill based and affective theories of learning outcomes to new methods of training evaluation. *Journal of Applied Psychology, 78,* 311–328.

Kram, K. E. (1983). Phases of the mentor relationship. *Academy of Management Journal, 26,* 608–625.

Kram, K. E. (1985). *Mentoring at work: Developmental relationships in organizational life.* Glenview, IL: Scott, Foresman.

Kravtiz, D. A., & Platania, J. (1993). Attitudes and beliefs about affirmative action: Effects of target and of respondent sex and ethnicity. *Journal of Applied Psychology, 78,* 928–938.

Kruger, J. A. (1992). *Racial/ethnic intergroup disputing and dispute resolution in the United States: A bibliography and resource guide.* (Available from Judith A. Kruger, P.O. Box 3, Collingswood, NJ 08108)

Kuhlmann, T. M., & Stahl, G. K. (1996). Fachkompetenz allein genugt nicht— Interkulturelle Assessment Center unterstutzen die gezielte Personalauswahl. *Personalführung Plus* [Specialized authority alone is not enough—An intercultural assessment center as the connecting piece in the purposeful choice of personnel] *96,* 22–24.

Kuhlmann, T. M., & Stahl, G. K. (1998). Diagnose interkultureller Kompetenz: Entwicklung und Evaluierung eines Assessment Centers. In C. Barmeyer & J. Bolten (Eds.), *Interkulturelle Personal-organisation* [Diagnosis for intercultural authority: Development and evaluation of an assessment center] (pp. 213–223). Berlin: Verlag Wissenschaft & Praxis.

Laurent, A. (1986). The cross cultural puzzle of human resource management. *Human Resource Management, 25*(1), 91–102.

Leonard, J. S., Levine, D. I., & Joshi, A. (2003). Do birds of a feather shop together? *The effect on performance of employees' similarity with one another and with customers.* Unpublished manuscript, University of California, Berkeley.

Lee, C. C. (1991). Promise and pitfalls of multicultural counseling. In C. C. Lee & B. L. Richardson (Eds.), *Multicultural issues in counseling: New approaches to diversity* (pp. 3–9). Alexandria, VA: American Association for Counseling and Development.

LeResche, D. (Ed.). (1993). Native American perspectives on peacemaking. *Mediation Quarterly, 10*(4).

Lewis, J. A., Lewis, M. D., Daniels, J. A., & D'Andrea, M. J. (1998). *Community counseling.* Pacific Grove, CA: Brooks/Cole.

Likert, R. (1961). *The human organization: Its management and value.* New York: McGraw-Hill.

Linnehan, F., & Konrad, A. M. (1999). Diluting diversity: Implications for intergroup inequality in organizations. *Journal of Management Inquiry, 8,* 399–414.

Locke, D. C. (1990). A not so provincial view of multicultural counseling. *Counselor Education and Supervision, 30,* 18–25.

Locke, E. A., Shaw, K. N., Saari, L. M., & Latham, G. P. (1981). Goal setting and task performance: 1969–1980. *Psychological Bulletin, 90,* 125–152.

London, M., & Sessa, V. I. (1999). *Selecting international executives: A suggested framework and annotated bibliography.* Greensboro, NC: Center for Creative Leadership.

Lopez, E. M. (2003, October 24). How embarrassing! New Buick's name means masturbation to French Canadians. *DiversityInc.* Retrieved February 25, 2004, from http://www.diversityinc.com

Lubove, S. (1997). Damned if you do, damned if you don't. *Forbes, 160*(13), 122–126.

Lund, B., Morris, C., & LeBaron-Duryea, M. (1994). *Conflict and culture.* Vancouver, BC: University of Victoria, Institute for Dispute Resolution.

Lynch, F. R. (1997). *The diversity machine: The drive to change the "White male workplace."* New York: Free Press.

Macdonald, K. M. (1995). *The sociology of the professions.* Thousand Oaks, CA: Sage.

Mai-Dalton, R. R. (1993). Managing cultural diversity on the individual, group, and organizational levels. In M. M. Chemers & R. Ayman (Eds.), *Leadership theory and research: Perspectives and directions* (pp. 189-215). San Diego, CA: Academic Press.

Martin, J. (2003). Multiple intelligences and business diversity. *Journal of Career Assessment, 11*(2), 187–204.

Mayer, J. D., & Salovey, P. (1993). The intelligence of emotional intelligence. *Intelligence, 17,* 433–442.

Mayer, R. E. (1975). Different problem-solving competencies established in learning computer programming with and without meaningful models. *Journal of Educational Psychology, 65,* 725–734.

Mayer, R. E. (1989). Models for understanding. *Review of Educational Research, 59,* 43–64.

McCall, M. W., Jr., & Hollenbeck, G. P. (2002). *Developing global executives.* Boston: Harvard Business School Press.

McFarlin, D. B., & Sweeney, P. D. (2003). *International management: Strategic opportunities and cultural challenges.* (2nd ed.). Boston: Houghton Mifflin.

McGehee, W., & Thayer, P. W. (1961). *Training in business and industry.* New York: John Wiley.

McGregor, D. (1960). *The human side of the enterprise.* New York: McGraw-Hill.

McGuire, W., McGuire, C., Child, P., & Fujioka, T. (1978). Salience of ethnicity in the spontaneous self-concept as a function of one's ethnic distinctiveness in the social environment. *Journal of Personality and Social Psychology, 36,* 511–520.

McIntosh, P. (1989, July/August). White privilege: Unpacking the invisible knapsack. *Peace and Freedom,* pp. 8–10.

McIntosh, P. (2002). White privilege and male privilege: A personal account of coming to see correspondences through work in women's studies. In C. Harvey & M. J. Allard (Eds.), *Understanding and managing diversity* (2nd ed., pp. 120–129). Upper Saddle River, NJ: Prentice Hall. (Original work published 1988)

McKenna, S. (1995). The business impact of management attitudes towards dealing with conflict: A cross-cultural assessment. *Journal of Managerial Psychology, 10*(7), 22–27.

Mehra, A., Kilduff, M., & Brass, D. (1998). At the margins: A distinctiveness approach to the social identity and social networks of underrepresented groups. *Academy of Management Journal, 41,* 441–452.

Mendenhall, M. E. (1999). On the need for paradigmatic integration in international human resource management. *Management International Review, 39*(2), 1–23.

Mendenhall, M. E., Jensen, R. J., Black, J. S., & Gregersen, H. B. (2003). Seeing the elephant: Human resource management challenges in the age of globalization. *Organizational Dynamics, 32*(3), 261–274.

Mentzer, M. S. (2002). How Canada promotes workplace diversity. In C. Harvey & M. J. Allard (Eds.), *Understanding and managing diversity* (2nd ed.). Upper Saddle River, NJ: Prentice Hall.

Meyer, M. (1994). *Ho'oponopono—To set right.* Unpublished manuscript, Harvard Graduate School of Education.

Miles, M. (2003). Negotiating with the Chinese: Lessons from the field. *Journal of Applied Behavioral Science, 39,* 453–472.

Milhouse, V. H. (1996). Intercultural communication education and training goals, content, and methods. *International Journal of Intercultural Relations, 20,* 69–95.

Miner, J. B. (1984). The validity and usefulness of theories in an emerging organizational science. *Academy of Management Review, 9,* 296–306.

Ministry of Public Management. (1995). Special tabulation on foreigners. Retrieved on November 25, 2004. from http://www.stat.go.jp/english/data/kokusei/1995/1518.htm

Mintzberg, H. (1980). *The nature of managerial work.* Upper Saddle River: NJ: Prentice Hall.

Miville, M. L., Gelso, C. J., Pannu, R., Liu, W., Touradji, P., Holloway, P., & Fuertes, J. N. (1999). Appreciating similarities and valuing differences: The Miville-Guzman Universality Diversity Scale. *Journal of Counseling Psychology, 46,* 291–307.

Mobley, M., & Payne, T. (1992). Backlash: The challenge to diversity training. *Training and Development Journal, 43*(12), 47.

Mueller, N. L. (1996). Wisconsin Power and Light's model diversity program. *Training and Development, 50*(3), 57–60.

Nelson, D. L., & Campbell Quick, J. (2003). *Organizational behavior: Foundations, realities, and challenges* (4th ed.). Mason, OH: Thomson South-Western.

Nemetz, P. L., & Christensen, S. L. (1996). The challenge of cultural diversity: Harnessing a diversity of views to understand multiculturalism. *Academy of Management Review, 21,* 434–462.

Noe, R. A. (2005). *Employee training and development.* Boston: McGraw-Hill–Irwin.

O'Connell, M. S., Lord, R. G., & O'Connell, M. K. (1990, August). *Differences in Japanese and American leadership prototypes: Implications for cross-cultural training.* Paper presented at the Academy of Management, San Francisco.

O'Connor, A. (2001). Understanding inequality in the late twentieth-century metropolis: New perspectives on the enduring racial divide. In A. O'Connor, C. Tilly, & L. D. Bobo (Eds.), *Urban inequality: Evidence from four cities* (Unnumbered volume, Multi-City Study of Urban Inequality series). New York: Russell Sage.

Oetting, G. R., & Beauvais, F. (1991). Orthogonal cultural identification theory: The cultural identification of minority adolescents. *International Journal of the Addictions, 25,* 655–685.

O'Hara-Devereaux, M., & Johansen, R. (1994). *Globalwork: Bridging distance, culture, and time.* San Francisco: Jossey-Bass.

Ohbuchi, K., & Takahashi, Y. (1994). Cultural styles of conflict management in Japanese and Americans: Passivity, covertness, and effectiveness of strategies. *Journal of Applied Social Psychology, 24,* 1345–1366.

Opotow, S. (1990). Moral exclusion and injustice: An introduction. *Journal of Social Issues, 46,* 1–20.

Ottavi, T. M., Pope-Davis, D. B., & Dings, J. G. (1994). Relationship between White racial identity attitudes and self-reported multicultural counseling competencies. *Journal of Counseling Psychology, 41,* 149–154.

Pack-Brown, S. (1999). Racism and White counselor training: Influence of White racial identity theory and research. *Journal of Counseling & Development, 77,* 87–92.

Panglinawan, L. (1972). *Ho'oponopono Project II.* Honolulu: Queen Lili'uokalani Children's Center, Cultural Committee.

Paris, S., & Winograd, P. (1990). How metacognition can promote academic learning and instruction. In B. Jones & L. Idol (Eds.), *Dimensions of thinking and cognitive instruction* (pp. 15–51). Hillsdale, NJ: Lawrence Erlbaum.

Patel, V. L., & Groen, G. J. (1991). The general and specific nature of medical expertise: A critical look. In K. A. Ericsson & J. Smith (Eds.), *Toward a general theory of expertise: Prospects and limits* (pp. 93–125). New York: Cambridge University Press.

Pavett, C. M., & Lau, A. W. (1983). Managerial work: The influence of hierarchical level and functional specialty. *Academy of Management Journal, 26,* 170–177.

Pearson, V. M., & Stephan, W. G. (1998). Preferences for styles of negotiation: A comparison of Brazil and the U.S. training section. *International Journal of Intercultural Relations, 22*(1), 67–83.

Pedersen, P. (1977). The triad model of cross-cultural counselor training. *Personnel and Guidance Journal, 56,* 94–100.

Pedersen, P. (1981). *Developing interculturally skilled counselors* (Final Report, NIMH Grant 1–724-MH-1552). Honolulu: Institute of Behavioral Science.

Pedersen, P. (1988). *Handbook for developing multicultural awareness.* Alexandria, VA: American Counseling Association.

Pedersen, P. (1997a). *Culture-centered counseling interventions* (pp. 25–26). Thousand Oaks, CA: Sage.

Pedersen, P. (1997b). Doing the right thing: A question of ethics. In K. Cushner & R. Brislin (Eds.), *Improving intercultural interactions: Vol. 2. Models for cross cultural training programs* (pp. 149–165). Thousand Oaks, CA: Sage.

Pedersen, P. (1997c). Recent trends in cultural theories. *Applied and Preventive Psychology, 6,* 221–231.

Pedersen, P. (1999). Intercultural understanding: Finding common ground without losing integrity. In D. Christie, D. Wagner, & D. Winter (Eds.), *Peace, conflict and violence: Peace psychology for the 21st century,* Prentice Hall.

Pedersen, P. (2001). Intercultural understanding: Finding common ground without losing integrity. In D. Christie, D. Wagner, & D. Winter (Eds.), *Peace, conflict and violence: Peace psychology for the 21st century.* Upper Saddle River, NJ: Prentice Hall.

Pedersen, P. B. (2000). *A handbook for developing multicultural awareness* (3rd ed.). Alexandria, VA: American Counseling Association.

Pedersen, P. B. (2004). *110 experiences for multicultural learning.* Washington, DC: American Psychological Association Press.

Pedersen, P. B., & Ivey, A., (1993). *Culture-centered counseling and interviewing skills.* Westport, CT: Greenwood.

Petersen, D. K. (2002). The relationship between unethical behavior and the dimensions of the ethical climate questionnaire. *Journal of Business Ethics, 41,* 313–327.

Peterson, M. F., & Hunt, J. G. (1997). International perspectives on international leadership. *Leadership Quarterly, 8,* 203–232.

Phillips, J. J. (1996, February). ROI: The search for best practices. *Training and Development,* pp. 42–47.

Phinney, J. (1990). Ethnic identity in adolescents and adults: Review of research. *Psychological Bulletin, 108,* 499–514.

Phinney, J., DuPont, S., Espinosa, C., Revill, J., & Sanders, K. (1994). Ethnic identity and American identification among ethnic minority adolescents. In F. van de Vijver (Ed.), *Proceedings of 1992 Conference of the International Association for Cross-Cultural Psychology.* Tilburg, The Netherlands: Tilburg University Press.

Phinney, J. S., & Onwughalu, M. (1996). Racial identity and perceptions of American ideals among African American and African students in the United States. *International Journal of Intercultural Relations, 20,* 127–140.

Phye, G. D. (1989). Schemata training and transfer of an intellectual skill. *Journal of Educational Psychology, 81,* 347–352.

Phye, G. D., & Sanders, C. (1994). Advice and feedback: Elements of practice for problem solving. *Contemporary Educational Psychology, 19,* 286–301.

Pike, R. (1966). *Language in relation to a united theory of the structure of human behavior.* The Hague, The Netherlands: Mouton.

Pinder, C. C. (1984). *Work motivation: Theory, issues, and applications.* Glenview, IL: Scott, Foresman.

Ponterotto, J. G. (1988). Racial/ethnic minority research in the *Journal of Counseling Psychology:* A content analysis and methodological critique. *Journal of Counseling Psychology, 3,* 410–418.

Ponterotto, J. G., & Pedersen, P. B. (1993). *Preventing prejudice.* Newbury Park, CA: Sage.

Powell-Hopson, D., & Hopson, D. (1992). Implications of doll color preferences among Black preschool children and White preschool children. In A. Burlew, W. C. Banks, H. McAdoo, & D. Azibo (Eds.), *African American psychology* (pp. 183–198). Newbury Park, CA: Sage.

President's Initiative on Race. (1997). *One America in the 21st century.* Washington, DC: Government Printing Office.

Pringle, J., & Scowcroft, J. (1996). Managing diversity: Meaning and practice in New Zealand organizations. *Asia Pacific Journal of Human Resources, 34*(2), 28–43.

Pritchard, K. H. (1999). *Introduction to competencies* (White Paper, Society for Human Resource Management). Retrieved on December 12, 2001, from http://www .shrm.org

Pukui, M. K., Hartig, E. W., Lee, C. A. (1972). *Nana I Ke Kumu (Look to the source).* Honolulu: Queen Lili'uokalani Children's Center.

Rabie, M. (1994). *Conflict resolution and ethnicity.* Westport, CT: Praeger.

Ragins, B. R. (2002). Understanding diversified mentoring relationships: Definitions, challenges, and strategies. In D. Clutterbuck & B. R. Ragins (Eds.), *Mentoring and diversity: An international perspective* (pp. 23–53). Oxford, UK: Butterworth-Heinemann.

Rashid, M. Z. A., Sambasivan, M., & Rahman, A. A. (2003). The influence of organizational culture on attitude towards organizational change. *Leadership and Organizational Development Journal, 25,* 161–179.

Reintzell, J. F. (1997). When training saves lives. *Training and Development, 51,* 41–42.

Rentsch, J. R., & Klimoski, R. J. (2001). Why do "great minds" think alike? Antecedents of team member schema agreement. *Journal of Organizational Behavior, 22,* 107–122.

Richard, O. C. (2000). Racial diversity, business strategy, and firm performance: A resource-based view. *Academy of Management Journal, 43,* 164–177.

Ridley, C. (1989). Racism in counseling as an aversive behavioral process. In P. Pedersen, J. Draguns, W. Lonner, & J. Trimble (Eds.), *Counseling across cultures* (3rd ed., pp. 55–79). Honolulu: University of Hawaii Press.

Rijsman, J. B. (1997). Social diversity: A social psychological analysis and some implications for groups and organizations. *European Journal of Work and Organizational Psychology, 6,* 139–152.

Robbins, S. P., & DeCenzo, D. A. (2004). *Fundamentals of management* (4th ed.). Upper Saddle River, NJ: Pearson Prentice Hall.

Robbins, S. P., & Hunsaker, P. L. (2003). *Training in interpersonal skills: Tips for managing people at work* (3rd ed.). Upper Saddle River, NJ: Prentice Hall.

Robinson, T. L., & Howard-Hamilton, M. (2000). *The convergence of race, ethnicity, and gender: Multiple identities in counseling.* Upper Saddle River, NJ: Merrill Prentice Hall.

Roberts, K., Kossek, E., & Ozeki, C. (1998). Managing the global workforce: Challenges and strategies. *Academy of Management Executive, 12*(4), 93–106.

Rodrigues, C. (2001). *International management: A cultural approach* (2nd ed.). Cincinnati, OH: South-Western College Publishing.

Ronen, S., & Shenkar, O. (1985). Clustering countries on attitudinal dimensions: A review and synthesis. *Academy of Management Review, 10,* 435–454.

Rosen, R., & Digh, P. (2001). Developing globally literate leaders. *Training and Development, 55*(5), 70–81.

Rosen, R., Digh, P., Singer, M., & Phillips, C. (2000). *Global literacies: Lessons on business leadership and national cultures.* New York: Simon & Schuster.

Rubin, J. Z., Pruitt, D. G., & Kim, S. H. (1994). *Social conflict: Escalation, stalemate and settlement* (2nd ed.). New York: McGraw-Hill.

Rynes, S. L., & Rosen, B. (1994, October). What makes diversity programs work? *HR Magazine, 39*(10), 67–73.

Rynes, S. L., & Rosen, B. (1995). A field study of factors affecting the adoption and perceived success of diversity training. *Personnel Psychology, 48,* 247–270.

Sagiv, L., & Schwartz, S. H. (1995). Value priorities and readiness for out-group social contact. *Journal of Personality and Social Psychology, 69,* 437–448.

Salovey, P., & Mayer, J. D. (1990). Emotional intelligence. *Imagination, Cognition and Personality, 9,* 185–211.

Sanders, R. E., Gonzalez, D. J., Murphy, M. D., Pesta, B. J., & Bucur, B. (2002). Training content variability and the effectiveness of learning: An adult age assessment. *Aging, Neuropsychology & Cognition, 9*(3), 157–174.

Sartorius, N., Pedersen, P. B., & Marsella, A. J. (1984). Mental health services across cultures: Some concluding thoughts. In P. B. Pedersen, N. Sartorius, & A. J. Marsella (Eds.), *Mental health services: The cross-cultural context.* Beverly Hills, CA: Sage.

Schein, E. (1992). *Organizational culture and leadership* (2nd ed.). San Francisco: Jossey-Bass.

Schendel, J. D., & Hagman, J. D. (1982). On sustaining procedural skills over a prolonged retention interval. *Journal of Applied Psychology, 67,* 605–610.

Schwartz, S. H. (1992). Universals in the content and structure of values: Theoretical advances and empirical tests in 20 countries. In M. Zanna (Ed.), *Advances in experimental social psychology* (Vol. 25, pp. 1–65). New York: Academic Press.

Schwartz, S. H., & Bilsky, W. (1987). Toward a psychological structure of human values. *Journal of Personality and Social Psychology, 53,* 550–562.

Schwartz, S. H., & Bilsky, W. (1990). Toward a theory of the universal content and structure of values. *Journal of Personality and Social Psychology, 58,* 878–891.

Schwartz, S. H., & Huismans, S. (1995). Value priorities and religiosity in four Western religions. *Social Psychology Quarterly, 58,* 88–107.

Schwartz, S. H., & Sagiv, L. (1995). Identifying culture-specifics in the content and structure of values. *Journal of Cross-Cultural Psychology, 26,* 92–116.

Scott, D. A., & Robinson, T. L. (2001). White male identity development: The key model. *Journal of Counseling & Development, 79,* 415–421.

Sellers, P. (2003). The trials of John Mack. *Fortune, 108*(4), 98–108.

Serving the multicultural customer. (2003). *Lodging Hospitality, 59*(10), 18.

Shank, R. C., & Abelson, R. P. (1977). *Scripts, plans, goals and understanding: An inquiry into human knowledge structures.* Hillsdale, NJ: Lawrence Erlbaum.

Shaw, G. B. (1919). *Man and superman: A comedy and a philosophy.* New York: Brentano's.

Shook, E. V. (1985). *Ho'oponopono*. Honolulu: University of Hawaii Press.

Siebert, H. (1999). *Globalization and labor*. Tübingen, Germany: Mohr Siebeck.

Sigelman, L., & Welch, S. (1991). *Black Americans' views of racial inequality: The dream deferred*. New York: Cambridge University Press.

Sims, R. R., & Brinkmann, J. (2002). Leaders as moral role models: The case of John Gutfreund at Salomon Brothers. *Journal of Business Ethics, 35,* 327–340.

Smith, E. (1991). Ethnic identity development: Toward the development of a theory within the context of majority/minority status. *Journal of Counseling and Development, 70*(1), 181–188.

Smith, E. M., Ford, J. K., & Kozlowski, S. W. J. (1997). Building adaptive expertise: Implications for training design strategies. In M. A. Quinones & A. Ehrenstein (Eds.), *Training for a rapidly changing workplace: Applications of psychological research* (pp. 89–118). Washington, DC: American Psychological Association.

Smith, P. B., & Peterson, M. F. (2002). Cross-cultural leadership. In M. J. Gannon & K. L. Newman (Eds.), *The Blackwell handbook of cross-cultural management* (pp. 217–235). Oxford, UK: Blackwell Business.

Solomon, C. (1996). Big Mac's McGlobal HR secrets. *Personnel Journal, 75*(4), 46–54.

Solomon, C. (1998, July). Today's global mobility. *Global Workforce*, p. 16.

Spengler, P. M., Strohmer, D. C., Dixon, D. N., & Shivy, V. A. (1995). A scientist-practitioner model of psychological assessment: Implications for training, practice and research. *Counseling Psychologist, 23,* 506–534.

Spreitzer, G. M., McCall, M. W., Jr., & Mahoney, J. D. (1997). Early identification of international executive potential. *Journal of Applied Psychology, 82,* 6–29.

Stahl, G. K. (2001). Using assessment centers as tools for global leadership development: An exploratory study. In M. E. Mendenhall, T. M. Kuhlmann, & G. K. Stahl (Eds.), *Developing global business leaders: Policies, processes, and innovations* (pp. 197–210). Westport, CT: Quorum.

Stewart, T. A. (1999). Leaders of the future: Have you got what it takes. *Fortune, 140*(7), 318–322.

Storti, C. (1989). *The art of crossing cultures*. San Francisco: Intercultural Press.

Strauss, J. P., & Connerley, M. L. (2003). Demographics, personality, contact and universal-diverse orientation: An exploratory examination. *Human Resource Management, 42*(2), 159-174.

Strauss, J. P., Connerley, M. L., & Ammermann, P. A. (2003). The "threat hypothesis," personality, and attitudes toward diversity. *Journal of Applied Behavioral Science, 39,* 32–52.

Stroh, L. K., & Caligiuri, P. M. (1998). Strategic human resources: A new source for competitive advantage in the global arena. *International Journal of Human Resource Management, 9,* 1–17.

Stuart, R. B. (2004). Twelve practical suggestions for achieving multicultural competence. *Professional Psychology: Research and Practice, 35,* 3–9.

Sue, D. W. (1991). A conceptual model for cultural diversity training. *Journal of Counseling and Development, 70,* 99–105.

Sue, D. W. (1999). Creating conditions for a constructive dialogue on "race": Taking individual and institutional responsibility. In J. Q. Adams & J. R. Welsch (Eds.), *Cultural diversity: Curriculum, classroom, & climate* (pp. 15–20). Chicago: Illinois Staff and Curriculum Developers Association.

Sue, D. W. (2001). Multidimensional facets of cultural competence. *Counseling Psychologist, 29,* 790–821.

Sue, D. W., Arredondo, P., & McDavis, R. J. (1992). Multicultural counseling competencies and standards: A call to the profession. *Journal of Counseling and Development, 70,* 477–486.

Sue, D. W., Berneir, J. E., Durran, A., Feinberg, L., Pedersen, P., Smith, E. J., & Vasquez-Nuttall, E. (1982). Cross-cultural counseling competencies. *Counseling Psychologist, 19*(2), 45–52.

Sue, D. W., Bingham, R., Porche-Burke, L., & Vasquez, M. (1999). The diversification of psychology: A multicultural revolution. *American Psychologist, 54,* 1061–1069.

Sue, D. W., Carter, R. T., Casas, J. M., Fouad, N. A., Ivey, A. E., Jensen, M., LaFromboise, T., Manese, J. E., Ponterotto, J. G., & Vasquez-Nuttall, E. (1998). *Multicultural counseling competencies: Individual and organizational development.* Thousand Oaks, CA: Sage.

Sue, D. W., Parham, T. A., & Bonilla-Santiago, G. (1998). The changing face of work in the United States: Implications for individual, institutional, and societal survival. *Cultural Diversity and Mental Health, 4,* 153–164.

Sue, D. W., & Sue, D. (1972). Counseling Chinese Americans. *Personnel and Guidance Journal, 50,* 637–645.

Sue, D. W., & Sue, D. (1999). *Counseling the culturally different* (3rd ed.). New York: John Wiley.

Sunoo, J. J. M. (1990, October). Some guidelines for mediators of intercultural disputes. *Negotiation Journal,* pp. 383–389.

Swerdlow, J. L. (1998, August). New York's Chinatown. *National Geographic,* pp. 58-77.

Szapocznik, J., Kurtines, W. M., & Fernandez, T. (1980). Bicultural involvement and adjustment in Hispanic-American youths. *International Journal of Intercultural Relations, 4,* 353–365.

Tajfel, H. (Ed.). (1978). *Differentiation between social groups.* London: Academic Press.

Tan, D. L., Morris, L., & Romero, J. (1996). Changes in attitude after diversity training. *Training and Development, 50*(9), 54–55.

Taylor, E. B. T. (1924). *Primitive culture.* Gloucester, MA: Smith. (Original work published 1871)

Taylor, T. S. (2002, December 29). What's in a name? Bias, sometimes. *Chicago Tribune,* Chicagoland Final Edition, p. 5.

Thomas, C. (1971). *Boys no more.* Beverly Hills, CA: Glencoe Press.

Thomas, D. A., & Ely, R. J. (1996, September-October). Making differences matter: A new paradigm for managing diversity. *Harvard Business Review,* pp. 79–90.

Thomas, K. W. (1976). Conflict and conflict management. In M. D. Dunnette (Ed.), *Handbook of industrial and organizational psychology* (pp. 889–935). Chicago: Rand McNally.

Thomas, K. W., & Schmidt, W. H. (1976). A survey of managerial interests with respect to conflict. *Academy of Management Journal, 19,* 315–318.

Thomas, R. R. (1990, March-April). From affirmative action to affirming diversity. *Harvard Business Review,* pp. 107–117.

Thompson, L. (1991). Information exchange in negotiation. *Journal of Experimental and Social Psychology, 27,* 161–179.

Thorndike, E. L., & Woodworth, R. S. (1901). (I) The influence of improvement in one mental function on the efficiency of other functions. (II) The estimation of magnitudes. (III) Functions involving attention, observation, and discrimination. *Psychological Review, 8,* 247–261, 384–395, 553–564.

Tichy, N. M., Brimm, M., Charan, R., & Takeuchi, H. (1992). Leadership development as a lever for global transformation. In V. Pucik, N. M. Tichy, & C. K. Barnett (Eds.), *Globalizing management: Creating and leading the competitive organization* (pp. 47–60). New York: John Wiley.

Ting-Toomey, S., & Cole, M. (1990). Intergroup diplomatic communication: A face-negotiation perspective. In F. Korsenny & S. Ting-Toomey (Eds.), *Communicating for peace: Diplomacy and negotiation* (pp. 77–95). Newbury Park, CA: Sage.

Todeva, E. (1999). Models for comparative analysis of culture: The case of Poland. *International Journal of Human Resource Management, 10,* 606–623.

Townsend, A. M., & Scott, K. D. (2001). Team racial composition, member attitudes, and performance: A field study. *Industrial Relations, 40,* 317–337.

Triandis, H. C. (1972). *The analysis of subjective culture.* New York: John Wiley.

Triandis, H. C. (1975). Cultural training, cognitive complexity and interpersonal attitudes. In R. Brislin, S. Bochner, & W. Lonner (Eds.), *Cross-cultural perspectives on learning* (pp. 39–78). New York: John Wiley.

Triandis, H. C. (1977). *Interpersonal behavior.* Monterey, CA: Brooks/Cole.

Triandis, H. C. (1993). *The contingency model in cross-cultural perspective.* San Diego, CA: Academic Press.

Triandis, H. C., Bontempo, R., Leung, K., & Hui, C. H. (1990). A method for determining cultural, demographic and person constructs. *Journal of Cross-Cultural Psychology, 21,* 302–318.

Trompenaars, F., & Hampden-Turner, C. (1998). *Riding the waves of culture: Understanding cultural diversity in global business* (2nd ed.). New York: McGraw-Hill.

Trubinsky, P., Ting-Toomey, S., & Lin, S. (1991). The influence of individualism-collectivism and self-monitoring on conflict styles. *International Journal of Intercultural Relations, 15,* 65–84.

Tseng, W. S. (2003). *Clinician's guide to cultural psychiatry.* New York: Academic Press.

Tung, R. L. (1993). Managing cross-cultural and intranational diversity. *Human Resource Management, 32,* 461–477.

Tung, R. L. (1997). International and intranational diversity. In C. S. Granrose & S. Oskamp (Eds.), *Cross-cultural work groups* (pp. 163–185). Thousand Oaks, CA: Sage.

Tung, R. L., & Miller, E. (1990). Managing in the twenty-first century: The need for global orientation. *Management International Review, 30,* 5–18.

U.S. Census. (2000). U.S. Census Bureaus. United States Department of Commerce. Retrieved March 16, 2002, from http://www.census.gov (under "QuickFacts").

U.S. Department of Commerce (2003, July). *Addressing the challenges of international bribery and fair competition: The fifth annual report under Section 6 of the International Anti-Bribery and Fair Competition Act of 1998.* Retrieved August 9, 2003, from www.export.gov/tcc

Useem, J. (2003). The 25 most powerful people in business. *Fortune, 148*(3), 74.

van Oudenhoven, J. P. (2001). Do organizations reflect national cultures? A 10-nation study. *International Journal of Intercultural Relations, 25,* 89–107.

Vinson, T. S., & Neimeyer, G. J. (2000). The relationship between racial identity development and multicultural counseling competency. *Journal of Multicultural Counseling and Development, 28,* 177–192.

Warr, P., Bird, M., & Rackham, N. (1970). *Evaluation of management training.* London: Gower.

Watkin, C. (2000). Developing emotional intelligence. *International Journal of Selection and Assessment, 8,* 89–92.

Watson, W. E., Johnson, L., & Merritt, D. (1998). Team orientation, self-orientation, and diversity in task groups: Their connection to team performance over time. *Group & Organization Management, 23,* 161–189.

Watson-Gegeo, K., & White, G. (Eds.). (1990). *The discourse of disentangling: Conflict discourse in Pacific societies.* Palo Alto, CA: Stanford University Press.

Wehrly, B. (1995). *Pathways to multicultural counseling competence.* Pacific Grove, CA: Brooks/Cole.

Wellner, A. (2000). How do you spell diversity? *Training, 37*(4), 34–38.

West, C. (2000, May 2). *Race and the American experience.* Presentation given to the IPI World Congress, Boston.

Westwood, R. (1997). Harmony and patriarchy: The cultural basis for "paternalistic headship" among the overseas Chinese. *Organization Studies, 18*(3), 445–480.

Wexley, K. N., & Latham, G. P. (2002). *Developing and training human resources in organizations* (3rd ed.). Upper Saddle River, NJ: Prentice Hall.

Wills, S., & Barham, K. (1994). Being an international manager. *European Management Journal, 12*(1), 49–58.

Workplace Visions. (2000). Globalization and the human resource profession (Issue 5).

World Economic Forum. (1997). *The global competitiveness report.* Geneva, Switzerland: Author.

Wrenn, C. G. (1962). The culturally encapsulated counselor. *Harvard Educational Review, 32,* 444–449.

Wrenn, C. G. (1985). Afterword: The culturally encapsulated counselor revisited. In P. Pedersen (Ed.), *Handbook of cross-cultural counseling and therapy* (pp. 323–329). Westport, CT: Greenwood.

Yeung, A. K., & Ready, D. A. (1995). Developing capabilities of global corporations: A comparative study in eight nations. *Human Resource Management, 34,* 529–547.

Zemke, R. (1999). Toward a science of training. *Training, 36*(7), 32–36.

Name Index

Subject Index

Learning styles, 63–65
Legislative action, 8–9
Lian (face), 141–142
Literacies, 71
Lockheed Martin, 25
Low-context cultures, 139–141, 146

Mack, John, 14
Managers, 13–14
Manufacturing techniques, 33
Maoris (indigenous citizens), 9
Ma, Peter, 16
Marginality, 48, 58, 83, 84
Marketing issues, 31–32
Masculinity, 42, 125, 171–173, 175
Massed versus spaced practice
    sessions, 102
Mastery goals, 101
Mattel, 46–47
McDonald's, 32–33
McIntosh, Peggy, 35
McKinsey, 11
Melting pot perspective, 23, 83
Mentoring relationships, 154–156
Metacognitive strategies, 100
Microskills training, 122
Minimization, 48
Minority population, 85
Minority populations,
    7–10, 57–59, 83–84
Moffat, Bob, 14
Monocultural organizations, 83
Monty, Jean, 14
Moral free space, 157
Motivational values, 43–44
Motor skills, 65
Mullainathan, Sendhil, 7
Multi-City Study of Urban
    Inequality, 34–35
Multicultural competencies, 69–88
    definition, 70
    global leadership skills, 70–74
    individual/personal levels, 80–82
    multicultural counseling
        competencies, 77
    multidimensional model for
        developing cultural competence
        (MMDC), 74–77, 80–85

obstacles, 80–85
    organizational levels, 82–84
    professional levels, 82
    societal levels, 84–85
    training objectives, 112–114
Multiculturalism:
    adjustment strategies, 3–4
    awareness benefits, 7–9, 77–80
    cultural constructs, 25–28
    mentoring relationships, 154–156
    multicultural perspectives, 25–28
    occurrences, 2
    three-stage developmental
        sequence, 49–51
    value, 9–13
Multiculture organizations, 84
Multidimensional model for developing
    cultural competence (MMDC),
    74–77, 80–85
Multiple intelligences, 62–63

National culture, 40–42
Nationality, 5, 15–16
Near transfer, 95
Needs assessments, 90–95, 112
Negative transfer, 95
Negotiation styles, 159–160
Nestlé, 2
Netherlands, 9
Neutral cultures, 43
New York Life, 2
New Zealand, 9
Nextel, 12–13
Nigrescence model, 59
Noncontact stage, 61
Nondiscriminatory organizations, 83
Nontraditional underrepresented
    groups, 62
Non-Western conflict resolution
    models, 30, 138–144
Nortel (Northern Telecom), 14
Northwest Airlines, 15
Novartis Consumer Health, 32

Ohana (extended family), 143
Opotow, S., 34
Optimal stage, 61
Organizational analysis, 90–91

About the Authors

Mary L. Connerley is an Associate Professor in the Department of Management, Pamplin College of Business at Virginia Tech. She received her PhD in Human Resource Management from the University of Iowa and her master's and undergraduate degrees in Industrial Relations and Psychology, respectively, from Iowa State University. She has taught a variety of courses at the undergraduate, MBA, and doctoral levels, including Managing Diversity in the Workplace, Training & Development, Staffing, and Human Resource Management. She has been an active researcher and has published more than 20 articles on aspects of multiculturalism and diversity, cross-cultural and expatriate issues, and the staffing process. She is a member of the Academy of Management and the Society for Industrial and Organizational Psychologists. She enjoys serving as a Multicultural Fellow at Virginia Tech and has chaired or been a member of the college's Multicultural Diversity Committee since 1996.

Paul B. Pedersen is a Visiting Professor in the Department of Psychology at the University of Hawaii. He has taught at the University of Minnesota, Syracuse University, University of Alabama at Birmingham, and for 6 years at universities in Taiwan, Malaysia, and Indonesia. He has authored, coauthored, or edited 40 books, 99 articles, and 72 chapters on aspects of multicultural counseling. He is a Fellow in Divisions 9, 17, 45, and 52 of the American Psychological Association.